UNIVERSITY LIBRARIES AND DIGITAL LEARNING ENVIRONMENTS

University Libraries and Digital Learning Environments

Edited by

PENNY DALE
Bournemouth University, UK

JILL BEARD
Bournemouth University, UK

MATT HOLLAND
North West Ambulance Service, UK

ASHGATE

Published by
Ashgate Publishing Limited
Wey Court East
Union Road
Farnham
Surrey, GU9 7PT
England

Ashgate Publishing Company
Suite 420
101 Cherry Street
Burlington
VT 05401-4405
USA

www.ashgate.com

British Library Cataloguing in Publication Data
University libraries and digital learning environments.
1. Education, Higher--Digital libraries. 2. Academic
libraries--Information technology. 3. Electronic
information resource literacy. 4. Education, Higher--
Digital libraries--Administration. 5. Education, Higher--
Digital libraries--Employees--Training of. 6. Academic
libraries--Relations with faculty and curriculum.
I. Dale, Penny. II. Beard, Jill. III. Holland, Matt.
027.7'0285-dc22

Library of Congress Cataloging-in-Publication Data
University libraries and digital learning environments / by Penny Dale, Jill Beard, and Matt Holland.
  p. cm.
Includes bibliographical references and index.
 ISBN 978-0-7546-7957-8 -- ISBN 978-0-7546-9897-5 (ebook)
1. Academic libraries--Effect of technological innovations on. 2. Academic libraries--Information technology. 3. Academic libraries--Collection development. 4. Libraries and electronic publishing. 5. Electronic information resources--Management. 6. Digital libraries. 7. Communication in learning and scholarship--Technological innovations. I. Dale, Penny. II. Beard, Jill. III. Holland, Matt.
Z675.U5U5475 2010
027.7--dc22

                                                                    2010035143

ISBN 9780754679578 (hbk)
ISBN 9780754698975 (ebk)

MIX
Paper from
responsible sources
FSC
www.fsc.org   FSC® C018575

Printed and bound in Great Britain by the
MPG Books Group, UK

Contents

List of Figures and Tables

Figures

Tables

Notes on Contributors

The Editors

Jill Beard is Library and Learning Support Manager at Bournemouth University, a service which includes librarians, learning technologists and specialists in academic skills development. She has written extensively over many years on a wide range of subjects. She was a project lead on the UK Higher Education Academy funded e-Res project looking at innovative e-learning with e-resources (Bournemouth University 2008). She is currently a member of the SCONUL working group on space, and since The Sir Michael Cobham Library at Bournemouth University won the SCONUL Library Design award in 2007 she has published and presented at conferences on libraries, space and pedagogy.

Penny Dale was until recently a Subject Librarian at Bournemouth University where she worked in a number of different roles with all academic schools over almost 20 years. She also contributed to projects integrating aspects of technology and learning in a digital environment into the curricula. She is a Chartered member of the Chartered Institute of Library and Information Professionals (CILIP) and a Fellow of the Higher Education Academy (HEA). Her professional interests include engaging students with information literacy, and mentoring Accreditation and Chartership candidates for CILIP. She has written journal articles and book chapters and was co-editor of *Subject Librarians: Engaging with the Learning and Teaching Environment* published by Ashgate in 2006.

Matt Holland has 20 years experience in library and information work in higher education and more recently in the NHS. His interests are in the areas of media, broadcasting archives, subject librarianship in higher education and institutional repositories. Matt is currently working for the North West Ambulance Service NHS Trust as an Outreach Librarian. He was an advisor and board member on a number of the Arts and Humanities Research Council (AHRC) and Joint Information Systems Committee (JISC) funded digitisation projects in radio and television history including: the *TV Times*, the IRN/LBC Archive, Independent Local Radio Programme Sharing Archive, the South Southern Local Radio Digitisation Project, the This Week Project and the BBC Radio 4 Analysis Project. He has published chapters in books and journal articles on a wide range of topics and was a co-editor of *Subject Librarians: Engaging with the Learning and Teaching Environment* published by Ashgate.

The Contributors

David Ball is Head of Academic Development Services at Bournemouth University. Under his leadership Bournemouth has become recognised as a leading library in terms of use of e-resources and integration with virtual learning environments (VLEs). In 2007 Bournemouth won the prestigious quinquennial SCONUL Library Design Award, and in 2009 the Times Higher Education Leadership and Management Awards for Outstanding Library Team.

He is recognised as a leading practitioner and speaker, particularly in the field of library purchasing, having led innovative tenders for e-books, books and journals, chairing national and regional library procurement organisations in higher education. Most recently he has led, on behalf of all the English universities, probably the most valuable and complex tender for books and e-books yet seen. He also has experience of procuring and implementing VLEs.

David is a member of various bodies, such as the Board of SCONUL and the JISC Journals Working Group, and chairs the Library and Information Research Group of CILIP. He has a strong record in leading research and digitisation projects, such as the Heritage Lottery Fund (HLF) funded Streets of Bournemouth, and the New Opportunities Fund (NOF) funded Dorset Coast Digital Archive. His publishing record includes a major book, *Managing Suppliers and Partners for the Academic Library*.

Angela Conyers is Research Fellow at Evidence Base, the evaluation and research unit within Library and Learning Resources at Birmingham City University. Her particular interests are in the measurement of use and impact of electronic information services in libraries. Before moving into research, she was Director of Library Services at Canterbury Christ Church University.

Sheila Corrall is Professor of Librarianship and Information Management at the University of Sheffield Information School, where she served as Head of Department from 2006 to 2010. Her research focus is the application of strategic management concepts and techniques to library and information services and her current research interests include professional roles and competencies in knowledge-based organisations, information literacy strategy development and collection management in the digital world. Her teaching areas include academic and national libraries, collection development and reference services, in addition to management and organisation behaviour.

In her earlier career, Sheila spent five years in the public library sector, ten years at the British Library and 13 years directing library and information services in universities, most recently as Director of Academic Services at the University of Southampton.

Sheila has published and lectured on professional and management issues and has undertaken consultancy assignments for educational institutions and professional associations in the UK, Ireland, Hungary, Iceland, Norway, Portugal and Spain. She has also served on the committees and working groups of many professional bodies; she was the founding Chair of the Information Services National Training Organisation (isNTO), a former government-sponsored body with responsibility for vocational qualifications and occupational standards for the sector, and recently served four years as Chair of the Heads of Schools and Departments Committee of the British Association for Information and Library Education and Research (BAILER).

In 2002 she was named in the *Independent on Sunday* as one the top ten librarians in the UK, in 2002–03 she served as the first President of CILIP, and in 2003 she was awarded the International Information Industries Lifetime Achievement Award for her contribution to the development of the information profession. She is one of the few librarians listed in *Who's Who*.

Emma Crowley joined Bournemouth University in 2008 as Subject Librarian for the School of Conservation Sciences. In addition to information literacy and resource acquisition she leads the library support and advocacy for the university-wide research community. This includes providing bibliometrics training, current awareness via the BU Research Blog, new e-theses submission protocols and advocacy for the university's institutional repository, Bournemouth University Research Online (BURO). Emma has managed BURO since April 2009.

Prior to her tenure at Bournemouth University, Emma's role was that of Senior Academic Services Librarian (Functional) at the University of Greenwich, where she introduced a number of innovative acquisitions processes, liaising and negotiating with numerous external library suppliers. Emma continues to work closely with prominent library vendors, influencing new system functionality and representing university libraries on several user groups.

Jacqui Weetman DaCosta is Director of Library Services at Georgian Court University in New Jersey, USA. Previously, she was Information Literacy Librarian at The College of New Jersey (TCNJ) where she managed an online information literacy course, which is compulsory for all incoming students. At TCNJ, she was responsible for the development of a new online tutorial and the redesign of the library web pages. She undertook extensive usability testing, which provided valuable information that influenced the final products.

Prior to moving to the USA in 2006, Jacqui's work experience was mainly in further and higher education libraries, where she held positions of increasing responsibility. At De Montfort University in Leicester, UK, she was awarded a Curriculum Development and Innovation Award for her work on creating an assessed information skills course within Blackboard.

Jacqui's research interests are deeply rooted in information literacy and include faculty perceptions of information literacy, active learning and online learning. Her work has been published both in the UK and USA. In 2009, she had a 'recipe' published in the Association of College and Research Libraries' (ACRL) *The Library Instruction Cookbook*, which became one of the ACRL's bestsellers. She has presented her research at academic and library conferences around the world. Jacqui has been active professionally for a number of years, in the UK and USA. She has chaired committees involved with information literacy. She is a member of the CILIP Information Literacy Group committee and was one of the founding members of the committee that organises the Librarians' Information Literacy Annual Conference (LILAC).

Tim Denning is the Project Manager for the Keele University Virtual Learning Environment (VLE) programme and a member of the Research Institute for Public Policy and Management.

During the last three years he has lead successful HEA-funded Benchmarking and Pathfinder projects at Keele, and is currently a work package leader for the Open Educational Resources project in Medicine, Dentistry and Veterinary Medicine (MEDEV), a subject centre of the HEA. He has also undertaken work funded by the Teacher Development Agency exploring frameworks for describing the 'learning purposes' associated with ICT use in the classroom and was part of a small team convened by the British Educational Communications and Technology Agency (Becta) to develop earlier work on profiling e-maturity in the teaching force as part of exemplifying the '21st Century Teacher'.

In recent years he has led a national evaluation project for Becta and the UK Department for Education and Skills (DfES) concerned with online professional development for secondary subject teachers, and a research team funded by the British Council developing an evaluation framework for the Jordan Education Initiative. He also completed an evaluation of multimedia teaching resources supporting Japanese, Latin and Mathematics teaching.

Rachel Geeson is Service Development Manager for Library and Learning Support (LLS) at Bournemouth University, where she has worked in different roles since 1998. Her responsibilities include evaluation and enhancement of service quality, managing virtual enquiry services and co-ordinating support for partner institutions. She is also the LLS copyright adviser and Copyright Licensing Agency (CLA) licence co-ordinator, managing the scanning and integration of library resources within the University's VLE.

Peter Godwin is Academic Liaison Librarian at the University of Bedfordshire in Luton, UK. Formerly he was Academic Services Manager at London South Bank University, in charge of subject support to all faculties. His interest in information literacy has focussed on support to academic staff in universities and the impact of Web 2.0 on information literacy in all information sectors. He has presented widely on Web 2.0 and how this affects the content and delivery of information literacy.

In 2008 he co-edited the pioneering book *Information Literacy meets Library 2.0* for Facet Publications, which is supplemented by a blog of the same name. Currently he is investigating how mobile devices will affect library services, and information literacy in particular. He draws on many years' experience in academic library management and has presented at conferences in Europe, Asia, the USA and Canada.

Sue McKnight is Pro Vice-Chancellor Learning Resources at the University of Canterbury where she is responsible for library services, information and communication technologies, and facilities management. Her major research interest is 'customer value discovery', especially as this relates to libraries and e-learning.

She is a Fellow of both CILIP (UK) and the Australian Institute of Management. Sue was named a National Teaching Fellow in June 2008 by the Higher Education Academy (UK) and was named Manager of the Year by the Australian Library & Information Association in 1999.

Before joining the University of Canterbury, she was Director of Libraries and Knowledge Resources at Nottingham Trent University in the United Kingdom. Prior to that Sue was Executive Director of Learning Services and University Librarian at Deakin University in Australia, and held senior posts at the University of Queensland Libraries. Sue also has special library and public library experience in Australia, as well as international consulting and facilitation experience.

She has served on, and chaired, many advisory groups including the International Federation of Library Associations (IFLA) and JISC.

Philip Payne is Librarian at Birkbeck, University of London, having previously worked at Leeds Metropolitan University, City of London Polytechnic, Lancaster University, and Hatfield Polytechnic. He has a particular interests in practitioner research and in performance measurement.

Claire Ross is a Research Assistant at University College London (UCL) on the JISC-funded LinkSphere project in collaboration with the University of Reading. It aims to develop a Virtual Research Environment (VRE) with Web 2.0 features, which will allow cross-repository searching across various digital collections and archives. Claire's research interests include usability studies, Web 2.0 applications, social media, museum e-learning, digital heritage and digital repositories. She focuses on user evaluation and user-centred design of social media applications, online collections and cross repository searching in order to produce a useful user interface for the VRE. Before coming to UCL she was E-Learning Development Project Manager of a collaborative project with the University of Exeter and Geevor Tin Mine Museum. She is a member of the committee of the Digital Learning Network.

Jane Russ is the Learning Resources and Student Support Manager at Kingston Maurward College, a land-based FE College near Dorchester in Dorset. She has worked in both Higher and Further Education libraries and is an enthusiastic supporter of widening participation and the delivery of Higher Education programmes in Further Education colleges.

Chris Spencer is Library Procurement and Systems Development Manager at Bournemouth University. He has been working in the UK library profession for 30 years with experience of both the academic and the commercial R&D sectors. Professional interests include procurement of electronic resources, their integration into existing business systems and the development of applications to aid search and discovery for the end user. He is a member of EBSCO's European Academic Advisory Board.

Alma Swan is a consultant working in the field of scholarly communication. She is a director of Key Perspectives Ltd and holds honorary academic positions in the University of Southampton School of Electronics & Computer Science and the University of Warwick Business School. Alma is Convenor for Enabling Open Scholarship, the organisation of universities promoting the principles of open scholarship in the academic community.

Her work covers market research and business modelling, project management and evaluation, research communication practices and behaviours, and the study and promotion of new forms of scholarly communication in the age of the Web. She writes and makes frequent presentations on scholarly communication issues.

She is an elected member of the Governing Board of Euroscience (the European Association for the Promotion of Science and Technology) and is the editor of its online magazine, *The Euroscientist*.

Melissa Terras is the Senior Lecturer in Electronic Communication in the Department of Information Studies, University College London, and the Deputy Director of the UCL Centre for Digital Humanities. With a background in Classical Art History and English Literature, and Computing Science, her doctorate (University of Oxford) examined how to use advanced information engineering technologies to interpret and read the Vindolanda texts. Publications include *Image to Interpretation: Intelligent Systems to Aid Historians in the Reading of the Vindolanda Texts* (Oxford University Press, 2006) and *Digital Images for the Information Professional* (Ashgate, 2008). She is a General Editor of *Digital Humanities Quarterly* (DHQ) and Secretary of the Association of Literary and Linguistic Computing. Her research focuses on the use of computational techniques to enable research in the arts and humanities that would otherwise be impossible.

Frank Trew is currently College Librarian at Rose Bruford College of Theatre and Performance and was previously University Librarian at Richmond: the American International University in London, where he worked for over 19 years. Both institutions have large cohorts of international student groups. At Richmond he founded the Information Literacy programme where every new student was required to complete a semester-long course in research skills and techniques, and is currently working on embedding information literacy into the curriculum at Rose Bruford. Frank has written previously on library induction and international students.

Liz Waller is Deputy Director of Library and Archives and Head of Strategic Planning at the University of York. She took up this post in 2009, having previously worked in a number of institutions. At Leeds Metropolitan University she led an initiative on information literacy which led to the adoption of an institutional information literacy policy. Later she ran a study skills website, created a face-to-face skills unit and became an institutional teacher fellow. She has previously contributed to the professional literature and conference circuit (including the HEA annual conference) on these topics. She now uses this expertise in teaching and learning to inform her interest in estates planning. At York she includes within her remit responsibility for strategic planning of estates, and is currently engaged with the refurbishment of the J.B. Morrell Library and the redevelopment of another large building to create an extended 21st-century library at York.

Liz went to York from the post of Head of Public Service Strategy at the University of Leeds, where she again had responsibility for estates planning, refurbishing the Health Sciences Library there in 2007 and 2008. Work on evaluating the redeveloped Health Sciences Library was the basis for a presentation The Library Chameleon: Changing Spaces for the 21st century at the International Conference on Information and Learning Commons: Enhancing its Role in Academic Learning and Collaboration held in Hong Kong in 2007. Liz has been a member of the SCONUL Working Group on Space Planning since 2009, and has contributed to briefings and seminars on learning spaces.

Claire Warwick is Director and founder of the UCL Centre for Digital Humanities, a Reader in Digital Humanities in the UCL Department of Information Studies and Vice Dean Research for the UCL Faculty of Arts and Humanities. Her research is on the use of digital resources in the humanities, especially electronic texts and digital libraries and on reading in physical and digital environments. She is a lead researcher of the Implementing New Knowledge Environments project (INKE), funded by the Canadian Social Sciences and Humanities Funding Council (SSHRC) which aims to produce new digital environments for reading and research in the humanities, and associate director of the JISC-funded LinkSphere project studying the use of social networking applications by humanities researchers. She serves on the advisory boards of several digital humanities research projects, including Synergies, an electronic publication infrastructure for Canadian Humanities and Social Sciences. She is a member of the UK AHRC Peer Review College and chaired its recent Digital Equipment and Database Enhancement for Impact (DEDEFI) funding panel.

Acknowledgements

The editors would like to acknowledge the help and support of colleagues across the higher education sector who have contributed to this book in various ways.

Special thanks are due to Roger Dale for proofreading, Louise Tucker for work on the formatting and the index, and to Kimberley Mills and Lee Anstey for help and advice with all sorts of technical questions.

Editors' Introduction

Penny Dale, Jill Beard and Matt Holland

When we commissioned the authors to write for our book we anticipated that these practitioners, operating at the forefront of their respective fields, would stimulate and provoke debate about academic libraries now and in the future. When we read the chapters as they were delivered we were not disappointed. We hope the reader will be struck by two seemingly disparate aspects of their content. On the one hand each chapter is highly individual, not only in style and content, but also in approach and reflection. On the other hand common themes emerge: notably the opportunity afforded by technology (especially mobile technology), the importance of training and development for library staff, and evaluation, as well as the interdependence of teaching and research and the role technology plays in bringing these even closer together. To focus these synergies and differences we decided to use word clouds to introduce each chapter. As we ran each chapter through *Wordle*[1] we saw themes and patterns emerging; we hope that readers of the book will find this a useful and stimulating contribution to each chapter and the book as a whole. A word cloud for the entire book has been created for the cover, demonstrating in a very graphic way the breadth and depth of the content.

The opening chapter by **Sue McKnight** describes the significant role that academic libraries have in creating, supporting and participating in digital learning environments, today and into the future. Throughout the book the contributing authors reflect from a wide range of viewpoints both where academic library services are today, and how they will deal with the challenges ahead to ensure that academic libraries remain a reality in the world of digital learning environments.

Sue highlights one of the central themes to emerge from this book, that of the pivotal role of staff working in our academic libraries. She identifies that the greatest challenge will be changing the mindsets of those staff and capitalising on the fact that academic librarians are blended professionals, with multi-faceted skills and responsibilities that transcend the physical and virtual library. As more and more learning becomes supported by blended and online modes of delivery, librarians have to move out of their traditional roles and engage not only in the virtual learning environment (VLE) and the post-VLE environment, but also the physical and virtual library. These skilled staff will develop new ways of working and new partnerships. The future will not recognise the silo of the academic library,

---

1 http://www.wordle.net/.

or an academic library and information technology converged service. The library's services, its staff and the resources that it manages and delivers will engage across the campus and be embedded into the curriculum and the administration of our universities.

Other contributors return to the theme of staff development throughout the book, notably Sheila Corrall in Chapters 4 and 15, and we have been heartened by the breadth and depth of the recognition of this important topic.

Peter Godwin gives his chapter a provocative title to focus on the phenomenon known as Web 2.0, now often referred to as social media. Peter gives a fascinating insight into the opportunities, and possible pitfalls, of Web 2.0 and leaves the reader to ponder what will happen when social media merge with mobile technology. The release of the Apple iPad in spring 2010, just as this book was being completed, is perhaps just a foretaste of what is to come with one device for accessing, communicating and creating content. As Peter points out, the increasing move to electronic publications has caused various voices to raise doubts over the need for physical library buildings in the future. Yet despite the move to e-resources, the higher education sector has continued to invest in its library buildings, understanding the continuing relevance of the physical library in the 21st century. The impact of mobile technologies as we move beyond the VLE and the effects of economic down-turns will undoubtedly cause further re-evaluation and debate. Liz Waller expands on this theme in Chapter 5.

Jacqui Weetman DaCosta provides both a comprehensive overview of information literacy in digital learning environments, and an exploration of the role of information literacy within digital environments. Some common definitions of 'digital literacy' are offered, along with a comparison to 'information literacy' and she discusses the digital library and its relationship to information literacy. The chapter reviews opportunities for information literacy development in academic libraries and the different ways in which these are practised in digital learning environments. Jacqui also considers staff development to enhance staff skills in information literacy and teaching. The chapter concludes with a review of recent digital initiatives and reports and the role that information literacy has (or has not) played in them.

In Chapter 4 **Sheila Corrall** discusses professional education, and the skills and knowledge needed to deliver successful library services in an increasingly digital world. She points out that professional education for library and information work is affected by numerous influences in the general global environment in addition to developments within our own education sector and in professional practice. She considers key drivers and themes including internationalisation, interdisciplinarity, technology and the economy. This chapter also describes contemporary trends in library education both in the UK and in the US.

To inform the discussion on physical space, **Liz Waller's** review uses four case studies at the Universities of Warwick, Edinburgh, Leicester and Nottingham Trent that in many ways summarise building and design trends in the United Kingdom during the first decade of the 21st century. Liz observes that what has become evident through these developments is a strategic response to specific institutional contexts. Institutions are not generic clones of each other; each institution learns from earlier examples and following customer consultation develops a space response to fit their own needs.

Liz concludes that evaluation of our learning spaces will be essential in ensuring that the spaces delivered within our libraries are contributing to the institutional mission, improving learning and research. In this area the JISC-funded Study of Effective Evaluation Models and Practices for Technology Supported Physical Learning Spaces project (JELS) sought to identify and review the tools, methods and frameworks used to evaluate technology supported or enhanced physical learning spaces. Liz makes the point that evaluation is an area in which the library sector will need to develop further in the immediate future; there is further detailed discussion of evaluation in Chapter 13 by Angela Conyers and Philip Payne.

Rachel Geeson's chapter blends the physical and virtual environments and looks at service delivery. Specifically she considers the issues involved with implementing and running a chat enquiry service, from choosing an appropriate product to staff training and publicity. The experiences of a number of UK Higher Education Institutions currently offering chat enquiry services are discussed at various stages. Aspects of more advanced use, such as web 'co-browsing' and virtual advice by appointment are also included. The chapter closes by considering what the future holds for virtual advice services and the potential impact of the growth in mobile technologies. The outcome of the proliferation of mobile technologies will surely be a step change in how we communicate with all our library users in the future.

The continuing role of the academic library supporting learning, teaching and research is by no means a foregone conclusion. This chapter by **Penny Dale** and **Jill Beard** looks at some examples from library history of services that have vanished because they have failed to respond to changes in user demands and expectations. It considers what the term 'reading for a degree' means in digital learning environments and looks at the partnerships needed to support students.

Reading lists have long been synonymous with printed books and journals. The authors take the experience at BU, where changes to the Copyright Licensing Agency rules have enabled book chapters and journal articles to be scanned and made available at unit level. This has enabled other enhancements to the blended learning environment to happen, for example the short loan collection to be replaced by more study spaces, and academic staff have been more involved with the possibilities of the digital library.

The next three chapters focus on research, and begin with a contribution by **Alma Swan** on institutional repositories (IRs). Alma points out that IRs are becoming essential tools for universities, to enhance the visibility and impact of their research on a national and international stage.

Alma identifies advantages for institutions in implementing IRs. If the whole research output is collected in the repository, then it becomes part of the university's management information system. Managers can see what is being produced, by whom, when, and where outputs are being formally published. Such analysis informs future planning activities and budget allocation decisions of research managers. In countries such as the UK, where there are national research assessment processes, repositories will provide a base layer of data to underpin research assessments.

There is a broader vision to explore as well. Repositories will form the data layer of the future – the layer where research articles, datasets and other digital items that support research will be located. This system will support the e-research (or e-science) agenda, facilitating the sharing of research data and their curation and preservation. New services will work on this data layer, aggregating, analysing and disseminating content, and providing researchers with the means to organise and display their own content in new ways.

Alma reflects on progress so far in technical, cultural and policy areas, discussing the barriers that have already been surmounted and those that threaten future progress.

Matt Holland and **Tim Denning** continue the research theme and consider the importance of IRs in support of research, focussing on three areas; how the IR fits with the university organisation; how to promote the use of the IR to end users and contributors; and how to secure long-term benefits for the broadest range of stakeholders. They incorporate two short case studies into the discussion, and include a description of the implementation of Bournemouth University Research Online (BURO).

Virtual research environments (VREs) are the subject of the next chapter by **Melissa Terras, Claire Warwick and Claire Ross**. Recent developments in online resources have led to the establishment of VREs: suites of applications, services, and resources which aim to enhance the research process by aiding scholars to carry out a range of complex research activities. The definition and concept of what constitutes a VRE continues to evolve, as developers attempt to create flexible and adaptable frameworks of resources to support both large- and small-scale research across a variety of disciplines. VREs are often integrated with digital library and virtual learning environments (VLEs), to allow users to analyse and manipulate existing digital research data.

To ensure the success of VREs, it is essential that developers liaise closely with the user community they are providing services for. This chapter discusses the potentials inherent in VRE technology, whilst addressing the relationship that such environments have to their users. A case study involving the JISC-funded Virtual Research Environment for Archaeology (VERA) project is presented to demonstrate that close integration with the relevant community is crucial if a VRE is to provide computational tools that reflect research practice. This chapter also stresses the necessity to include users into a systems design process, and highlights the opportunities that exist for librarians to become more involved in the creation, management, and curation of VREs and their related research data.

Moving from the space, students and research agenda in HE to supporting degree-level students in Further Education (FE), **Jane Russ** reminds us that the concept of studying a Higher Education programme at a Further Education Institution (FEI) in the UK is not new. In partnership with Higher Education Institutions (HEIs), FEIs have been delivering Foundation Degrees, the most recent manifestation of HE in FE, for nearly ten years. Many colleges are now delivering top-up programmes for their Foundation Degrees with considerable success. At Kingston Maurward College, for example, it is now possible in some disciplines for students to start college on a day release or a diploma programme at 14 and continue to study at the college until they graduate with a BSc Honours Degree. Many of these Foundation Degree and Honours graduates go on to find highly specialised professional careers or move on elsewhere to undertake postgraduate studies.

In the early days of Foundation Degrees, there was much discussion about the practicalities of delivery, such as ensuring access to resources, and the more esoteric aspects of delivery, such as the student perception of identity with the partner HEI. Libraries and Learning Resources Centres have always played a key role in these discussions.

This chapter reviews briefly how many of the initial concerns relating to delivering resources in the HE and FE environment have been tackled and, for the most part, overcome. It goes on to explore the opportunities and challenges faced by the emerging use of virtual learning environments.

International students are increasingly important to HE, and **Frank Trew** looks at the support offered to international students by library services at UK academic institutions, with some mention of services at US and Australian universities as points of comparison. He describes a range of projects and support services, and asks 'What are we doing for international students?' During the course of the research for this chapter Frank found himself confronted by the question 'Why are we doing it?' and writes about this experience, and his changing thoughts on an answer to that question.

The book returns to one of the themes identified in the opening chapter and referred to by several other contributors, that of evaluation and performance measurement. **Angela Conyers** and **Philip Payne** agree that libraries and their services to support learning and teaching are being transformed as dependence increases on electronic resources. They observe that previous perspectives on library quality are being challenged in the search for new measures of use and performance. The rapid transition for libraries in the digital world calls for a stronger evidence base to inform change management.

As we invest increasing sums in e-services and digital infrastructure, we need to know that this represents value for money. This chapter considers such questions as: How can we show that our services are cost-effective? What e-measures exist and how can we use them to evaluate the library's performance? How do e-measures differ from traditional input and output measures for libraries? The student experience, and the student perspective, are increasingly important to our institutions. In a student-centred environment, it is not just about finding out whether students are happy with our services (although this is important). It is increasingly a matter of how we can involve students and staff in the design and development of services and gather their perspectives on what we are doing.

Measurement of cost-effectiveness and satisfaction are valuable to us in managing our libraries. However, there is an increasing pressure for libraries to demonstrate their impact. Angela and Philip ask what approaches and methods can be adopted to help us show that our performance in the digital age makes a direct contribution to learning and teaching.

The possibilities of the digital future require new models for procurement, innovation and exploitation. **Emma Crowley** and **Chris Spencer** describe the skills staff need to deliver resources in hybrid and digital environments. The chapter demonstrates the innovative ways that librarians use to procure and exploit the wealth of resources available in a digital world. They also describe the technological developments that can be adopted to improve workflow processes and they highlight the challenges faced on this fascinating journey.

We end with two chapters that look to the future. Staff development has been a recurrent theme of this book and in her second chapter **Sheila Corrall** discusses continuing professional development (CPD) and workplace learning in electronic environments. She points out that CPD has become even more important than before in the changing digital environment as shown by the introduction by professional bodies of formal schemes for recording progress. Information schools are offering both open programmes and bespoke courses to meet needs for updating and training in new specialties, and employers and practitioners are using a variety of methods to meet their ongoing educational and development needs. Work-based learning, leadership development programmes and on-the-job learning in the workplace are now recognised as convenient, cost-effective and flexible methods that can be offered to staff at all levels.

Mentoring schemes, reflective writing and portfolio building have also become more common as their value has been demonstrated through formal incorporation into professional qualifications and active promotion through supporting workshops. Several of our contributors have identified the vital role that staff training and development has in the digital future, and this chapter shows the reader some excellent examples of what is being done, giving some pointers for provision needs in the near future.

Finally **David Ball** quotes from Karl Marx to challenge views about the third ICT revolution. He signposts that we are on the threshold of the third, electronic ICT revolution and that its effects will be as fundamental as those of the previous revolution – the invention of printing.

The links in the information value chain are discussed – creation, publication, aggregation, access and use – with a particular focus on the differences between print and electronic formats for scholarly communication. There follows an analysis of the costs of scholarly communication through journals and monographs, and of the trends in pricing and negotiation, particularly the effect of the big deal. It is noted that the largest cost is in the time of users of information, not in subscriptions: savings here could far outweigh any potential savings through big deals.

David points out that the electronic age has the potential to turn academic library practice on its head: a library will collect all the research outputs of its own scholars, and make them available to the wider academic community, instead of collecting, storing and disseminating the research outputs of other universities. He highlights a number of measures to facilitate change, particularly in terms of repositories and open access journals.

In our opening remarks we anticipated that the practitioners we had asked to contribute to our book would stimulate and provoke debate about academic libraries now and in the future. We hope the result presents the reader with an exciting journey through the development of the digital learning environments in academic libraries, and a clearer vision of the immediate future. Along this journey we hope readers will find many points of reflection and debate to inform their practice now and into the future.

Chapter 1
Here Today and Here Tomorrow

Sue McKnight

Introduction

This book describes the significant role that academic libraries have in creating and supporting digital learning environments, and participating in them today and into the future. This chapter will outline the evolution of the academic library over time, demonstrating the resilience and adaptability of library services and library management.

Many previous authors have focussed on what the future might look like, offering glimpses of possibilities envisaged given the knowledge and experience at a particular time. Looking to the future is a positive process, as creating a vision of what might be possible helps to define the steps that can be taken to turn aspirations into reality. Even if the prophecies are not always accurate, establishing a goal to head towards ensures that the library service will be moving in the desired direction. Imagining a utopia of excellent services to support learners, teachers and researchers will encourage those coming behind to make the envisaged services a reality. For example, Bush (1945) wrote about the Memex, a technology that would be used to access, organise and contribute to the store of human knowledge, which anticipated the development of Web 2.0 type collaborative and joined up information services at least 60 years before its time.

The other chapters of this book provide insights into specialist areas of academic library practice, focusing on digital services and resources. Therefore, the observations in this introductory chapter focus more on where academic libraries are today, in a general sense, and where academic library services may go in the future, and the challenges ahead for academic librarianship in making the future a reality.

The future will be built upon a solid base. 'The library is the heart of the university', attributed to Charles William Eliot who was President of Harvard University from 1869–1909, is an often-heard phrase and, until recently, it was an earnestly held belief by many in academic libraries and universities generally. It even appears on library buildings, such as at Sterling Memorial Library at Yale. However, as Lorcan Dempsey (2008) posted in his blog, this assertion is beginning to be challenged from a variety of fronts.

The debate as to whether libraries are at the heart of their university can be unsettling for academic librarians. Because of the move to digital information and online services, it is argued by some that the library can no longer be the heart of a university, because many of its most valued services and resources are now located in a virtual library environment. This perception presumes that the heart has to be a physical manifestation and downplays the very important responsibility of the library in actually making the virtual library an easy-to-use space, complementing the physical spaces already occupied. The academic library can be a physical and virtual heart of a campus.

As a great deal of the existing and future services and resources of academic libraries belong in a virtual environment, then our brand associated with an iconic building at the heart of the campus is no longer as relevant. Today, there is much discussion on future learning spaces, and a great deal of this discussion revolves around re-conceptualising the lecture theatre or tutorial room, rather than embracing the substantial role that can and is being played by the library in a world where students learn in a social networked environment. Over the past decade, there have been great advances in establishing physical libraries as a location of choice for students who undertake group assignments, online learning and 'traditional' library study, through the establishment of learning commons, such as at the University of Guelph[1] and the University of University of Massachusetts Amherst[2], learning grids such as at the University of Warwick[3], and learning hubs (for example the one under development in early 2010 at the University of Adelaide). While we can still remain the heart of the university, our challenge will be to take information and knowledge services to an entirely different place, not constructed on the concept of a library per se, but taking the wealth of information, data and knowledge accumulated in academic libraries and enabling it to be accessed, consumed and remixed in the personal places of tomorrow's scholars, teachers and researchers.

However, perhaps the greatest challenge will be changing the mindsets of staff in academic libraries and capitalising on the fact that academic librarians are blended professionals, with multi-faceted skills and responsibilities that transcend the physical and virtual library. As more and more learning becomes supported by

---

1   http://www.learningcommons.uoguelph.ca/.
2   http://www.umass.edu/learningcommons/.
3   http://www2.warwick.ac.uk/services/library/grid.

blended and online modes of delivery, the library and the librarians have to move out of their silos and engage in the virtual learning environment, as well as the physical and virtual library. These skilled staff will develop new ways of working and new partnerships.

The future will not recognise the silo of the academic library, or even an academic library and information technology converged service. The library's services, its staff and the resources that it manages and delivers will engage across the campus and be embedded into the curriculum and the administration of our universities.

Evolution (and Revolution) of Academic Libraries

Academic libraries have moved a long way from the early beginnings at institutions like Oxford University in the 1400s. The contents of libraries have diversified from hand crafted parchments and illuminated manuscripts, through a revolution brought about by the invention of the printing press and movable type, which resulted in the mass production of printed books. Today, academic libraries collect books, pamphlets, newspapers, journals, indexing and abstracting resources, multi-media resources (film, audio, image) on a range of technological platforms (tapes, compact discs, digital video discs, microforms etc). The libraries seek to preserve and maintain collections of the past, while embracing the multiplicity of formats that information is published in today, with an increasing emphasis on creating digital versions of collections already held.

The management of information resources has also seen a vast amount of change over the years, moving from limiting access by chaining books and gating stack areas to keep people away from the collections, to book catalogues, card catalogues, and today's online public access catalogues to help academic library customers to find the resources available.

The advent of affordable computers, personal computers for individual use and the development of the Internet have transformed the ways libraries operate (Billings 2003). Today, there are discovery aids such as federated search engines enabling access to a multiplicity of data sources, both local and remote. Even more technologically advanced is the capacity for a scholar to embed library-supplied catalogue search widgets in their preferred digital space, such as Facebook and MySpace, so that searching the library's catalogue does not have to be done from the library's home page, but from their personalised portal. So, rather than restricting access to a library's physical and digital collections, academic libraries are providing the tools for individuals to find useful information regardless of where it is held. With the development of the new generation of search engines, academic libraries can make available resources that are not normally associated with academic libraries, such as organisational data, in-house web pages, and primary research data.

Not only has the content of our academic libraries changed over time, access to information resources has been transformed. Today's students and academic staff want easy access to information resources, and this is fulfilled through extended opening hours, 24/7 access to digital resources from anywhere with an internet connection, self-service loans and book returns, virtual reference desks and real-time chat to a librarian, as well as through physical access to print and multi-media resources. In addition, academic libraries facilitate access to the myriad of digital resources by providing vast numbers of networked PCs and by providing wireless networking and power sockets in libraries so that visitors can use their own laptops. Whereas many libraries today lend laptops for in-library use, in the future, portable digital book readers will be available for loan. Greater emphasis is being placed on rendering library digital content, including web pages providing access to online services, to formats that can be used by mobile devices, such as smart phones and personal digital assistants. Easy access to information will, most likely in the future, also make use of geo-spatial tags so that an item in the catalogue can be located in the library through the wonders of global positioning systems.

The type of scholars accessing academic libraries has also changed significantly over time. Where once there was little diversity in the students or mode of study (male students and face-to-face learning), today we have a broad range of learners: male and female students; school leavers and mature students; international and local students; on-campus and distance students; full-time and part-time students; students with disabilities; students sitting for foundation degrees, undergraduate degrees, post-graduate taught and research degrees; students studying for continuing professional development and academic curiosity; and the list could go on. Today academic libraries are serving students and staff who have vastly different experiences of and skills in working with digital technologies. Sweeney (2005, p. 165) emphasises the impact of digital natives on libraries:

> … They make up the demographic tsunami that will permanently and irreversibly change the library and information landscape.

However, it would be wrong to focus on this demographic (those born from 1982 onwards), as we all have expectations of the web and what it will offer us.

> While we frame digital natives as a generation 'born digital,' not all youth are digital natives. Digital natives share a common global culture that is defined not by age, strictly, but by certain attributes and experiences in part defined by their experience growing up immersed in digital technology, and the impact of this upon how they interact with information technologies, information itself, one another, and other people and institutions. Those who were not "born digital" can be just as connected, if not more so, than their younger counterparts. (Digital Natives, n.d.)

This diversity, which will only increase in the near future, adds a complexity to the way academic libraries deliver services and resources, especially in areas of academic literacy, which will be discussed elsewhere in this chapter and in detail in a later chapter.

Emerging Digital Technologies and Academic Library Futures

There can be a sense of déjà vu reading some accounts of the more recent history of academic libraries and the projections for the future. For instance, Holley (1999), looking back on 25 years of academic librarianship in the United States of America, wrote of the challenges of trying to keep up with the output of scholars and spiralling costs of serials, and the financial challenges faced by libraries in 1976 when there were pay freezes and staff cuts, which are realities being faced by academic libraries in the United Kingdom and elsewhere in 2010.

Lyman (1991) wrote of a system of scholarly communication in crisis and the emergence of the digital library. These two themes appear to have a long tail. People are still speaking of the crisis in scholarly communication. And the digital library is still be become a reality in many developing economies (Harle 2009).

Dougherty and Hughes (1991; 1993) reported on the outputs of a series of workshops with academic library directors that were aimed at identifying preferred library futures. There was a view that there would be a scholars' workstation that would deliver a myriad of information to the desktop, but the leaders at that time were unsure how this was going to be achieved, except through an understanding that leadership would be a key enabler. They recognised the need for innovation in the development of demonstration projects, and the need for 'long-term, strategic reallocation of resources if the vision of the future is to be more than a mirage' (Dougherty and Hughes 1993, p. 1). Again, these themes are as relevant today as they were almost 20 years ago: leadership, innovation and reallocation of resources towards new services.

Hawkins (1994) recognised the potential wonders of an electronic, information-rich environment, and the realisation of the dream seemed imminent with the advent of the 'information superhighway', a term today that seems almost quaint. Hawkins envisaged the electronic library supporting distance learning and life-long learning: 'a library is not a place and is about much more than books' (Hawkins 1994, p. 27).

He correctly emphasised the need to define technical standards, and to develop tools to organise and search massive amounts of information. Developments of the semantic web, enterprise search engines, data mining of research, standards for open educational resources etc. have occurred since Hawkins' article.

Hawkins also envisaged the library portal:

> The library of the future will be less a place where information is kept than a portal through which students and faculty will access the vast information resources of the world. (Hawkins 1994, p. 46)

Lombardi (2000) wrote a challenging article highlighting that, regardless of the fact that digital library portals are available,

> ... Students have little patience with the formal organizational structure of the library and the authority of the librarian.

Ten years later, academic libraries are still developing and maintaining portals, and the very real challenge still being faced is that of developing the academic literacy skills of learners, so that they should not rely solely on the search services of Google and Wikipedia and the like.

A seminal work on the future of academic librarianship was edited by Lancaster (1993), which collected essays on the library of the 21st century. One paper, in particular, resonated with the situation today, in that it advocated a focus more on the services delivered and not on the assets controlled (Penniman 1993). With the reality of the digital library, academic librarians are able to concentrate on what is required for supporting research and teaching regardless of where the information is held.

The 1990s was a decade of huge developments in digital technologies and digital information resources. However, not everyone saw the advent of these as a panacea. Crawford and Gorman (1995) cautioned that there was no real need to go 'all digital' and to avoid 'technolust' in favour of technology as a tool that may be able to perform functions more efficiently. Going 'all digital' seems to be a trend today, with growing numbers of libraries moving from print to digital information resources if these are available. The use of technology as an efficiency tool has been embraced for a range of library services: from backroom processes in acquisitions and cataloguing to front line services such as self-service borrowing and renewals.

Another dissenting voice was that of Mann (2001, p. 268) who claimed 'Although libraries must continue to provide electronic resources, the distinctive strength of research libraries lies mainly in their ability to provide free access to preservable book collections that facilitate understanding of lengthy textual works that cannot be tapped into from anywhere, at any time, by anyone'. The Google initiative to scan both out-of-copyright and copyright works to create an international library of digital books certainly challenges this assertion. The *Google Book Settlement* is still not settled so how large and what impact this mass digitisation of print-based collections will have is yet to be seen. But tomorrow's academic libraries must focus on the value-adding that can be delivered by the librarians and the contextual knowledge they have of their organisation's teaching and research profile, rather than on what information they control.

New Partnerships – A New Future

None have gone so far as to predict the death of the academic library, although there are conflicting predictions, such as an exchange reported in *Inside Higher Ed* (2009) in an article on libraries of the future:

> Daniel Greenstein, vice provost for academic planning and programs, University of California System was quoted as saying 'the university library of the future will be sparsely staffed, highly decentralised, and have a physical plant consisting of little more than special collections and study areas.' ... Deborah Jakubs, vice provost for library affairs at Duke University countered 'I see the exact opposite happening, that libraries are taking on new roles [such as] working with faculty in introducing technology into teaching... there's a lot more intersection with libraries and faculty than he would lead you to believe'.

The above exchange highlights the dichotomy between those who see the library as the physical entity, as opposed to those who see the benefits of partnerships required to maximise services and resources. Clearly, digital technologies have changed the way academic libraries do and can operate.

Foo et al. (2002) emphasise the importance of new partnerships and new endeavours in addressing the opportunities offered by a future in which digital technologies are dominant. They speak, in passing, of the convergence of libraries and information technology departments as a way of the future. Certainly, many libraries and IT departments have converged. And today, some are de-converging, such as at the University of Melbourne in Australia and the University of Birmingham in the United Kingdom. There is a risk in assuming that because IT underpins the digital services that are offered in today's academic libraries, it is necessary to work in a single organisational unit. Today, almost all functions of a university are supported by technology, not just the library's services.

Libraries are about information, data and knowledge and the services that underpin these, whether located physically, virtually, onsite or somewhere else in the world. There may have been an argument that librarians were not trained to manage hardware and software as effectively as the IT experts. However, with the advent of 'software as a service' and cloud computing, libraries can benefit from applications and services that are not hosted locally, thus removing the need to be database and system administrators etc. There are a growing number of externally hosted library services, for example Ex Libris' PRIMO Direct and the Talis Aspire resource list service that are managed in the cloud. The majority of e-books and digital full-text journals are remotely managed. So, why would we join with the IT department? Perhaps for some organisational efficiencies and to instill an ethos of customer service that is often seen as lacking, with the library staff translating the needs of end users for their technical colleagues.

The new partnerships are unlikely to be with the IT professionals, but with the academics, student support professionals, educational developers and e-learning technologists who are creating and working in online learning spaces. McKnight (2010) describes the concept of an academic services hub, bringing together colleagues who can transform students' learning experiences:

> Imagine tutors who deal with remedial support (e.g. maths support; academic writing support; English language support) working with liaison librarians who gather appropriate resources to support the remedial work that might be required and also the reading list resources for a course. The librarians would also provide just-in-time online tutorials in using the resources. This coalition of professionals then work with an academic team to incorporate testing of a student's ability to cope with the concepts required of the unit of study so that if early intervention is required, it is quickly identified and students guided to the support. Then add the educational developers to the mix to help design the VLE learning room that incorporates all these value adding features from the start of a student's enrolment in that course. Finally, add input from the team responsible for supporting students with special needs (e.g. dyslexia, visual or manual impairments) who can advise on the overall accessibility of the learning room (design, online resources, online tutorials, assessment practices, etc). (McKnight 2010, pp. 177–8)

This assertion of new partnerships is also supported by Bangert (2009) who said:

> Future academic libraries will blend traditional professional practice with an increased external response to the larger institution and community.

The future will be multidimensional and complex, and take place in both physical and virtual spaces. Lowry et al. (2009) also point to new partnerships and collaborations, predicting an increasingly diverse and talented library staff, with new leadership and technical skills, and new relationships with library customers.

Toby Bainton, Secretary of the Society of College, National and University Libraries (SCONUL) said 'the digital revolution in the late 1990s transformed – and is still transforming – everything' (Tickle 2009). Bainton's emphasis also focussed on the complexity of the digital landscape, and on some of the technical skills, such as negotiating and legal expertise, required of today's academic librarians.

Another theme that is prevalent in the literature of digital libraries and academic librarianship into the future is the need for an increased level of competency in teaching information literacy skills. As the complexity of information in libraries developed, so too did the notion of bibliographic instruction, which became information literacy and, today, more focussed on academic literacy. While this is not a new development in academic libraries, there is a greater urgency to make sure that students have these skills so that they are aware of the potential for useless and misleading information on the web (Foo et al. 2002).

Academic librarians need skills in developing and delivering online information literacy skills tutorials, in particular, as more and more student learning is done in virtual learning environments, such as Desire2Learn, Moodle and Blackboard. Embedding these tutorials into the curriculum, so that the skills development is placed in the context of a discipline specific assignment, requires two important factors. Firstly, there needs to be an acknowledgement that information literacy skills have to be considered as a formal part of the curriculum, not an optional add-on but a mandatory requirement for credit within the course. Secondly, librarians need to demonstrate appropriate skills as teachers in order to design activities that achieve stated learning outcomes, and the ability to evaluate and provide constructive feedback to students.

Traditional library and information science education does not cover these skills. Academic librarians need to commit to securing additional qualifications, for example teaching qualifications, so as to be confident in taking on these additional responsibilities. In my own institution, librarians are facilitated to undertake post-graduate teaching qualifications. Not only are the librarians providing training in traditional information literacy skills (using the catalogue, federated search software, and bibliographic management tools, as well as evaluating the quality of the information discovered), they are also training and supporting academic staff by teaching them to use the virtual learning environment's learning object repository, the ePortfolio tool, and in using plagiarism detection tools. This is as well as supporting them with advice on open access publishing options, and on accessibility issues for supporting students with disabilities. In addition, the library has assumed responsibility for making sure that students (and academic staff) can use the basic digital technologies (operating a personal computer; using word processing and presentation applications; navigating through the virtual learning environment; storing, managing and retrieving files, etc.) at a competent level.

New technical competencies will be required to maximise the potential of managing, sharing and re-purposing digital research data. Expertise in data mining, data analysis and digital curation are new skills for the academic library professional. In addition, as the digital environment becomes even more complex, discipline-specific skills and research skills in general will be valued in the academic library. The librarian of the future will be a multi-skilled professional, utilising the traditional skills of librarianship with new media, and delivering new services because of the wealth of digital information at their fingertips.

Bainton, as already mentioned, highlighted the legal complexities of the digital environment (Tickle 2009). As academic libraries become more engaged in managing learning assets (lectures, lecture materials, learning objects etc.), the need to understand and be able to advise on and manage intellectual property rights, copyright, performance rights and moral rights will become vital skills for librarians.

Leadership

Many authors have highlighted the need for strong and visionary leadership to steer the future of academic librarianship in the digital age. Libraries, learning centres or whatever they are called, will be staffed by multi-functional and multi-skilled professional teams, so the leaders will have to be able to create a vision for a new future in this ever increasingly complex environment.

Skills in negotiating the new partnerships and collaborations will be required, in what Blackwell and Kandiko (2009) describe as leadership across new boundaries. To leverage greatest value from the knowledge assets they manage, academic library leaders will have to be competent in working across disciplines and organisational silos. This does not mean that there has to be convergence of services, but an acknowledgement that library leaders have to influence beyond their own organisations. Influencing and persuading are more difficult than managing.

As was ever true, library leadership must not make assumptions about service developments, as Sapp and Gilmour (2003) highlight:

> for planning purposes, it is necessary to ask what are the users' needs and how are they changing.

Assumptions are made about customer expectations, and these are not always correct (McKnight 2009a). This was also highlighted by the recent report commissioned by the British Library on digital skills and research methods which overturns the common assumption that the 'Google Generation'– youngsters born or brought up in the Internet age – is the most web-literate (CIBER 2008). Leaders and managers must actively engage in a dialogue with academic library customers so that decisions regarding resourcing and services can be made on accurate information about service excellence from the viewpoint of the customer. Library management-developed survey instruments, such as LibQUAL, have a place, but must not be relied upon to yield valuable information about the changing expectations (and capabilities) of the academic community.

Perhaps the biggest challenge for leading libraries into the future is about re-positioning the library staff to think beyond acquiring, managing and making accessible information resources. The future is taking data, information, and knowledge and making it meaningful in a variety of contexts, whether it is in a discipline-specific learning room in a virtual learning environment, in a researcher's portal, or an administrator's desktop. It is about taking the stuff to where it is needed and likely to be used by individuals in the digital spaces that they choose to work in, rather than having it 'in the library', whatever that means in a digital world.

Strength of Association

Academic libraries across the globe are supported by a great deal of research undertaken by professional associations to help libraries prepare for the increasingly complex information environment. Just a few of the many research exercises, reports and services offered are listed here as an indication of what is available.

In the United Kingdom, SCONUL established a Task and Finish Group on Learning and Teaching to identify the 'value add' that academic libraries provide students and their parents, academic staff, employers, the library community, government and sector agencies, the broader library and professional communities, as well as the parent institution. This group presented at the 2009 SCONUL Conference, using the context of the student journey to highlight the value-adding provided by academic libraries from before a learner starts at university to when they have graduated and beyond (McKnight 2009b).

The evidence, and the gaps in evidence, identified by the SCONUL Learning and Teaching Task and Finish Group, has been forwarded to the 'Academic Libraries of the Future' project. The project partners are the British Library, the Joint Information Systems Committee (JISC), Research Information Network (RIN), Research Libraries UK (RLUK) and SCONUL. 'Academic libraries of the future' is an 18-month project being undertaken by Curtis+Cartwright Consulting Ltd, a technology and management consultancy that helps public sector organisations make best use of current and emerging technologies. The project aims to explore future scenarios for academic libraries and information services, particularly in the context of a rapidly-changing technological environment. It will help higher education institutions and organisations look at the challenges faced from a fresh focus and formulate strategies to ensure the sector continues to be a leading global force.

Our colleagues in North America provide a wealth of thoughtful, and often thought provoking, information on the environment today and where it is heading in the future. The Association of College and Research Libraries (ACRL) in the USA published the *ACRL 2009 Strategic Thinking Guide for Academic Librarians in the New Economy* that listed 'technology' as one of the future drivers: cloud computing, signalling a move away from locally supported services and towards open source, with growing concerns regarding security; mobile and 'smart' devices for delivering learning content; distributed and diffused content and opportunities to create and share content (Web 2.0 tools and social networking); growth in blended and e-learning; the evolution of institutional repositories beyond pre- and post-print article dissemination to include a wide range of content types, clients and service needs; and the identification that vendors of web-based products for libraries are beginning to market these directly to students (Deiss and Petrowski 2009, pp. 7–8). All of these and the latter, in particular, require leaders to contemplate what these developments mean for their library services and resourcing decisions.

The Association of Research Libraries publishes a regular environmental scan to assist with strategic planning, with the leading theme in the 2009 report being that 'libraries need to change their practices for managing traditional content and develop new capabilities for dealing with digital materials, but especially new forms of scholarship, teaching and learning resources, special collections (particularly hidden collections), and research data' (Lowry et al. 2009).

Research Data: Unseen Opportunities is a recently published awareness toolkit commissioned by the Canadian Association of Research Libraries (Shearer 2009) that makes it clear that academic libraries have to provide stewardship in research data management and the associated policy and infrastructure challenges associated with this important area of new endeavour.

Conclusion

Academic libraries are here today, and academic libraries will be here tomorrow. They have survived many changes over the centuries and, in the majority of cases, prospered in the new eras each significant change brings. Since the 1990s, digital libraries have provided great opportunities as well as a suite of challenges, and academic libraries have demonstrated that they are up to the task.

This chapter has demonstrated the capacity of libraries, and the librarians that work in them, to adapt and capitalise on the changes that technologies have offered. Others in this book will elaborate on, amongst many things, social networking tools, research data management, libraries as publishers, working in virtual learning environments, and the challenge of educating learners and teachers about the myriad of information resources and services that are available.

However, it will be important for academic library leaders, and the staff who work with them, to scan the horizon well beyond the library and even the institution that it serves. There will be opportunities (and threats) coming from publishers, system vendors, entertainment providers and broadcasters, to name a few. The financial crisis gripping the world at this time will also help to focus minds on envisaging new ways of working, and with new partners, as we grapple with doing more with less resources.

It feels, though, with the rapidly changing technological environment and the increasing expectations of stakeholders and customers of academic libraries, that we are on the cusp of the next significant event in the evolution of academic libraries. The challenge and opportunity lies in moving our resources and services and know-how beyond the physical and digital library to the spaces where our customers want to work and study and socialise.

References

Bangert, S.R., 2009. *Thinking Boldly! College and University Library Mission Statements as Roadsigns to the Future*, Chicago: American Library Association. Available from: http://www.ala.org/ala/mgrps/divs/acrl/publications/whitepapers/nashville/bangert.cfm (accessed 1 February 2010).

Billings, H., 2003. *The Wild-card Academic Library in 2013*, College and Research Libraries, March, 105–109.

Blackwell, P. and Kandiko, C., 2009. *Leadership Across Boundaries*, Engage, Autumn, 10–11.

Bush, V., 1945. As we may think, *The Atlantic Monthly* 176(1), 101–108.

CIBER, 2008, *Information Behaviour of the Researcher of the Future*, University College, London. Available from: http://www.bl.uk/news/pdf/googlegen.pdf (accessed 1 February 2010).

Crawford, W. and Gorman, M., 1995. *Future Libraries: Dreams, Madness and Reality*, Chicago: American Library Association.

Deiss, K. and Petrowski, M.J., 2009. *ACRL 2009 Strategic Thinking Guide for Academic Librarians in the New Economy*. Association of College and Research Libraries. Available from: http://www.ftrf.org/ala/mgrps/divs/acrl/issues/value/acrlguide09.pdf (accessed 1 February 2010).

Dempsey, L., 2008. *The Heart of the University*, Lorcan Dempsey's Weblog, posted 13 May. Available from: http://orweblog.oclc.org/archives/001636.html (accessed 17 January 2010).

Digital Natives. (no date) *Are All Youths Digital Natives?* Available from: http://www.digitalnative.org/#about (accessed 28 January 2010).

Dougherty, R. and Hughes, C., 1991. *Preferred Futures for Libraries: A Summary of Six Workshops with University Provosts and Library Directors*, Mountain View, CA: Research Libraries Group.

Dougherty, R. and Hughes, C., 1993. *Preferred Library Futures II: Charting the Paths*, Mountain View, CA: Research Libraries Group.

Foo, S., Chaudhry, A.S., Majid, S.M. and Logan, E., 2002. *Academic Libraries in Transition – Challenges Ahead*, Proceedings of the World Library Summit, Academic Library Seminar, National Library Board, Singapore, 22–26 April. Available from: http://www3.ntu.edu.sg/home/assfoo/publications/2002/02wls_fmt.pdf (accessed 28 January 2010).

Harle, J., 2009. *Unlocking the Potential: New Opportunities for Commonwealth Libraries*, London: Association of Commonwealth Universities.

Hawkins, B.L., 1994. Creating the library of the future: Incrementalism won't get us there! *Serials Librarian*, 24 (3/4),17–47.

Holley, E.G., 1999. Academic libraries over twenty-five years, *Journal of Academic Librarianship*, 25 (2), 79–81.

Inside Higher Ed, 2009. *Libraries of the Future*, Available from: http://www.insidehighered.com/layout/set/print/news/2009/09/24/libraries (accessed 17 January 2010).

Lancaster, F.W., ed. 1993. *Libraries and the Future: Essays on the Library in the Twenty-first Century*, Binghamton, NY: Haworth Press.

Lombardi, J.V., 2000. Academic libraries in a digital age, *D-Lib Magazine*, 6 (10), 1–11. Available from: http://dlib/october00/lombardi/10lombardi.html (accessed 17 January 2010).

Lowry, C.B., Adler, P. Hahn, K., Stuart, C., 2009. *Transformational Times: An Environmental Scan Prepared for the ARL Strategic Plan Review Task Force, Association of Research Libraries, Washington*. Available from: www.arl.org/bm~doc/transformational-times.pdf (accessed 17 January 2010).

Lyman, P., 1991. The library of the (not-so-distant) future, *Change*, 23 (1), 34–44.

McKnight, S., 2009a. Bridging the gap between service provision and customer expectation, *Performance Measurement and Metrics*, 10 (2), 79–93.

McKnight, S., 2009b. *Backing the Winners: Libraries Adding Value*, Presentation to the SCONUL 2009 Annual Conference, Bournemouth. Available from: http://www.sconul.ac.uk/events/agm2009/presentations/McKnight.ppt (accessed 1 February 2010).

McKnight, S., 2010. Adding value to learning and teaching. In McKnight, S. ed. *Envisioning Future Academic Library Services: Initiatives, Ideas and Challenges*, London: Facet Publishing, 174–87.

Mann, T., 2001. The importance of books, free access, and libraries as places – and the dangerous inadequacy of the information science paradigm, *Journal of Academic Librarianship*, 27 (4), 268–81.

Penniman, W.D., 1993. Shaping the future for libraries through leadership and research. In Lancaster, F.W. ed. *Libraries and the Future: Essays on the Library in the Twenty-first Century*, Binghamton, NY: Haworth Press, 5–16.

Sapp, G. and Gilmour, R., 2003. A brief history of the future of academic libraries: predictions and speculations from the literature of the profession, 1975–2000 – part two, 1990 to 2000, portal: *Libraries and the Academy*, 3 (1), 13–34.

Shearer, K., 2009. *Research Data: Unseen Opportunities*, CARL, Ottawa, Available from: http://www.carl-abrc.ca/about/working_groups/pdf/data_mgt_toolkit.pdf (accessed 1 February 2010).

Sweeney, R.T., 2005. Reinventing library buildings and services for the millennial generation, *Library Administration and Management*, 19 (4),165–75.

Tickle, L., 2009. *Academic Libraries are Undergoing a Quiet Revolution, Guardian*. Available from: http://www.guardian.co.uk/education/2009/aug/18/university-librarians-recruitment/ (accessed 1 February 2010).

Chapter 2

It's All About Social Media, Stupid!

Peter Godwin

Introduction

The election campaign of Barack Obama marked a watershed in how to influence and motivate people. The UK election campaign in spring 2010 saw both major parties clamouring to harness the new media in January as the poll battle began (Helm 2010). Social media are here to stay in politics, business and also, I believe, in libraries. But what are social media and do they represent the golden key? Is it all hype? I shall examine how Web 2.0 has evolved into social media and what this has meant for academic libraries. I shall chart the huge growth in interest from librarians both for their own modes of working and their outreach to users in promotion, marketing, communication, and service delivery. However I shall conclude that while social media represent an opportunity that libraries ignore at their peril, they are still additional to existing modes of promotion and delivery. They are still young and evolving tools. As they mature it is reasonable to ask how their success can be measured, so an important part of this chapter has been devoted to begin a discussion of social media metrics. The literature is not yet adequate to make evidence-based decisions (Boxen 2008). Librarians not only need surveys which tell us how many libraries are using social media, but exactly what kind of benefits these are bringing.

From Web 2.0 to Social Media

When Tim O'Reilly coined the term 'Web 2.0' to describe what he considered to be a second generation Web, he could not have predicted the arguments about what it actually was, or the revolution that has occurred. I believe it represented a new manifestation of the web allowing users to create, exchange and share information, by using a changing collection of freely available tools with the Web as their platform. The term 'Library 2.0' derives from Mike Casey's LibraryCrunch blog[1] in 2005 and has become synonymous with Web 2.0 services in academic libraries (McManus 2009). This is the same approach I adopted in discussing Library 2.0 and Information Literacy (Godwin and Parker 2008). The recent *Guide to Using Web 2.0*[2] from the Chartered Institute of Library and Information Professionals (CILIP) in Libraries says that Web 2.0 reflects 'changes in how we use the web rather than describing any technical or structural change'. Many Web services (social networking, video and photo sharing, blogging, microblogging, social bookmarking, wikis and resource organising) are now referred to as social media, because of their ability to assist communication and create online communities.

The Climate has Changed

Web 2.0 has often been used by online advertising, e-commerce and other online business activities, but has not been engaged so enthusiastically by librarians (Maness 2006). The climate has changed from just early adopters and Web 2.0 concepts have become mainstream. Surveys are beginning to record more interest. Linh (2008) shows that 32 out of 47 Australasian university libraries employ at least one Web 2.0 technology, and the most used technologies were RSS, blogs, instant messaging (IM) and podcasts. Xu, Ouyang and Chu (2009) believe:

> academic libraries are quickly becoming the major players in adopting and incorporating Web 2.0 applications into their services compared with other types of libraries.

In their survey of 81 academic libraries in New York state they found that 42% employed one or more Web 2.0 applications. Bejune and Ronan (2008) in their survey of Association of Research Libraries (ARL) report a huge growth in usage, from just two institutions in 1998 to 63 in early 2008, and expansion from two types. The JISC TILE (Towards implementation of Library 2.0 and the e-Framework) survey of UK Higher Education libraries found that 47 were delivering Web 2.0 services and 36 more considering it, from 100 responses (Chad and Chowcat 2008). Blogs, podcasts, RSS feeds and wikis were the most popular. These were felt to be relatively easy to implement, with no input required from Library

---

1   http://www.librarycrunch.com/2005/10/working_towards_a_definition_o.html.
2   http://www.slainte.org.uk/files/pdf/web2/Web2GuidelinesFinal.pdf.

Management Systems or institutional IT structure. Librarian supporters of Web 2.0 are beginning to detect a sort of trust between the users and the library through the use of Library 2.0 techniques. Taken to the extreme the Library 2.0 model could replace traditional, one-directional service (Peltier-Davis 2009). Another approach is to try to take advantage of the stream of new technologies which could be incorporated into staff work schedules. Rogers (2009a) concludes:

> to put it bluntly, libraries need to stop performing tasks that are no longer needed and take on new tasks available through social media in order to promote, market, and transparently manage libraries.

What About the User Perspective?

Before I become overexcited by the progress of 2.0 concepts we must examine the context in which librarians operate: the attitudes of both the general public and our users.

How is Our Public Taking to the New Technologies?

In the USA the latest Educause Centre for Applied Research (ECAR) study (Smith et al. 2009), derived from over 30,000 responses from undergraduates, found 44.8% contribute to video websites, 41.9% to wikis, 37.3% to blogs and 35.0% use podcasts. Social network sites (SNS) (90.3%) and texting (89.8%) have grown at the expense of instant messaging. Most significant is the greater use of SNS by older age groups: over the past four years a 236% increase for ages 30–39 and 326% for 40 and over. Much research has been undertaken by the CIBER group at University College, London, and many myths exposed about the Google generation. Many of their so-called characteristics are exhibited by older persons. Herther (2009) describes research done with volunteers aged 55 to 76 to see whether there is any evidence that their brains work differently to those of young persons. Those with prior internet experience had greater activation in the brain than non-internet searchers. After only a week of training the brain circuitry of the non-internet searchers was found to be similar to the more experienced searchers. The research suggested it was more about experience and choice rather than generational difference.

A study in 2009 by Anderson Analytics estimated that 60% of the US population use SNS and of those who were non-users through lack of time, 22% said they would start to start to use it within three months and 27% within a year (Perez 2009b). The growth of SNS will continue. The age groups using the main SNS are changing. The median use for Facebook went from age 26 in May 2008 to 33 in October 2009. Twitter is now used by 37% of 18–24 year olds and 31% of 25–34 year olds (Perez 2009a). The generational gap relating to technology is closing, as all ages begin to socialise and communicate in the same trusted places. Parr (2009) summarises recent Nielsen data about use of the web by seniors and surprisingly their number three is Facebook compared to number 45 a year ago. At the other end of the age spectrum, Laurie (2010) reports a recent National Literacy Trust survey of 3,000 children in the UK which found a positive correlation between literacy and engagement with social media.

How is this Affecting our Library Users?

The importance of knowing the student body cannot be overstated (Farkas 2007, Booth 2009). What would work in one place may not work in another, so knowledge of the age group, background, subject breakdown etc. is crucial. Then finding out their attitudes to Web 2.0 can give real insight into what should be trialled. An investigation at Kent State University, Ohio, featuring a brief survey and focus groups, with a total of 26 freshers and sophomores in teens or early 20s, was undertaken in autumns 2007 and 2008. Most had used Wikipedia and YouTube, and were heavy users of texting and Facebook. They saw a separation between personal and academic sites and preferred library sites to be linked via Blackboard rather than Facebook. There was not evidence of great enthusiasm for the Web 2.0 ideas proposed, with only one student who had edited Wikipedia. Following the exercise the library was able to prioritise its activity, for example, spending less time on Facebook pages, and instead bringing in 2.0 features into their existing web pages, OPAC and links within Blackboard.

Do our users actually want to communicate with librarians via social media? Some users are technophobes; some resent the institution invading "their space"; and some are put off by the library trying to appear "cool". The study by Anderson Analytics referred to above, concluded that non-users of SNS were less likely to be technophobic than simply time poor, think it is stupid or have security concerns (Perez 2009b). The ECAR studies confirm a consistent pattern of innovators, early adopters, mainstream adopters, late adopters and laggards, with about half being mainstream adopters (Smith et al. 2009). It is important to keep a sense of proportion and realise that social media do not have universal appeal.

A survey at the University of Loughborough in 2008 of Department of Information Science students, which elicited 82 replies, found less than half had heard of the concept of Library 2.0. In general there was only a mildly positive response to what Library 2.0 could offer them. RSS feeds, podcasting, and instant messaging were the most popular, and social networking was not thought to be particularly useful. Also they were not keen to share material if others did not. The latest ECAR study shows despite the high usage of SNSs only 27.85% said they used them for their course work, with 5% using podcasts, 6% video-creation software, and 5% audio-creation software during the semester of the survey (Smith et al. 2009).

We must remember the Jakob Nielsen 'rule' that in most online communities, 90% of users are lurkers who do not contribute, 9% contribute a little and 1% account for most of the action (Nielsen 2006). Wikipedia has demonstrated this.

Its growth peaked in 2007 with about 60,000 new articles per month, declining to about two-thirds of that today. The number of active users peaked at 820,000 in March 2007 and has been between 650,000 and 810,000 since then. Most edits are now done by a small group of enthusiasts, and it is reckoned that 50% of the edits are done by 1% of the editors. This has raised the questions of whether this increases the possibilities of bias (Landgraf 2009).

The University of Aberdeen set up a social bookmarking/sharing initiative using PageFlakes but received "indifference from users" with no contributions from users "so far" (Chad and Chowcat 2008). This echoes experience of using Delicious at the University of Bedfordshire and the need to ensure that it is firmly embedded and supported by academic staff. The OCLC (2007) report also found that students did not find libraries' use of social networking useful and saw it as an invasion of their personal space. It should be noted that this worldwide survey was taken from December 2006 to February 2007 and the increase in users might give a very different response today. However this view is not always accepted and Chad and Chowcat (2008) reported a library which had found no such negative response.

The JISC report from the University of Central Lancashire, derived from surveys at four different kinds of UK HE institutions, was rather dismissive of social networking, with 'The few students who do use social networking to find research content tend[ing] to be 22–50 years old'. They found that less than 2% in their surveys used podcasts (Hampton-Reeves 2009). Amongst academics a survey by Elsevier in 2008 showed an expectation that social media would be important in coming years. Nevertheless academics are a rather conservative group who despite the potential benefits of new technologies are reluctant to risk the status quo (Stuart 2009a). Xu, Ouyang and Chu (2009) conclude that 'librarians often appeared more keen and active than the end users in employing or incorporating Web 2.0 tools in academic libraries'.

The Librarian Perspective

Social Media and the New Librarians

It has been said that social media are not included in a systematic way into professional development (Chad and Chowcat 2008). Murphy and Moulaison created a brilliant set of social networking competencies based on the Association of College and Research Libraries (ACRL) Information Literacy Competency standards to meet the needs of the modern librarian, which should be required reading for all library school administrators. This would ensure that today's librarian understands how to search and navigate SNS effectively, knows how to interact with patrons via the various channels of communication (e.g. mobiles, e-mail, texting), is confident to teach these skills to library patrons and users, is able to adopt SNS sites for quality delivery of services as appropriate, is able to be flexible enough to deploy skills for use with new SNS tools as they appear and finally be able to look ahead, visualise, create, and manage robust library services in full consideration of and within social networking sites (Murphy and Moulaison 2009).

Of course some librarians have already been doing this. An examination of Facebook for social search by Scale (2008) demonstrated that Facebook as available then was inadequate for timely and relevant results. This will be altering with real-time search availability via Google and Bing[3].

There has been huge progress throughout the world in updating library staff about Web 2.0, for example Learning 2.0 from Charlotte and Mecklenburg County Public Library[4] has played a major role. Some libraries have created their own programme, as at Liverpool John Moores University (Appleton 2009).

The old ways of working were about holding on to what we had and the new is social and collaborative. This is a major cultural change, which each university will have to tackle (Chad and Chowcat 2008). Email is being replaced by Short Message Service (SMS) for our patrons, but internally is still prevalent. We will need to look at the various means by which we are contacted, and consider streamlining our practices to reduce overload. Email worked for us when we were logging on and off but with continuous access via mobile or at a desk, SMS can answer many of the questions, and emails which get stuck with attachments may be supplanted by Google Wave.

Wikis can be used as an alternative to an intranet. San Diego State University created one and as a result use increased, with updating easier and more evenly distributed among staff (Dworak and Jeffery 2009).

Blogs, assisted by Really Simple Syndication (RSS), are a great social communication tool for librarians to update their knowledge, news, and discuss issues (Draper and Turnage 2008). Chen (2009) tells how a staff blog can assist in conversation and collaboration within a technical services department in a university library, this leading to greater participation in framing new policies and initiatives.

Ning[5] provides a kind of walled garden approach for librarians to create a forum to post and discuss their particular concerns. As such this can be a valuable staff development tool, which allows anyone to create their own new social networking site, with a certain amount of design control, and the means to open and control membership and access.

---

3   http://www.bing.com/.
4   http://plcmcl2-about.blogspot.com.
5   http://www.ning.com.

Social Media for Reaching Out

Over the past three years librarians have either been grasping the 2.0 mantra with enthusiasm by experimenting, or ignoring it. It is in the area of promotion and marketing that most interest has been shown. Academic libraries must embrace the electronic information revolution and relate to students who are time-poor and struggling to cope with the mass of material available to them. We can no longer wait for our users to come to us. We have to go to them, wherever they are, find out their needs and adapt our services accordingly. In practice this means we supplement existing services with new ways of marketing and new online services: 'We need to employ social media tools to communicate the library's mission more broadly' (Rogers 2009a).

They are just another way of getting our message out, in addition to posters, bookmarks, guides and all the other tried and trusted means. The message seems to have reached the participants in the second Rogers (2009b) larger survey with 92.7% agreeing the importance of Web 2.0 tools for marketing and promotion. One library responded:

> Web 2.0 tools are such a part of marketing strategy at our library that this has become an irrelevant question … They are simply part of the daily equipment we use to tell the story. The important thing to remember is that they are not appropriate tools for every audience nor every message.

The most popular tool used was Facebook (74.7%), followed by blogs (53.1%) and Twitter (50%). Rogers (2009a) emphasises the expansion in use of online video viewing sites. Facebook can introduce the subject librarian to a new cohort of overseas students (Lawson 2007). The University of Warwick Library is a good example of how to set up a Facebook page and had 1,084 fans by the end of April 2009 (Widdows 2009). Some libraries are using YouTube to promote their services and events, e.g. Library of Congress since October 2007.

Blogs can be useful marketing tools, but they themselves need to be marketed and librarians have not always been very good at this (Draper and Turnage 2008). Librarians would do well to consider marketing considerations at every stage of development. Draper and Turnage draw attention to an article in which Jill Stover draws a matrix based on the 4Ps of marketing (Product, Place, Price and Promotion) in relation to blogs. In their survey 70% said they were using blogs for marketing the library.

David Lee King (2009) posted about an interesting way of reaching users via Facebook which derived from seeing how companies are sometimes quoting their Facebook sites' addresses rather than a home site. The implications are that by using your Facebook demographics you then target this group by using your Facebook address, gaining new fans who are likely to be the interactive type of users who can help you develop your site and services.

Social Media for Service Delivery

How can the librarian move on from using Web 2.0 for marketing to actually deliver library core services and involve the user?

Randy Reichardt (2008), librarian for the Faculty of Engineering at the University of Alberta tells the story of how he moved from onsite departmental help through blogs, instant messaging, Facebook, and creating links with WebCT. By making communication location neutral, the librarian can be receptive, adapting to users' means of communication. Norah Xiao (2008), Science and Engineering Librarian at the University of Southern California demonstrates the success of using Web 2.0 tools for reaching out to new students for orientation. McMaster University, Ontario, developed a Library Experience wiki as a one-stop shop to help new students orientate themselves, find out about tours and workshops and add advice for their peers (Trzeciak 2008). Relevance to the user depends on moving into their space, whether Facebook or using texting. Chad Boeninger, at Ohio University Library, created one of the first wiki subject guides and this BizWik[6] has become an exemplar. Chu (2009) found in a survey of 60 libraries in Asia, Australasia and the US that the main uses for wikis were to help construct library web pages, assist information sharing among librarians, archive several versions of a document, and speed up editing of web pages. Delicious can be used to store and make available subject resources (Widdows 2009). Subject blogs can help meet user needs, by providing news, links to new resources, recommended web sites, blog posts and can encourage users to become familiar with RSS as the glue to link all their subscriptions together.

Improving Access

We have to begin to make our websites less formidable, and more adaptable to personal and course requirements. Despite the accuracy and scholarly qualities present in library sites, Google, Amazon, eBay, YouTube, flickr, Facebook and Delicious all play their part in shaping user expectations. The librarian can no longer claim that information retrieval is complex, requiring sophisticated interfaces and search facilities. That is the road to oblivion. There are several ways to approach this. Liu (2008) examined the home pages of ARL members in the USA. He is concerned that home pages focus on library functions; with numerous links for access, huge numbers of options, and a single design that does not recognise individual needs. There was also little opportunity for users to create and share their own content. He proposes that the library website becomes adaptable according to the needs of the user. By selecting an option for their particular user group, the patron could then enter basic user information, set up a profile and create their own Library Space. This could link to their blogs, portfolios, institutional Virtual Learning Environment (VLE) and RSS aggregator.

---

6   https://www.library.ohiou.edu/subjects/bizwiki/index.php/Chad_Boeninger.

Another approach is for librarians and academic staff to provide pathfinders for their students, made up of RSS feeds from blogs, news services, YouTube videos, twitter feeds from reputable journalists, and mashups with Google maps to illustrate a topic (Hamilton 2009).

Some students already use Delicious to store and share their bookmarks, Netvibes, iGoogle or PageFlakes as their home page, and Facebook as their main channel of communication. Why not encourage them to access our services via these rather than to insist that they all have to go though our more unattractive and clunky VLEs? We have already seen that forcing them to use an institutional e-mail system has been problematic and some universities are now using Google accounts instead. There is clear evidence that students do use VLEs for course information and the challenge will be to integrate this with Web 2.0 services in the future (Chad and Chowcat 2008). Librarians should also realise that users see us as a source which should be put into the spaces and applications which they use for social and learning activities. We will never become their home page or a major gateway of choice: a lesson I learnt at London South Bank University many years ago.

We need to make access to our databases and catalogues as easy and painless as possible. A prime purpose for a Facebook site is to make the library catalogue available via this route. This need not be an arduous task. The University of Warwick say that this took only half a day by using code found on a library management system discussion board (Widdows 2009).

Use of social tagging from major services like LibraryThing[7] may play a part in improving subject access to our collections. Lawson (2009) concluded:

> by examining … and using it to enhance subject access in library catalogue records we can make catalogue records more inclusive and helpful to improve the overall library experience of our users.

Reference and Communication

Social media can be a better way for some users to ask us questions. Second Life (SL) has been put forward as a source for virtual reference services. It gives users who do not want to approach a desk in a physical library another way of getting help. A Second Life Reference Desk was begun in January 2007, with volunteers from the USA, Europe and Australia. It helped users to see libraries as a global service and aided librarian career development (Hill and Lee 2009). Experience of using SL has been mixed. Condic (2009) remarked:

> this author has devoted four hours in SL and can barely fly and teleport properly.

---

7   http://www.librarything.com/.

Furthermore there were the problems of lack of nonverbal cues, and the need for fast computers. A survey of the Library and Information Technology Association and the SL Librarians Group in summer 2008 elicited 161 responses of a possible 2710. It highlighted the perceived lack of buy-in from library administration and inadequate computers as the major obstacles (Blankenship and Hollingsworth 2009). The ability to respond to user feedback, both good and bad, via SMS, is valuable. This can help librarians to know their clientele better. Comments picked up via Twitter give libraries an opportunity to both become aware of user concerns and answer criticism.

Instant messaging (IM) has been adopted by many libraries as a way for users to contact us (McManus 2009). Librarians' attitudes to running these services are well documented in a recent survey by Gronemyer and Deitering (2009). However in recent months it has clearly been overtaken by SMS texting, as mobile devices become ubiquitous. Elizabeth Bagley at Agnes Scott College, Georgia found that IM had increased 300% between 2006–9. A user consultation has shown that 72% would prefer a text alternative. According to Kolowich (2010), texting reference services are on the ascendant. In China a survey of 46 Chinese libraries found 32 offering IM reference services, but it was concluded that that they ought to follow the users and move to texting SMS (Cao 2009).The limitations of IM in discovering the depth of a user query might be felt to be more acute with the 160 character limit of SMS. This may not be a problem as users seem able to accept multiple text exchanges (Kroski 2009a). The mobility granted to the librarian in dealing with queries, and the popularity of texting with users, may outweigh any considerations of message brevity.

Instruction and Information Literacy

Screencasting software has been used to replace instructions and can show users how to undertake an activity. It can appeal to all learning styles as it can contain visual, auditory and hands-on elements (Farkas 2009). This has therefore been a major area for libraries to follow up and the University of Cardiff have been trendsetters in this (University of Cardiff Information Services 2009).

Libraries have adopted "how to" videos, as a means of explaining databases and the intricacies of library use. We have already seen the huge growth in online video usage. The use of tools like Camtasia and Captivate have made the addition of video material much easier, which can be embedded on websites. How far it actually supports student learning requires more empirical research. Sutton-Brady et al. (2009) do provide some positive evidence of learning benefits, from podcasts in the Faculty of Economics and Business in the University of Sydney. Users favour short focussed videos (Buczynski 2009). This has been the thought behind our own series of *Just a Minute* videos at the University of Bedfordshire. Ten one-minute videos have been produced for Autumn 2009, covering topics from basic catalogue searching to self-issue machines (University of Bedfordshire, Learning

Resources 2010). For case studies on how Web 2.0 tools can be applied to helping the delivery of Information Literacy see Godwin and Parker (2008).

Social Media: Toward a Strategic Approach

The JISC TILE project found that few libraries were getting involved in Web 2.0 initiatives in a planned strategic way. It was still the result of individual initiatives and experimentation (Chad and Chowcat 2008). The same conclusion had been reached by an international review of Web 2.0 use in HE (Armstrong and Franklin 2008).

As the adoption of social media has moved beyond innovators and enthusiasts in business, just as in libraries, the need for a social media strategy is being debated. It is easy to say that it requires a clear vision of service which is innovative, collaborative and connects to its users. It should put people first and then find the right technology (Li 2009). However I believe that social media themselves are not a strategy, rather a means to an end, so social media will be employed as part of other plans to achieve institutional objectives.

A clear social media policy can be useful to guide staff in their use of SNS, especially as the distinction between personal and professional use is becoming blurred. A policy can assist staff who have to post on behalf of the library. Users also need to know what is acceptable and what is unacceptable. Some examples include Western Kentucky University. Kroski (2009b) has suggested a number of areas that might need to be covered: use of a disclaimer; avoid sharing sensitive or proprietary information; don't be anonymous; respect copyright; avoid online battles; post accurate information.

Social Media Metrics and Roads to Success

If libraries are to go beyond the experimentation and the early adopter phase, and develop a social media policy, then they need hard evidence to convince sceptics. This could begin with Rogers' second survey of 545 individuals (25% academic libraries) in November 2009 (Rogers 2009b). This reveals a division between library administrators on the merits and benefits of social media for libraries.

How can a business case be made based on current practice? What are the benefits as opposed to the costs involved? What is the return upon investment? These are questions being asked in business use of social media too. Fisher (2009) sees return on investment becoming even more of a bone of contention as use of social media increases and the recession bites. Is it more about return on engagement or return on influence? Measurement is hard because it involves qualitative rather than just quantitative measurement. We need to look at the buzz: the opinions and experiences that users are sharing about the product. Wheeler and Omundson (2010) provide an interesting set of metrics to help gauge the reliability, importance and influence of social media for information professionals. They identify five influence attributes: reach, buzz, engagement, content and audience. Using metrics to measure against each attribute (e.g. retweets for buzz) they were able to score a product against each attribute, and also a composite score. Chad and Chowcat (2008) note the difficulty of measuring success; a library reporting no comments on a blog, another university saying it was too early to tell, the need for better feedback mechanisms. There is a need for more sharing of good practice, evaluating whether the services are meeting their objectives. Chad and Chowcat (2008) highlight this need to share innovation and good practice and The Library Success[8], a best practices wiki, is a well known attempt to help with this problem, albeit mainly about the USA. However, the problem is more about trying to understand how to measure success. Li (2009) said at the Online 2009 Conference in Olympia 'We tend to overvalue the things we can measure and to undervalue the things we cannot'.

In a thoughtful post Schmidt (2009) decries libraries relying on circulation figures and recommends the use of a Library Made icon (cf. Creative Commons) which could demonstrate when and by whom content had been created, and the library resources consulted to achieve it. It is hard to find valid statistics, partly because the costs are more about staff time than money. Success is measured over time, and the return on investment depends on the starting point (Ojala 2008). This is the crucial understanding: decide exactly what the social media are intended to do, and then consider how well they are performing, and whether there are any sustainability issues. Another technique before adopting SNS would be to undertake a SWOT analysis. Fernandez (2009) gives an interesting introduction into how this could be applied.

The various social media offer individual opportunities and problems in measurement. These measurements are called social media metrics. Blogs are provided by companies like Blogger or WordPress and these contain code which can show visitor behaviour (Stuart 2009b). Blog comments, reactions and blogrolls all give some indication of the impact of the blog. RSS readers give details of the number of subscribers to a blog. The importance of each metric depends upon the purpose of the blog. If it was to get feedback then comments would be the important metric. Wikis can be measured by number of pages created, number of editors, amount of edits and again importance is determined by the purpose of the wiki. Social network sites give varying amounts of information about visitors. For example, YouTube gives detailed information about users. Microblogs like Twitter are more complex to evaluate as a large number of followers is not necessarily the best indicator. Retweeting can push a tweet around a huge network of followers. Tweetstats and URL shortening services like bit.ly provide extra information. The Twitter API can itself provide data automatically if library staff are prepared to put in the time to extract it. Finally it may be possible to set benchmarks against similar services from other institutions. Fichter and Wisniewski (2009) recommend use of Delicious to see how many people have bookmarked your sites; Twitter

---

8   http://www.libsuccess.org/index.php?title=Main_Page.

for mentions of your library; setting up Google Alerts to monitor mentions of a service and the use of Google Analytics or Clicky Web Analytics to help monitor social media (Fichter and Wisniewski 2009).

Conclusion

Social media are not the panacea for all our library ailments. There has been a danger of too much hype. This does not mean that we should agree with the extreme views of Michael Gorman, former President of the American Library Association:

> I don't believe that social networking sites provide any real, practical advantage to library services ... the bottom line is that users of Twitter and Facebook are the victims of a massive advertising scam, and libraries perhaps more than anyone, are best out of it.

As we have seen from the foregoing analysis Web 2.0 concepts are here to stay. Library websites will become more personalised providing valuable opportunities for user participation. In the ability to connect wherever and whenever required provided by mobile technologies may lie the most powerful bond with social media in the future. We will be helping users to create their own personal learning networks, and employing social media as a means to plug into the best library content and services.

References

Appleton, L., 2009. Learning 2.0 @ LJMU: a staff development programme for learning and information service staff. *SCONUL Focus*, 46, 59–63.

Armstrong, J. and Franklin, T., 2008. *A Review of Current and Developing International Practice in the Use of Social Networking (Web 2.0) in Higher Education.* Available from: http://www.franklin-consulting.co.uk/Reports.html#Topic5 (accessed 6 January 2010).

Bejune, M. and Ronan, J., 2008. Social software in libraries. Association of Research Libraries, *Spec kit* 304. Available from: http://www.arl.org/bm~doc/spec304web.pdf (accessed 6 January 2010).

Blankenship, E.F. and Hollingsworth, Y., 2009. Balancing both lives: issues facing librarians working in Second Life and real life worlds. *New Library World*, 110 (9/10), 430–40.

Booth, C., 2009. *Informing Innovation: Tracking Student Interest in Emerging Library Technologies at Ohio University.* Chicago: ACRL.

Boxen, J.L., 2008. Library 2.0: a review of the literature. *Reference Librarian*, 49(1), 21–34.

Buczynski, J.A., 2009. Video clip reference: the medium is the message. *Internet Reference Services Quarterly*, 14, 37–43.

Burhanna, K.J., Seeholzer, J. and Salem, J., 2009. No natives here: a focus group study of student perceptions of Web 2.0 and the academic library. *Journal of Academic Librarianship*, 35(6), 523–32.

Cao, D., 2009. Chinese Library 2.0: status and development. *Chinese Librarianship: An International Electronic Journal*. 27. Available from: http://www.white-clouds.com/iclc/cliej/cl27cao.htm (accessed 24 January 2010).

Chad, K. and Chowcat, I., 2008. *TILE 03: Library 2.0 – Perceptions and Responses in UK Higher Education*. JISC. Available from: http://www.sero.co.uk/assets/ JISC-TILE/TILE%2003%20-%20Survey%20&%20Interview%20Analysis. pdf (accessed 4 January 2010).

Chen, S., 2009. Can blogging help cataloguing? *Library Resources and Technical Services*, 53(4), 251–60.

Chu, S.K-W., 2009. Using wikis in academic libraries. *Journal of Academic Librarianship*, 35(2), 170–76.

CIBER, 2008. *The Information Behaviour of the Researcher of the Future*, Report prepared for the British Library and JISC. Available from: http://www.bl.uk/ news/pdf/googlegen.pdf (accessed 19 April 2010).

Condic, K.S., 2009. Using Second Life as a training tool in an academic library. *Reference Librarian*. 50, 333–45.

Draper, L. and Turnage, M., 2008. Blogmania: blog use in academic libraries. *Internet Services Quarterly* 13(1), 15–55.

Dworak, E. and Jeffery, K., 2009. Wiki to the rescue: creating a more dynamic intranet. *Library Hi Tech* 27(3), 403–10.

Farkas, M. 2007., *Social Software in Libraries: Building Collaboration, Communication, and Community Online*. Nedford, New Jersey: Information Today.

Farkas, M., 2009. Your desktop; the movie. *American Libraries*. Nov. 33.

Fernandez, J., 2009. A SWOT analysis for social media in libraries. *Online*. Sept./ Oct. 35–7.

Fichter, D. and Wisniewski, J., 2009. Social media metrics: tracking your impact. *Online*, Jan/Feb. 54–7.

Fisher, T., 2009. ROI in social media: a look at the arguments. *Database Marketing and Customer Strategy Management*, 16(3), 189–95.

Godwin, P. and Parker, J., 2008. *Information Literacy Meets Library 2.0*. London: Facet.

Gronemyer, K. and Deitering, A.M., 2009. "I don't think it's harder, just that it's different." Librarians' attitudes about instruction in the virtual reference environment. *Reference Services Review*, 37(4), 421–34.

Hamilton, B., 2009. *Integrating Social Media as Authoritative Information into Research Pathfinders*. Unquiet Librarian. Blog. Available from: http:// theunquietlibrarian.wordpress.com/2009/07/02/integrating-social-media-as-authoritative-information-into-research-pathfinders/ (accessed 29 September 2009).

Hampton-Reeves, S., 2009. *Students' Use of Research Content in Teaching and Learning: A Report for the Joint Information Systems Council.* University of Central Lancashire. Available from: http://www.jisc.ac.uk/media/documents/aboutus/workinggroups/studentsuseresearchcontent.pdf (accessed 24 January 2010).

Helm, T., 2010. Parties race to harness new media as poll battle begins. *Observer* 13 Jan. 8.

Herther, N.K., 2009. Digital natives and immigrants: what brain research tells us. *Online.* Nov/Dec. 15–19.

Hill, V. and Lee, H.J., 2009. Libraries and immersive learning environments unite in Second Life. *Library Hi Tech*, 27(3), 338–56.

King, D.L., 2009. *Widening your Nets, Decentralizing Your Web Services*, David Lee King, blog. Available from: http://www.davidleeking.com/2009/12/09/widening-your-nets-decentralizing-your-web-services/ (accessed 6 January 2010).

Kolowich, S., 2010. Text generation. *Inside Higher Ed.* Available from: http://www.insidehighered.com/news/2010/01/08/texting (accessed 8 January 2010).

Kroski. E., 2009a. Text message reference: is it effective? Stacking the tech. *Library Journal.* Available from: http://www.libraryjournal.com/article/CA6701869.html (accessed 11 November 2009).

Kroski, E., 2009b. Should your library have a social media policy? *School Library Journal*, October, 44–6.

Landgraf, G., 2009. Wikipedia growth slows. *American Libraries.* Nov. 27.

Laurie, M., 2010. *How Social Media has Changed Us. Mashable, the Social Media Guide.* Available from: http://mashable.com/2010/01/07/social-media-changed-us/ (accessed 24 January 2010).

Lawson, D., 2007. Taking the library to users: experimenting with Facebook as an outreach tool, in Cohen, L., ed. *Library 2.0: Initiatives in Academic Libraries.* Chicago: Association of College and Research Libraries, 145–55.

Lawson, K.G., 2009. Mining social tagging data for enhanced subject access for readers and researchers. *Journal of Academic Librarianship*, 35 (6), 574–82.

Li, C., 2009. *The Impact of Social Media in your Organization.* Presentation at Online Information Conference, London, 3 December 2010. Available from: http://www.slideshare.net/charleneli/the-role-of-social-media-in-the-organization (accessed 24 January 2010).

Linh, N.C., 2008. A survey of the application of Web 2.0 in Australasian university libraries. *Library Hi Tech*, 26 (4), 630–53.

Liu, S., 2008. Engaging users: the future of academic library web sites. *College and Research Libraries*, 69 (1), 6–27.

Maness, J.M., 2006. Library 2.0 theory: Web 2.0 and its implications for libraries. *Webology.* Available from: http://www.webology.ir/2006/v3n2/a25.html (accessed 6 January 2010).

McManus, B., 2009. The implications of web 2.0 for academic libraries. *Journal of Academic and Special Librarianship* 10(3) Available from: http://southernlibrarianship.icaap.org/content/v10n03/mcmanus_b01.html. (accessed 6 January 2010).

Murphy, J. and Moulaison, H., 2009. *Social Networking Competencies for Librarians: Exploring Considerations and Engaging Participation.* Proceedings of the 14th National Conference of the Association of College and Research Libraries. Chicago: ACRL. Available from: http://eprints.rclis.org/16219/1/ Social_networking_Literacy_for_librarians.pdf (accessed 6 January 2010).

Nielsen, J., 2006. *Participation Inequality: Encouraging More Users to Contribute.* Jakob Nielsen's Alertbox. Available from: http://www.useit.com/alertbox/ participation_inequality.html (accessed 25 January 2010).

OCLC, 2007. *Sharing, Privacy and Trust in our Networked World.* OCLC. Available from: http://www.oclc.org/reports/sharing/ (accessed 6 January 2010).

Ojala, M.D., 2008. E*valuating New Technologies: Getting Management Buy-in.* Available from: http://sla-sd.typepad.com/Seminar2008/2008OjalaPresentation. pdf (accessed 24 January 2010).

Parr, B., 2009. *What do Seniors do Online? Visit Facebook and YouTube of Course.* Mashable, blog. Available from: http://mashable.com/2009/12/10/seniors-online-habits/ (accessed 6 January 2010).

Peltier-Davis, C., 2009. Innovative services for sustainable libraries. *Computers in Libraries.* Nov/Dec, 16–21.

Perez, S., 2009a. *As Facebook Ages, Gen Y turns to Twitter.* ReadWriteWeb blog. Available from: http://www.readwriteweb.com/archives/as_facebook_ages_ gen_y_turns_to_twitter.php (accessed 6 January 2010).

Perez, S., 2009b. *Who Uses Social Networks and What are They Like?* ReadWriteWeb blog. Available from: http://www.readwriteweb.com/archives/who_uses_social_ networks_and_what_are_they_like_part_1.php (accessed 6 January 2010).

Reichardt, R., 2008. How may I help thee? *Internet Reference Services Quarterly*, 13(2–3), 271–80.

Rogers, C., 2009a. *Social Media, Libraries and Web 2.0: How American Libraries are Using New Tools for Public Relations and to Attract New Users.* Available from: http://www.slideshare.net/crr29061/social-media-libraries-and-web-20-how-american-libraries-are-using-new-tools-for-public-relations-and-to-attract-new-users (accessed 6 January 2010).

Rogers, C., 2009b. *Social Media, Libraries and Web 2.0: How American Libraries are Using New Tools for Public Relations and to Attract New Users,* second survey November 2009. Available from: http://www.slideshare.net/crr29061/ social-media-libraries-and-web-20-how-american-libraries-are-using-new-tools-for-public-relations-and-to-attract-new-users-second-survey-november-2009 (accessed 6 January 2010).

Scale, M.S., 2008. Facebook as a social search engine and the implications for libraries in the twenty-first century. *Library Hi Tech* 26(4), 540–56.

Schmidt, A., 2009. *Libraries Should Become Better with Use.* Available from: http://www.walkingpaper.org/2399 (accessed 8 January 2010).

Smith, S. D., Salaway, G. and Caruso, J.B., 2009. *The ECAR Study of Under-graduate Students and Information Technology, 2009.* Available from: http://www.educause.edu/Resources/TheECARStudyofUndergraduateStu/187215 (accessed 6 January 2010).

Stuart, D., 2009a. Web 2.0 fails to excite today's researchers. *Research Information.* Oct/Nov. Available from: http://www.researchinformation.info/features/feature.php?feature_id=236 (accessed 6 January 2010).

Stuart, D., 2009b. Social media metrics. *Online*, Nov. Available from: http://www.infotoday.com/Online/nov09/Stuart.shtml (accessed 8 January 2010).

Sutton-Brady, C., Scott, K.M., Taylor, L., Carabetta, G. and Clark, S., 2009. The value of using short-format podcasts to enhance learning and teaching. *Open and Distance Education and eLearning*, 17(3), 219–32.

Trzeciak, J.G., 2008. McMaster University Libraries 2.0: transforming traditional organisations. *SCONUL Focus*, 44, 4–9.

University of Bedfordshire, Learning Resources, 2010. *Just a Minute videos.* Available from: http://lrweb.beds.ac.uk/libinfo/videos (accessed 19 April 2010).

University of Cardiff Information Services, 2009. *Updated Podcast Series Now Available.* Available from: http://www.cardiff.ac.uk/insrv/news/podcast.html (accessed 19 April 2010).

Westwood, R., 2010. Extremely human: Library heroes: Michael Gorman. *Library and Information Gazette*, 14–27 January, 20.

Wheeler, E. and Omundson, S., 2010. Evolution in source evaluation: using social media data. *FUMSI Focus*, Jan. Available from: http://web.fumsi.com/go/article/find/4435 (accessed 23 January 2010).

Widdows, K., 2009. Web 2.0 moves 2.0 quickly 2.0 wait: setting up a Library Facebook presence at the University of Warwick. *SCONUL Focus*, 46, 54–9.

Xiao, N., 2008. Web 2.0 as catalyst: virtually reaching out to users and connecting them to library resources and services. *Issues in Science and Technology Librarianship.* Fall. Available from: http://www.istl.org/08-fall/article2.html (accessed 24 January 2010).

Xu, C., Ouyang, F. and Chu, H., 2009. The academic library meets Web 2.0: applications and implications. *Journal of Academic Librarianship*, 35 (4) 324–31.

Chapter 3

Information Literacy in the Digital Environment

Jacqui Weetman DaCosta

Introduction

This chapter will explore the role of information literacy within the digital environment. The concept of information literacy predates the 'digital age' but, like other academic library resources and services, it has embraced (and been embraced by) the digital environment.

There can be many reasons why an institution may turn to the digital environment as a medium for developing students' information literacy skills, and some of these are discussed in this chapter. Examples will be reviewed of the opportunities for information literacy development in academic libraries and the varied ways in which these are practised in digital learning environments.

One of the most often quoted reasons for using digital initiatives to develop information literacy skills and support students' learning needs is the comfort level of in-coming generations with technology. Whether they are called the Google Generation, Millennials or Digital Natives, it is commonly felt that they bring different skills and expectations to their academic studies. An interesting report was produced by the Centre for Information Behaviour and the Evaluation of Research (CIBER) Group at University College London in 2008. *Information Behaviour of the Researcher of the Future* (CIBER 2008) outlines the results of a study, commissioned by the British Library and the Joint Information Systems Committee (JISC), on how young people search for information and what libraries may need to do to support their research needs. The report states that, when using digital information, the behaviour characteristics of our in-coming students are:

- Horizontal information seeking – skim reading and not staying with one document for very long
- Navigation – where people spend as much time locating information as they do reading it
- Squirreling – storing downloads without necessarily reading the information
- Speed checking – assessing authority and establishing trust in a matter of seconds.

The report lists some themes, with which many librarians are all too familiar:

- the information literacy of young people has not improved with the widening access to technology: in fact, their apparent facility with computers disguises some worrying problems
- internet research shows that the speed of young people's web searching means that little time is spent evaluating information, either for relevance, accuracy or authority
- young people have a poor understanding of their information needs and thus find it difficult to develop effective search strategies
- as a result, they exhibit a strong preference for expressing themselves in natural language rather than analysing which key words might be more effective. (CIBER 2008, p. 12)

These sentiments were echoed by Lynne Brindley (2009a), Chief Executive of the British Library and a former university librarian, when she said 'Google Generation students are technologically savvy but not digitally literate'.

Definitions and Standards

Opinions differ as to the origins of the concept of information literacy. This debate ranges from its inception in 1876, 'when Melvil Dewey urged librarians to become educators' (Zhang 2001, p. 141), to the 1980s, when Bloom and Deyrup (2003) felt that it was only with the advent of the Internet that information literacy was truly born. It is said that Paul Zurkowski was the first person to use the term 'information literacy' (Webber and Johnston 2000), in the 1970s, in his proposal to the US National Commission on Libraries and Information Science. It appears that national debate on the subject first came into prominence in the United States in the late 1980s, Australia in the early 1990s and the United Kingdom in the late 1990s.

The American Library Association (ALA) was the first professional body to produce an agreed definition of information literacy in its 1989 Presidential Committee on Information Literacy. This Final Report (ALA 1989) said that an information literate person is one who can:

... recognize when information is needed and have the ability to locate, evaluate, and use effectively the needed information.

For many years, this was the definition used within the United Kingdom until a group of information literacy devotees, mainly from higher education libraries, got together to produce a definition for the Chartered Institute of Library and Information Professionals (CILIP). This definition went a step further by incorporating the ethical use of information, stating that:

Information literacy is knowing when and why you need information, where to find it, and how to evaluate, use and communicate it in an ethical manner (CILIP 2004).

Initially, it was the Society of College, National and University Libraries (SCONUL) that started promulgating the information literacy 'cause' in the United Kingdom when they convened a task force on the topic in 1999. This task force produced the 'Seven Pillars of Wisdom model' (SCONUL 1999) which outlined the relationship between information and IT skills and their potential progressive development within the higher education curriculum. Many higher education institutions have made use of the model as a way of providing a framework or benchmarks for information literacy development and assessment (DaCosta 2009).

Even though the SCONUL model for information literacy has experienced widespread acceptance within many British academic libraries, and is known internationally, it has not yet achieved the level of 'clout' of the Association of College and Research Libraries' Information Literacy Competency Standards for Higher Education (ACRL 2000) in the United States. These standards are used by many American academic libraries for assessment and accreditation. However, it is thought that they are a little over-complicated and do not translate so easily for working with academic staff (Gullikson 2006).

While 'information literacy' is well documented, 'digital literacy' is a newer concept, on which there is less written. David Bawden offers a review of both concepts, along with others such as media and computer literacy, in an article from 2001. Definitions of 'digital literacy' focus more on the medium and the fact that required skills include the ability to decipher images and sounds, and to understand multimedia texts. However, it could be argued that digital literacy skills, along with many other literacies brought about by the widespread use of technology, are already accounted for in characteristics of information literacy listed by recognised scholars in this area, such as Christine Bruce (1994) and Hannelore Rader (1991). Digital literacy could simply be defined as the ability to perform information literacy tasks within a digital environment. As Bawden (2001, p. 251) concludes:

It is not of importance whether this is called information literacy, digital literacy, or simply literacy for an information age. What is important is that it be actively promoted as a central core of principles and practice of the information sciences.

Moreover, as written in Barack Obama's (2009) Presidential Proclamation on Information Literacy:

> Rather than merely possessing data, we must also learn the skills necessary to acquire, collate, and evaluate information for any situation ... The ability to seek, find, and decipher information can be applied to countless life decisions, whether financial, medical, educational, or technical.

Information literacy skills are core to lifelong learning and need to be developed to equip students to manage information in whatever format it is presented.

Teaching

Increasingly, information literacy skills are being taught and supported within the digital environment, whether it is through the use of online tutorials, virtual learning environments or blended learning. The digital environment presents many opportunities to develop students' information literacy skills and may be chosen to support distance learning, to provide 24/7 tuition, to make learning more interactive or simply because the course leader does not want to hand over much of their class time to the library. Whatever the reason, it is down to the librarian to ensure that the information literacy teaching remains pedagogically sound, regardless of the medium.

Many librarians have looked to online tutorials as a means of providing 24/7 instruction and to appeal to the different learning styles of the Google Generation. Some academic libraries have created online tutorials because they are a good thing to have but others have responded to circumstances within their own institutions, for example to provide information literacy teaching in areas where they are not invited into the classroom. Some libraries have developed subject or task specific tutorials, such as citation or plagiarism. Some tutorials serve as the course material where assessment may be involved. However, many are generic in nature and can easily be utilised or customised to suit the needs of other institutions.

If one is looking for ideas on the types of tutorials available or to try to find one to customise, there are some good places to start. Firstly, there is a book which provides a guide to the state of this particular art as it stood in 2007. *Information Literacy Programs in the Digital Age: Educating College and University Students Online*, compiled by Daugherty and Russo (2007) provides details of 24 tutorials from American colleges, across the spectrum of general, subject specific, credit-bearing and those embedded into courses. For a more regularly updated resource, librarians could consult the PRIMO[1] database, which stands for Peer-Reviewed Instructional Materials Online and is produced by the Instruction Section of the ACRL. Tutorials and other online materials are reviewed twice a year, with the most exemplary being selected for inclusion in the database. A similar resource, although not limited to just library instruction and materials, is MERLOT[2] (Multimedia Educational Resource for Learning and Online Teaching). This is an ever-growing collection where a keyword search can be used to find materials related to information literacy or library skills in general, and sub-divided by subject area, if desired. Materials sourced could be online tutorials, quizzes and tests, presentations or reference materials.

Many librarians have taken the opportunity to incorporate library resources and support within their institutional virtual learning environments (VLE), known as course management systems (CMS) in the United States. Some libraries have only been able to add links to resources, or contact details for subject librarians, but others have been able to develop information literacy instruction, some within credit-bearing courses. It all depends on the level of control exerted by institutions over their VLE content, or sometimes just being in the right place at the right time. DaCosta and Jones (2007) describe how they were able to take the opportunity of De Montfort University's adoption of Blackboard to turn a previous classroom based course into one where much of the learning and assessment transferred into the online environment. Jefkins (2009) recounts how Moodle was used at University College London to supplement the library's other information literacy efforts. Where librarians have only been able to link to resources, many have taken advantage of Intute's Virtual Training Suite[3], funded by the Joint Information Systems Committee (JISC), in order to provide quality web materials. Sadly, at the time of writing, the future of Intute beyond August 2010 is unknown and it may need to become a subscription-based service.

Assessment

The digital environment has provided one of the biggest ways forward for the assessment of information literacy. When librarians are only offered a small amount of time within a course to work with students on information literacy, they have not always been able to allocate much of that time to assessment. The assessment of information literacy skills is desirable to test whether students are learning anything from your teaching or to inform you as to which teaching methods work best. However, in some institutions, it is required for accreditation or quality assurance purposes.

---

1   http://www.ala.org/ala/mgrps/divs/acrl/about/sections/is/projpubs/primo/index.cfm.

2   http://www.merlot.org/merlot/index.htm.

3   http://www.vts.intute.ac.uk/.

The number of commercial assessment packages is increasing at a steady pace. Some form part of general institutional assessment management software, while others have been designed to focus on library and/or information technology skills. The downside, for British academic libraries, is that many of these have been developed by American companies or libraries. While the skills to be tested do not differ across the Atlantic, the terminology does and librarians may have a harder time convincing managers of the value of these packages. The most popular of the commercial packages within the United States are SAILS, TRAILS and iSkills.

- Project SAILS[4] was launched in 2001, by the Kent State University in Ohio, USA. Their team of librarians, test designers, data analysts and programmers produced a Standard Assessment of Information Literacy Skills (SAILS) in 2006. The test measurements used are based on the ACRL Information Literacy Competency Standards for Higher Education. The tests, in the form of multiple-choice questions, are available online or on paper and are charged at a per student rate.

- TRAILS[5] (Tool for Real-time Assessment of Information Literacy Skills) is another initiative out of Kent State University and was also made available in 2006. It is aimed more at school libraries but has had some success in community colleges in the United States, which are comparable to British further education colleges. The multiple-choice questions are based on standards produced by the American School Librarians' Association and Ohio State. TRAILS is free to use but has limited flexibility for customisation.

- The iCritical Thinking Certification[6] replaced iSkills in late 2009. Both tests were developed by the American Educational Testing Service (ETS), which is perhaps better known in the United Kingdom for the problems associated with the administration of SATS, or the national curriculum tests, in 2008. The previous iSkills test was criticised by some librarians for having too great a focus on information technology. However, this does make it more appropriate to the digital environment (Katz 2007). Rather than being based on the ACRL Information Literacy Competency Standards, the iCritical Thinking test is described as being 'aligned to' the standards. There is a fee per student to administer the test.

Although the commercial products can help save time and provide a professional looking packaging of assessment results, they are prohibitively expensive for many academic libraries. Some librarians have turned to their institutional virtual learning environments to provide an assessment platform (DaCosta and Jones 2007). While this requires a lot more preparation up-front, it can easily allow for customisation to fit the course's information literacy learning outcomes. In

---

4   www.projectsails.org.
5   http://www.trails-9.org/.
6   www.certiport.com/iCriticalThinking.

the absence of a VLE, it is perfectly possible to take advantage of open source software to create assessments, such as Google Docs or SurveyMonkey[7]. The most challenging aspect of creating your own assessments is devising appropriate questions. The British Information Literacy Group, which is one of the CILIP Special Interest Groups, has been talking about developing a centralised bank of questions that would be suitable for the testing of information literacy skills. At the time of writing, this is just in the aspiration stage. However, at the time of reading, it may have become a reality so it would be worth checking their website.[8]

Learning Styles

Whether or not information literacy is developed and supported in the digital environment, librarians should always pay attention to the diverse learning styles of students. Many librarians share the learning style associated with reading and writing (an occupational hazard!). However, when we are teaching Art or Engineering students, it is unlikely that they are going to respond well to that same style. We have to climb out of our comfort zones to deliver our teaching in a range of styles and this is where the digital environment can help. Remember:

- We are all different learners.
- We are all different information gatherers.
- We receive information in different ways.

Much has been written on learning styles over the years covering theories and questionnaires for individuals to discover their own styles (Honey and Mumford 2006, Kolb 2005). There are many different names associated with the most commonly discussed styles but, simplistically, they boil down to four main types:

- Visual – preference for pictures, colour, graphics and videos. These learners may take lots of notes.
- Auditory – preference for lectures, podcasts and audio books. These learners take few notes.
- Read/Write – preference for reading lines of text and taking lots of notes.
- Kinesthetic – preference for activities and problem-solving. These learners take lots of notes.

Learning styles have been a topic for discussion and research long before the Google Generation came along. Their arrival has provided more challenges.

---

7 www.surveymonkey.com.
8 http://www.informationliteracy.org.uk/.

> Whereas lecture appeals to auditory learners, hands-on activities reach kinesthetic or experiential learners. Lecture may be very appropriate for older students; however, students in Gen Y may prefer hands-on activities (Willis and Thomas 2006, p. 438).

The arrival of these students is one of the reasons why librarians have turned to online tutorials as a way of incorporating more hands-on activities into information literacy instruction. Whereas many librarians may prefer to teach and provide information in a linear structure, today's students are more inclined to want to dart from one thing to another, spending little time on something that does not give them immediate answers. For this reason, a variety of digital media and formats may be more appealing to students looking for information.

Another characteristic of the Google Generation is that they have a great deal of confidence in their ability to do things on their own (Foster and Gibbons 2007). This confidence is thought by many educators to be overestimated and misplaced. Today's students are less likely to learn their information literacy skills at the enquiry desk or at a voluntary workshop, since they are less inclined to think that they need help. For this reason, librarians need to take advantage of any and every opportunity to help students to develop their information-seeking skills, and particularly utilise the opportunities presented by the digital environment.

Web Guides

Gone are the days when libraries provided numerous guides and instruction sheets on row upon row of display shelves. The Google Generation does not consist of many students who like to sit and work laboriously through written instructions to find out how to use a database. This is the trial and error generation – if something does not work immediately then they move onto another method very quickly. If today's students want to know something, they do not look for a printed guide, they go online and 'Google it'. If you have managed to get your message across, as their librarian, then your students may turn to your web pages for guidance on using library-related resources. At Wartburg College in Iowa, they talk about using the library website to provide 'stealth instruction' (Gremmels and Mashek 2007, p. 261), acknowledging that just as much thought needs to go into planning the content and desired learning outcomes of information on the Web, as when creating a lesson plan.

In keeping with the range of learning styles discussed above, guidance to students via library web pages is often provided in a variety of formats: iPods or MP3 players can be used for audio tours; podcasts can be used to give short explanations on procedures; interactive tutorials can be used to get students practising research skills. In 2008, the University of Huddersfield Library developed a website called

The Basics[9] in order to convey induction information to students in short FAQ style, utilising podcasts, Adobe Captivate demos, tutorials, graphics and hypertext links. Many libraries have responded to the students' need for immediate gratification by providing chat reference services, via instant messaging.

Many academic libraries in the United States have chosen to make use of LibGuides, which are provided on a Web 2.0 platform and are easy to create. They allow for multimedia content to be incorporated, as well as widgets and applications compatible with FaceBook, Twitter and other social networking software. Many American libraries have chosen LibGuides for their general and course specific guides, websites and portals, and also for library instruction. The ease with which they are created has encouraged librarians to prepare a guide, rather than a handout, to supplement teaching and to even add to the guides during class sessions. LibGuides are hosted on a server controlled by Springshare, which is an advantage to libraries that are unable to access their own institutional server. There is a small annual fee charged for this service, customisation and support.

As well as discarding printed library subject guides, students are also turning to the Internet for their citation referencing. They are not choosing to access guides to help them create their own citations but the even easier option of having the citation put together for them. Regardless of their accuracy, students just want the quick fix offered to them by sites such as: BibMe[10], EasyBib[11], Son of Citation Machine[12] and Neil's Toolbox[13].

Learning, Fun or Both

The digital environment presents more opportunities for students to experience the lighter side of learning through interactive games and social networking. Increasingly, librarians and instructors are using digital initiatives in the hope that students will engage more deeply in their learning, if they find the medium to be fun.

Sheila Webber, at the University of Sheffield, Esther Grassian, at the University of California Los Angeles, and professors at the Graduate School of Library and Information Science, University of Illinois, have done a lot of experimentation with information literacy within Second Life – the 3D virtual world used for socialisation and making connections. An Infolit iSchool has been created in Second Life, which is used with students at the University of Sheffield's Department of Information Studies and as a discussion forum for librarians from around the world. There was even an Information Literacy Week in Second Life,

---

9   http://www2.hud.ac.uk/cls/thebasics/index.php.
10   http://www.bibme.org/.
11   http://www.easybib.com/.
12   http://citationmachine.net/.
13   http://www.neilstoolbox.com/.

in November 2009, for which a blog was created, which has continued as a forum for discussion on this topic.[14]

Manchester Metropolitan University (Whitton and Jones 2009) have been experimenting with Alternative Reality Games (ARGs) as a supplement to traditional library induction and to introduce students to resources. ARGs are collaborative, problem-based computer games that utilise blogs and other social networking software, which makes them much easier to develop than the typical high-tech computer game. The focus on problem-based learning makes them more suitable for the educational sector. The ARGOSI Project, at Manchester Metropolitan University[15] did not determine that games of this nature should replace traditional teaching but that they could serve as a complement to engage students, who prefer this style of learning.

Some libraries have created YouTube videos to help teach information literacy skills to students, using these in classes or uploading them onto websites. Whilst the educational benefits of YouTube are still up for debate, this medium appeals to some students and is always worth trying as another digital enhancement to traditional teaching methods (Ayres 2008).

No-one is yet claiming that information literacy teaching is more effective within a virtual world but many are having fun experimenting with this form of learning without the real life limitations of budget constraints or room availability!

Staff Development

One of the most common complaints about library school courses around the world is that they do not prepare librarians adequately to teach information literacy skills. Many librarians just pick up what they can, doing the job and observing colleagues. Some librarians opt to take extra courses to learn the skills or benefit from in-house programmes. However, training for library staff to learn more about information literacy, and to equip librarians to teach the skills, is now available courtesy of the digital environment. The UK's Information Literacy Group has developed two online training packages:

- Lollipop[16] is an online tutorial that aims to enhance the information literacy skills of library enquiry desk staff. Tutorials have been developed for the Higher Education sector and are available under the Creative Commons Licence.
- SirLearnalot[17] – is an online tutorial and discussion forum to help develop librarians as teachers, with units on Understanding Learning and the Tools

---

14   http://infolit-week-in-sl.ning.com/.

15   www.argosi.playthinklearn.net.

16   http://www.lobelollipop.com/.

17   http://courses.informationliteracy.org.uk/course/view.php?id=13.

for Learning. It is freely available through the Information Literacy Group's Moodle site and, at the time of writing, is a work in progress. General users can log-on as guests.

Cardiff University has produced an excellent Handbook for Information Literacy Teaching (2009), which is available from their website under a Creative Commons Licence. This handbook is especially useful for new and inexperienced teachers of information literacy since it covers many aspects of teaching from the planning stage through to activities to engage students, assessment and evaluation.

National Digital Initiatives and Information Literacy

As many librarians know, information literacy has been woefully neglected by British governments despite its role within education. Perhaps the greatest success story has been in Scotland where the Scottish Information Literacy Project[18] has captured the attention of more 'movers and shakers'. At the time of writing, the project team based at Glasgow Caledonian University have almost completed a National Information Literacy Framework, which transcends primary, secondary and tertiary education by also encompassing lifelong learning.

Information literacy is in danger of becoming the overlooked Cinderella of the literacies, as government and other national agencies pay attention to the more 'sexy' digital and media literacies. The much-heralded Digital Britain (DCMS 2009) report mentions media literacy and basic literacy but does not talk of information literacy despite the fact that CILIP made a formal response to the draft report outlining the importance of information literacy. Information literacy did fare better in the JISC report on Higher Education in a Web 2.0 World (Melville 2009) but then the Committee of Inquiry into the Changing Learner Experience, which produced it, did include a librarian. This report commends how Web 2.0 tools help to enrich the educational experience because of their association with active learning. However, as with the CIBER report from 2008, it recognises that students look for a quick fix when searching for information, paying little attention to evaluation and ethical issues:

> It has also led them to impatience – a preference for quick answers – and to a casual approach to evaluating information and attributing it and also to copyright and legal constraints. (Melville 2009, p. 9)

The report recommends that:

> HEIs, colleges and schools treat information literacies as a priority area and support all students so that they are able, amongst other things, to identify,

---

18   http://www.gcal.ac.uk/ils/.

search, locate, retrieve and, especially, critically evaluate information from the range of appropriate sources – web-based and other – and organise and use it effectively, attributed as necessary, in an appropriate medium. (Melville 2009, p. 10)

As governments across the world start to show an interest in the digital environment, and its role within education, librarians should take the opportunity to emphasise the role of information literacy within the digital environment and the importance of the associated skills.

Conclusion

We live in an ever-changing world, which means that we must remain vigilant to the needs and demands of our users. The format in which information is presented, continues to change at an alarming pace. Because of this, students need information literacy training now more than ever. The proliferation of information that is available within the digital environment has generated a greater need for information skills. Our in-coming students generally:

- assume that search engines understand what they are looking for, without any regard for developing an effective search strategy;
- find the likes of Google and Yahoo to be a great deal more intuitive than many library websites;
- think that they are expert information searchers.

In order to combat this, librarians need to look at ways in which their web pages and library catalogues can be simplified. If instructions are needed on how to search the OPAC then the battle is already lost. The information that students need should be displayed prominently and in basic terms. There needs to be some bait to lure students and create a desire within them to spend a little more time using the library resources. Some libraries have turned to games, social networking and entertainment as a way to entice and motivate students. However, these need to continue to be evaluated for their pedagogical benefits:

> If the erratic behaviour we are seeing in digital libraries really is the result of failure at the library terminal, then society has a major problem. Information skills are needed more than ever and at a higher level if people are to really avail themselves of the benefits of an information society. (CIBER 2008, p. 32)

Project Information Literacy is an American study on students' information-seeking behaviours, competencies and challenges faced when conducting research in the digital age. Their interim report *How College Students Seek Information in the Digital Age* (Head and Eisenberg 2009) found that:

- Almost all of the respondents relied on the same few information resources regardless of the context.
- Students favoured sources that provided brevity, consensus and currency.
- About 80% of the students surveyed did not consult a librarian for help when doing course-related research.

Librarians need to be aware of these additional challenges posed by the Google Generation and work even harder to convince them of the importance of information literacy and the wider context of information resources.

Librarians, who have been around since before the Internet, know that students have always required instruction in order to formulate search strategies, develop keywords and evaluate sources. This has not changed just because more of the information is now available electronically. Students still require the training but librarians now have the additional option of providing instruction and guidelines in digital format. We need to continue to research the learning styles and preferences of our students, and to keep a watchful eye on what is working and what is not. Many librarians have fallen into the trap of thinking that they know what their users want without actually doing the research. Talk to students, survey them, and conduct focus groups and usability testing:

> The digital age offers huge opportunities, but the decline of information literacy skills risks robbing a generation of the ability to fully utilize these. (Brindley 2009b, p. 3)

Librarians need to work harder than ever to ensure that students of the 21st century are equipped with the information literacy skills to make the best of what the digital environment offers them.

References

American Library Association (ALA), 1989. *Presidential Committee on Information Literacy: Final Report*. Chicago, IL: ALA. Available from: http://www.ala.org/ala/mgrps/divs/acrl/publications/whitepapers/presidential.cfm (accessed 29 January 2010).

Association of College and Research Libraries (ACRL), 2000. *Information Literacy Competency Standards for Higher Education*. Available from: http://www.ala.org/ala/mgrps/divs/acrl/standards/standards.pdf (accessed 29 January 2010).

Ayres, P., 2008. *YouTube for Fun and Education*. Available from: http://www.intute.ac.uk/blog/wp-content/uploads/2008/12/allis_youtubedoc.pdf (accessed 29 January 2010).

Bawden, D., 2001. Progress in documentation – information and digital literacies: a review of concepts. *Journal of Documentation*, 57 (2), 218–59.

Bloom, B. and Deyrup, M., 2003. Information literacy across the wired university. *Reference Services Review* 31 (3), 237–47.

Brindley, L., 2009a. The digital paradoxes we face. *Library and Information Update*, September 2009, 21.

Brindley, L., 2009b. Challenges for great libraries in the age of the digital native. *Information Services and Use* 29 (1), 3–12.

Bruce, C., 1994. Portrait of an information literate person. *HERDSA News*, 16(3), 9–11.

Cardiff University, 2009. *Handbook for Information Literacy Teaching*. Cardiff: University of Cardiff. Available from: http://www.cardiff.ac.uk/insrv/ educationandtraining/infolit/hilt/ (accessed 29 January 2010).

Chartered Institute of Information Professionals (CILIP), 2004. *Information Literacy: A Definition*. Available from: http://www.cilip.org.uk/get-involved/ advocacy/learning/information-literacy/Pages/definition.aspx (accessed 29 January 2010).

Centre for Information Behaviour and the Evaluation of Research (CIBER), 2008. *Information Behaviour of the Researcher of the Future*. Available from: http:// www.jisc.ac.uk/media/documents/programmes/reppres/gg_final_keynote_ 11012008.pdf (accessed 29 January 2010).

DaCosta, J.W. and Jones, B., 2007. Developing students' information and research skills via Blackboard. *Communications in Information Literacy*, 1(1), 16–25. Available from: http://www.comminfolit.org/index.php/cil/article/view/ Spring2007AR2/12 (accessed 29 January 2010).

DaCosta, J.W., 2009. How passion and perseverance steered the course towards a university's Information Literacy Framework. In *Uncharted Waters: Tapping The Depths of Our Community to Enhance Learning: Thirty-fifth National LOEX Library Instruction Conference Proceedings*, San Diego (CA), May 3–5, 2007. Ypsilanti, MI: Eastern Michigan University.

Daugherty, A. and Russo, M.F., eds. 2007. *Information Literacy Programs in the Digital Age: Educating College and University Students Online*. Chicago, IL: Association of College and Research Libraries.

Department for Culture, Media and Sport (DCMS), 2009. *Digital Britain: The Final Report*. London: DCMS. Available from: http://www.culture.gov.uk/ images/publications/digitalbritain-finalreport-jun09.pdf (accessed 29 January 2010).

Foster, N. F. and Gibbons, S. eds. 2007. *Studying Students: The Undergraduate Research Project at the University of Rochester*. Chicago, IL: ACRL.

Gremmels, G. and Mashek, K.B., 2007. Wartburg College: planful deployment. In: *Information Literacy Programs in the Digital Age: Educating College and University Students Online*, Daugherty, A. and Russo, M.F., Chicago, IL: ACRL.

Gullikson, S., 2006. Faculty perceptions of ACRL's Information Literacy Competency Standards for Higher Education. *Journal of Academic Librarianship*, 32 (6), 583–92.

Head, A.J. and Eisenberg, M.B., 2009. *Lessons Learned: How College Students Seek Information in the Digital Age: Project Information Literacy Progress Report*. Seattle, WA: University of Washington. Available from: http://projectinfolit.org/pdfs/PIL_Fall2009_Year1Report_12_2009.pdf (accessed 29 January 2010).

Honey, P. and Mumford, A., 2006. *Learning Styles Questionnaire 2006: 80 Item version*. Maidenhead: Peter Honey.

Jefkins, A., 2009. UCL subject librarians get WISE in Moodle. *SCONUL Focus*, 45, 45–47. Available from: http://www.sconul.ac.uk/publications/newsletter/45/13.pdf (accessed 29 January 2010).

Katz, I.R., 2007. Testing information literacy in digital environments: ETS's iSkills assessment. *Information Technology and Libraries*, 26 (3), 3–12.

Kolb, D., 2005. *The Kolb Learning Styles Inventory*. London: Hay Resources Direct.

Melville, D., 2009. *Higher Education in a Web 2.0 World*. London: JISC. Available from: http://www.jisc.ac.uk/media/documents/publications/heweb20rptv1.pdf (accessed 29 January 2010).

Obama, B., 2009. *National Information Literacy Awareness Month, 2009*. By the President of the United States of America: A Proclamation. Available from: http://www.whitehouse.gov/assets/documents/2009literacy_prc_rel.pdf (accessed 29 January 2010).

Rader, H., 1991. Information literacy: a revolution in the library. *RQ*, 31 (1), 25–29.

Society of College, National and University Libraries (SCONUL), 1999. *Information Skills in Higher Education: A SCONUL Position Paper*. Available from: http://www.sconul.ac.uk/groups/information_literacy/papers/Seven_pillars2.pdf (accessed 29 January 2010).

Webber, S. and Johnston, B., 2000. Conceptions of information literacy: new perspectives and implications. *Journal of Information Science*, 26(6), 381–97.

Whitton, N. and Jones, R., 2009. Alternative Reality Gaming to support information literacy. *ALISS Quarterly*, 4(4), 18–21.

Willis, C.N. and Thomas, W.J., 2006. *Students as Audience: Identity and Information Literacy Instruction. Portal: Libraries and the Academy*, 6 (4), 431–44. Available from: http://muse.jhu.edu/journals/portal_libraries_and_the_academy/v006/6.4willis.pdf (accessed 29 January 2010).

Zhang, W., 2001. Building partnerships in liberal arts education: library team teaching. *Reference Services Review*, 29 (2), 141–9.

Chapter 4

Professional Education for a Digital World

Sheila Corrall

Introduction

Professional education for library and information work is subject to the same social, technological, economic and political forces as other university activities. Key drivers and trends in higher education in the 21st century include the internationalisation of educational programmes, as institutions compete in the global marketplace; growth in postgraduate provision, as individuals seek a competitive edge in the job market; development of interdisciplinary programmes, as new specialisms emerge at the boundaries of established professions; demand for flexible delivery, as workers need or want to combine study with employment; and the impact of information and communication technologies on both curriculum content and delivery modes. The digital environment has influenced programme and module content, the learning and research resources available to students and the methods of interaction and delivery for both on-campus and distance learners. National education and skills policies have also affected academic provision, reinforcing the importance of employability, connecting education to the workplace and promoting the need for lifelong learning. This chapter reviews developments in initial professional education in relation to practice in university libraries, with particular reference to the impact of technology on content and delivery.

Professional Education in the Information Society

Education for librarianship has evolved in response to changes in professional thinking and practice, employment patterns and market demand, as well as being subject to the requirements of academic institutions, professional bodies and government agencies responsible for quality assurance and assessment. Within the UK, the two key professional and academic reference points are the Body of Professional Knowledge (BPK) published by the Chartered Institute of Library and Information Professionals (CILIP 2004) and the subject benchmark statement for Librarianship and Information Management (LIM) published by the Quality Assurance Agency for Higher Education (QAA 2007). Both documents indicate the specialised subject knowledge and understanding that programmes in the field are expected to cover, along with more generic skillsets that are also important, though not unique, to the discipline. The CILIP BPK is central to the professional accreditation of educational programmes and thus potentially a significant influence on course content. The QAA benchmark is also intended to guide academic institutions in the design of their courses, but in addition is seen as potentially relevant to prospective students and employers. (The current benchmark formally covers only bachelor's degrees, but in practice also serves as the reference point for master's programmes; the academic community plans to produce a master's statement in 2010–11.)

Although the presentation styles of the CILIP (2004) and QAA (2007) statements are quite different, their interpretations of the domain are broadly similar. Both statements were developed with input from practitioners and academics, but their value as a current delineation of the nature and extent of the discipline is limited because they provide only high-level descriptions of the subject field. However, some indication of how the field has developed is shown by the fact that information literacy is more prominent in both statements than in the equivalent previous documents produced by both organisations; for example, the previous benchmark statement contained only a bullet point related to the need for information skills and information literacy, whereas the current statement uses the term as the heading for a section containing three points on the subject (QAA 2000; QAA 2007). The main headings used for the subject-specific knowledge and understanding and the generic skills and abilities sections of the QAA (2007) benchmark statement are shown in Table 4.1.

Other political, economic and social factors have been instrumental in the shift that has been evident as a global phenomenon over the past four decades from professionally-accredited courses in librarianship/library science provided by 'library schools' to a situation where such courses represent only a small minority among a multiplicity of other programme titles that are now typically offered by schools based on broader groupings of academic/professional disciplines, usually with 'information' in their collective title, although other disciplinary links are also evident (notably with business schools in UK universities). Within the UK, the most common library-related degrees now are the MSc in Information and Library

Table 4.1   Subject knowledge and generic skills for library and information management

Subject knowledge and understanding	Skills
• Information resources and collection management • Information retrieval and knowledge organisation • Information literacy and user support • Information services and intermediary roles • Information agencies and professional institutions • Information environment and policy context	• Knowledge acquisition and study • Management and organisational behaviour • Communication and interpersonal skills • Information and communications technology

Management and MSc in Information and Library Studies, followed by the MA in Library and Information Management or Studies; only two universities (Sheffield and City University London), offer specific Masters in Librarianship or Library Science. In the US, a higher proportion (around one-third) of professionally-accredited programmes have retained the Library Science title, but the most common degree is Library and Information Science (LIS). However, the more significant point is that in many cases the majority of programmes offered by the school where LIS is taught may not be accredited by a library association or equivalent body.

The iSchools movement is the latest manifestation of this trend towards expanding the disciplinary field and has typically extended subject groupings beyond library/information management and information systems/technology to computer science. The formal iSchools organisation was founded in 2005 by 'a collective of Information Schools dedicated to advancing the information field in the 21st Century'.[1] Its website explains that these schools and departments 'have been newly created or are evolving from programs formerly focused on specific tracks such as information technology, library science, informatics, and information science' and that they 'share a fundamental interest in the relationships between information, people, and technology'. Originally a US-based association, the membership of 27 now includes a few institutions in Europe (for example, the University of Sheffield) and Asia. Key membership criteria include a substantial track record in sponsored research and an active doctoral programme. LIS programmes are thus now offered alongside Masters in Information Management and/or Information Systems, in addition to more specialised variants typically offered in collaboration with other schools, such as Sheffield's MA in Multilingual Information Management and the dual Law (Doctor of Jurisprudence) and Master of Library Science (MLS-JD) at Indiana University Bloomington.

---

1   http://www.ischools.org/site/about/.

Some academic and professional commentators have viewed the emergence of iSchools and moves to define a new 'iField' as a threat to the library world, but others see these developments as a chance to re-brand and reposition a profession with a low profile and an image problem. In the United States, there has been a strange antipathy to the association of librarianship with information science, which pre-dates the arrival of the iSchools, typified by Gorman's (2004, p. 377) assertion:

> What we used to call library schools have, perforce, become hosts to information science and information studies faculty and curricula. These disciplines (if they exist at all) are, at best, peripheral to professional library work and, at worst, inimical to it.

However, examination of the activities and programmes of the iSchools reveals that despite the near-universal absence of the word 'library' from their names and the widely-publicised closure of a few well-known MLS degrees, most iSchools continue to offer library science degrees and to promote library education on their websites (Wallace 2009). While the iSchools do have an explicit interest in information technologies and their application, the movement is concerned to promote an interdisciplinary approach and the primary focus is on information, specifically on 'the uses and users of information', with 'a core commitment to concepts like universal access and user-centered organization of information'. A key issue here is the position of librarianship within the larger group: some library educators have expressed concern about forced alliances with other disciplines that have progressively led to librarianship becoming 'nothing more than a discipline stream, or even just a single course, within a school within a faculty' (Hallam and Calvert 2009, p. 292). This can restrict the scope for developing electives on library specialties, as reported by Middleton and Hallam (2001) in their review of the situation in Australia; however, it can also widen the choice of electives in other subjects that may be of interest and relevance to LIS students (e.g. modules with a focus on information systems or technology).

Connecting Professional Education with Library Practice

From a university library perspective, these developments in information schools generally parallel the movement within the information services sector that has brought many academic libraries closer to academic computing and information technology services, where cross-functional working and multi-professional teams in academic services correspond to the interdisciplinary interests and multi-disciplinary expertise that characterise contemporary information schools. The convergence of library, information technology, media and related services over the past two decades is well documented across multiple dimensions, including the formulation of integrated information strategies, evolution of new organisational models, creation of technology-rich learning spaces, discussion of changing professional roles and investigation of extended hybrid skillsets (Abbott 2003; Allen and Wilson 1996; Bennett 2009; Corrall and Lester 1996; Hanson 2005). The landscape has continued to change as institutions experiment with different service configurations, notably in relation to supporting learners, with specialist tutors and educational developers becoming other likely partners, in addition to or instead of information technologists (McKnight 2010).

The skillset needed by academic librarians in contemporary digital learning environments also continues to expand, demanding a breadth and depth of knowledge beyond the requirements assumed in the early days of hybrid libraries. Several practitioners note the need to blend librarianship expertise with both technological and pedagogical competencies (Allen 2005; Biddiscombe 2002; Bell and Shank 2007). Other commentators confirm the continuing importance of partnerships with IT services in addition to the development of collaborations with other agencies such as university presses and research offices in relation to emergent library roles in publishing peer-reviewed work (journals and books) and managing research data (Hahn 2008; Lewis 2010). The blended skillsets identified for roles in research data management are particularly challenging, with domain expertise/subject knowledge highlighted in addition to library and information science expertise, more advanced technical skills, personal and managerial abilities (Gabridge 2009; Henty 2008).

The scale and pace of change in the library environment and beyond has presented challenges for library educators, who have been criticised for inadequate coverage of both established subjects and contemporary topics. Gorman (2004) argues that concentration on technology has resulted in topics regarded as central by employers, such as cataloguing, reference work and collection development no longer having a central place in LIS curricula, which is confirmed by Lynch (2008) in her US-based review of developments in professional education. The situation in the UK has moved in the same direction, with most schools teaching these subjects as part of more broadly-based modules, but specific modules on collection management and on cataloguing and classification are provided in around one-third of the relevant programmes. Owens and Leonhardt (2009, p. 551–2) note that interdisciplinarity and the perceived move away from established core subjects has meant more choice for students in North America:

> more electives and fewer required core courses that, along with an increased interdisciplinary approach to LIS education, allow students to tailor programs to suit their individual needs. Information technology and courses addressing the Web and the Internet were identified ... as new clusters of courses that are new to LIS curricula over the past ten years or so.

Similar trends are evident in the UK, with schools such as Sheffield continually expanding their range of modules, but some UK programmes offer few or no electives. Owens and Leonhardt (2009) also note the growth in distance delivery (synchronous, asynchronous or hybrid) of LIS programmes, with the Web-based Information Science Education (WISE) consortium of 15 universities enabling schools that do not offer their own distance learning programmes to participate in collaborative distance education. WISE is US-led but includes members in Canada, Australia, New Zealand and the UK.[2]

While Lynch (2008) observes that the demotion of cataloguing has been especially hotly contested, inadequate coverage of information literacy has become the current focus for practitioner criticism, particularly in relation to the teaching roles of academic librarians (Dale et al. 2006; Peacock 2001; Walter 2006), a complaint that is repeated in this book. Information literacy is a key area of activity for university libraries that has expanded and diversified with the development of digital learning environments, with teaching now a large part of many liaison librarian jobs (Bewick and Corrall 2010). The current situation is not as unsatisfactory as the anecdotal evidence suggests. A recent survey in North America of ALA-accredited programmes reported 'great strides since the 1970s in acknowledging the importance of information literacy' and that '[elective] classes in information literacy instruction are common at most MLIS programs and had even increased since the last study' (Aproles et al. 2008, p. 207). Mbabu (2009) found 49 out of 57 (86%) programmes offered at least one course dedicated to instruction theory and practice. In the UK, the websites for CILIP-accredited Masters show a mixed picture and suggest that overall coverage is inferior to the US provision. Information literacy is listed among the topics covered by most institutions, but only three universities – Liverpool John Moores, Loughborough and Sheffield – provide core modules with information literacy in the title and only Sheffield offers electives enabling students to specialise in information literacy instruction as part of a generalist librarianship programme.

However, it is worth noting here the significant variation, not only in programme titles, but also in module titles and programme configurations among CILIP-accredited LIS courses, which makes it hard to compare offerings. In addition, the contents of academic programmes and their constituent modules are generally subject to a continuous process of review and renewal, with adjustments made annually to reflect research and developments in the field, as well as feedback and suggestions from students and employers. Such modifications are often not immediately apparent to external observers, if changes are made in the topics covered or delivery methods in ways that do not require amendment of formal unit descriptions, even though cumulatively such developments can amount to substantial change over time. For example, at Sheffield, we have altered the focus, content and delivery of our core module on 'Information resources and information literacy' incrementally over the past five years to such an extent that it is now radically different to what was offered before, but the title and description on our website have stayed the same. The module aims to develop an understanding of information literacy from both theoretical and practical perspectives, in addition

---

2   http://www.wiseeducation.org/.

to skills in searching for, evaluating and packaging information in response to a query from a client, but now also has a strong focus on preparing students for roles as information literacy educators. The following are examples of new elements:

- 'Search/teach task' – students work in pairs over four weeks to create a short instructional guide to using a specific aspect of a particular database. They also have to provide a list of links to recommended sources of information (guides, tutorials, evaluations) about the database and publish this using a Web 2.0 tool.
- Learning theories – in preparation for the search/teach task, a lecture session introduces students to theories about learning styles and principles of learning design. The session also provides guidelines on designing user documentation to support learning.
- Critical evaluation – following on from the production of their own database guide, students then have to evaluate one of the guides produced by their classmates.
- 'Practitioners' seminar' – students are given the opportunity to work on the development of their teaching skills in a half-day workshop with two expert practitioners. The workshop is modelled on events delivered to practitioners in the field and is currently led by the authors of a leading text on teaching information skills (Webb and Powis 2004).

At Sheffield, students keen to build on their learning from this core module, can take the elective module on 'Educational informatics', which provides more in-depth coverage of learning theories in the specific context of e-learning and different learning technologies. Practical exercises enable students to experiment with and evaluate technology applications for learning through the use of virtual environments, such as WebCT/Blackboard, Wimba, Second Life and wikis. Assessment tasks include working in small groups on the development of learning materials and evaluation of tools. Students can also take a seminar-based elective on 'Information literacy research', which considers research problems in information literacy and methods of investigating them. Seminars are led by members of the Centre for Information Literacy Research and researchers from other institutions (including academics and practitioner-researchers).

Generalist versus Specialist Programmes and Pathways

Middleton and Hallam (2001) note the tradition in LIS to offer generic education as preparation for both generalist and subject-specialist roles in library and information work, though they observe that the desirability of specialist provision has been debated among law librarians; it has also been discussed in the health sector (Petrinic and Urquhart 2007). While Middleton and Hallam (2001) see continuing value in broadly-based professional curricula, they recognise the need for some specialised education, but report that in Australia the amalgamation of library schools with other subjects has reduced the opportunity for offering modules on library specialties. They suggest specialist education could be delivered through collaborative provision (e.g. a module developed by one institution being offered to students at another via distance learning) or pursued later as continuing professional development (CPD). Petrinic and Urquhart (2007, p. 174–5) similarly highlight the importance of structured CPD for health librarians, acknowledging that it is not realistic to expect all LIS departments to provide a health information module (though several do so), but suggest that curricula:

> should encourage students to appreciate the need for domain knowledge in their future career, and provide opportunities for developing some specialist subject knowledge, and relevant skills, in the dissertation, at least.

Sector-specific modules on academic libraries are common in the US, where student numbers are more likely to support specialised provision, but relatively rare in the UK and other countries. Recent research by Bailey (2010) revealed that three-quarters of ALA-accredited schools in the US offered courses in academic librarianship, but evidence from UK websites indicates that only Sheffield and the University of the West of England currently offer academic library electives. However, examination of the US syllabi showed that such courses typically include a mix of specialist subjects directly related to university libraries (such as the higher education sector, scholarly communication and academic library standards) and other topics of general relevance to librarians (such as collection management, budgeting/finance and human resources), presumably presented in an academic library context. In addition, Bailey (2010) notes that several topics identified as essential or important by academic librarians (e.g. information literacy, instruction/ teaching and technology/Web 2.0) are more likely to be covered by other courses in their programmes, so even where specialist academic library courses exist, aspiring university librarians and their advisers need to look beyond these classes when assessing whether programmes will meet their particular needs.

Bailey (2010, p. 41) consequently argues that 'A single course in academic librarianship ... cannot be expected to develop pedagogical or technological competency' and suggests that schools could improve the advice on course selection (module choice) offered to students aspiring to work in academic libraries, and 'Perhaps ... should create an academic track with prescribed courses'. However, the increasingly specialist nature of professional work in university libraries arguably requires identification of not just one, but several different specialised academic library tracks or potential pathways through generalist programmes, to help students select the most suitable configuration of units from the wide range of electives now offered by many schools, particularly those within the more broadly-based iSchools community, whose portfolios typically include modules designed for information managers and information systems professionals that may appeal to more technically-oriented university librarians. In the UK, the iSchool at Sheffield has recently defined specialised pathways through its MA Librarianship programme for aspiring information literacy educators and digital library managers.

Table 4.2 shows how students at Sheffield can opt for either a generalist academic library education, by combining the academic libraries module with a varied mix of materials-based, subject-specific or technology-related electives, or a specialised academic library pathway, by selecting from designated clusters of modules. Students wanting to specialise in information literacy education can choose two electives from 'Information literacy research', 'Educational informatics' and 'Information storage and retrieval research' to build on the introductions to these subjects provided in their core modules (which must also include one sector-specific module, covering services in academic libraries, in public libraries or to young people). Similarly, students wanting to specialise in digital library management can select their two optional modules from two other clusters, offering different blends of content related to information, systems and technology.

The emergence of whole programmes for new entrants or established practitioners wanting a specialised education in these and other areas is one of the significant developments of the past decade. Specialist offerings of potential interest to university librarians include programmes based solely in information schools or equivalents, such as University College London's MA in Electronic Communication and Publishing, and Sheffield's MA in Information Literacy and MSc in Electronic and Digital Library Management, in addition to degrees offered jointly with other departments, such as Sheffield's MSc in Health Informatics (in partnership with the School of Health and Related Research), MSc in Information Systems Management (with the Management School) and MSc in Information Systems (with the Department of Computer Science) and City University London's MSc in Electronic Publishing (a partnership between the Department of Information Science and Department of Journalism) and MSc in Information, Communication and Society (a partnership between the Department of Sociology and Department of Information Science). Dual degrees with business and law schools are a common example of this phenomenon in North America (Owens and Leonhardt 2009).

Educating Professionals for Digital Library Environments

Technological impacts on collections, services, roles and skills dominate the top ten trends in academic libraries identified by the Association of College and Research Libraries (ACRL 2010). Technology has similarly pervaded LIS curricula. Traditional topics such as collection development and reference services are now taught in the context of electronic resources and digital delivery. At Sheffield, the module on information retrieval taken by Librarianship and Information Management students now has the sub-title 'Search engines and

Table 4.2   Generalist and specialist academic library pathways

Core modules (semesters 1 and 2)	Optional activities (semesters 1 and 2)

• Libraries, information and society 1
• Information resources and information literacy
• Information retrieval: search engines and digital libraries
• Libraries, information and society 2: Academic and research libraries
• Management for library and information services (double-length module)
• Research methods
• Dissertation
	• Library visits:
	  □ Research-led university library
	  □ Teaching-led university library
	• Information literacy practitioners seminar
	• UKSG serials roadshow
	• CILIP student conference
	• Essential professional skills
	• Essential computing skills

Academic Librarian Generalist Programme (semester 2: two electives from any area)

• Business intelligence • E-business and e-commerce • Legal information resource management • Independent study	• Archives and records management • E-government information • Healthcare information • Independent study	• Information literacy research • Educational informatics • Information storage and retrieval research	• Digital multimedia libraries • Educational informatics • Information storage and retrieval research	• Content management systems • Database design • Human computer interaction and user interface design

Information Literacy Educator	Digital Library Manager

Academic Librarian Specialised Pathways (two electives from selected specialty) digital libraries', showing how digital environments have given new meanings to the term 'library', which extend beyond traditional settings. Managing information systems and technology now occupies two sessions of the core management module in Sheffield's MA Librarianship programme and several new technology-based electives have also been offered to librarianship students in recent years (e.g. Content Management Systems, Digital Multimedia Libraries and Educational Informatics). Many librarianship students are choosing technology-related topics for their dissertations; recent examples at Sheffield include virtual reference services, next-generation library catalogues, institutional repositories, RFID technology, digital video archives and image retrieval. Owens and Leonhardt (2009) comment on new clusters of courses related to the Internet and the Web emerging in the past decade, and Ray (2009, p. 358) notes that 'Many LIS schools have or are developing tracks in digital libraries, archives, digital curation, and museum informatics' to meet the need for 'digitally savvy information professionals'.

However, commentators have criticised the treatment of digital library topics in LIS programmes. Varalakshmi (2009) analysed digital library course content of master-degree programmes in India, reporting that all the departments studied included basic aspects of digital libraries, both theoretical and practical, in the core curriculum, but the course components were rudimentary in nature, needing further expansion to gain the required depth of knowledge and skills in the particular areas of specialisation. He concludes with a detailed specification of recommended elements for both core and advanced elective units to give graduates the competence and confidence to handle the digital environments of the new millennium. Dahlström and Doracic (2009) discuss provision of digitisation education in Scandinavian programmes, noting limited coverage, mainly as elective modules, with many courses covering digitisation as part of a larger topic (e.g. electronic publishing) and more emphasis on theory than hands-on practice. Sheffield's innovative module on Digital Multimedia Libraries has been designed to meet the identified need for practical experiential learning; it is a core unit for the specialist MSc in Electronic and Digital Library Management, but is also offered as an elective for the MA in Librarianship and available as a standalone one-week CPD course. Other writers, such as Choi and Rasmussen (2006), argue that professional education for digital librarians should place more emphasis on management (especially project management) and interpersonal skills (particularly teamwork and communication) in preparing students for digital library roles.

There is a continuing debate on the specialist requirements of digital library environments, including the question of whether a library or computer/IT background is better preparation for jobs in libraries with a systems/technology focus, in addition to the issue of coverage in core and elective modules of LIS curricula. In the UK, provision has generally developed incrementally, with new topics and modules introduced into existing portfolios as needs and opportunities arise, but with a few new programmes also emerging through such a process. In the US, national funding has facilitated the development of specialist courses to meet emerging needs. The National Science Foundation supported the development of model curricula related to digital libraries through a collaborative project involving two institutions, and the Institute of Museum and Library Studies has funded projects to develop new courses and programmes in digital curation at several universities (Ray 2009). Thus, the University of Illinois at Urbana-Champaign[3] has developed a new Data Curation Education Program (DCEP) as a specialisation (a formal pathway) within its existing LIS Master of Science that offers:

> a focus on data collection and management, knowledge representation, digital preservation and archiving, data standards, and policy, providing the theory and skills necessary to work directly with academic and industry researchers who need data curation expertise.

DCEP includes specialist core units on 'Foundations of data curation' and 'Digital preservation', alongside existing units with an information systems/technology focus designated as core and elective courses. It is also available as an online distance learning programme and additional units are planned, including courses on humanities data curation. In addition, the University of North Carolina at Chapel Hill has revised one existing module and developed two new units to offer a postgraduate Certificate of Digital Curation that can be awarded in conjunction with its existing Masters in Library or Information Science on completion of additional credits for three digital curation-related courses (to be available from 2010–11).

Roles and Preparation for Data Management

US educational innovation for the digital environment has taken place alongside significant service development in US university libraries, evidenced by Gold's (2007) discussion of the current state of data librarianship and Walters' (2009) reference to several US academic libraries that 'have taken entrepreneurial steps to extend beyond their traditional digital assets and include managing scientific and scholarly research data' to become 'digital information management centers'. A need for more specialist education in data curation has also been identified in Australia and the UK, where the role of university libraries in managing research data has been debated in relation to e-research developments (Henty 2008; Lewis 2010; Swan and Brown 2008), although there are fewer current examples of data librarianship at present. Provision in UK LIS curricula is similarly limited, but Loughborough's MA/MSc in Information and Library Management includes an elective on digital curation and the University of Glasgow[4] offers a specialised programme in MSc in Information Management and Preservation (Digital) that

---

3   http://cirss.lis.illinois.edu/CollMeta/dcep/imlsSci.htm.

4   http://www.hatii.arts.gla.ac.uk/imp/page5.htm.

aims to equip students 'to work as archivists, records managers, and digital curators'.

Most commentators recognise that libraries have a role in facilitating access to data sets as an important part of the research knowledge base, but there is less certainty about exactly what it should be. Hey and Hey (2006, p. 526) note that many scientific fields have national repositories for research data, but suggest that university libraries may need to assist in managing smaller datasets generated by research groups or individuals, concluding that 'the e-Science revolution will put libraries and repositories center stage in the development of the next generation research infrastructure'. Swan and Brown (2008) agree that e-research offers strategic opportunities for university libraries, suggesting potential roles in raising data awareness among researchers, providing data archiving and preservation services through institutional repositories and developing data librarianship as a new strand of professional practice. However, Gold (2007) offers a counter-argument, highlighting the issue that domain expertise is sometimes seen as 'essential' for effective working with researchers and also important in providing 'credible expert help with data management problems or tools'. She notes the argument that

> it makes much more sense to train domain experts in data management and curation skills than it does to try to teach nonscientist librarians to understand the infrastructure and service needs of a domain.

The literature identifies several distinct but overlapping roles in the research data arena, with different and inconsistent labels, for example: data creators/ authors, data scientists/specialists, data curators/custodians/managers/stewards, data librarians/archivists and data users/re-users. These roles can be undertaken by practitioners from various backgrounds, including researchers, computer scientists, information technologists, information scientists and librarians (Swan and Brown 2008). Lewis (2010) notes that the field of research data management suffers from the terminological problems that often beset an emerging area of practice. The many continual, sequential and occasional action stages identified in the Digital Curation Centre's Curation Lifecycle Model (Higgins 2008; Lewis 2010) illustrate the pluralism and complexity of the field. Yakel (2007) discusses and dissects the concept of digital curation, noting different treatments of the concept in seminal reports and the different aspects emphasised in published definitions, highlighting their dual focus on active intervention and future usage. She concludes that digital curation has become an umbrella term for several related concepts, namely digital preservation, data curation, electronic records and digital asset management.

Writing from a UK perspective, Lewis (2010) discusses the need to resolve what exactly should be done locally, nationally and internationally to manage research data, but suggests nine strategic and operational areas where libraries should get involved, mostly working in partnership with other campus agencies, such as IT services and research offices. His pyramid of responsibilities includes:

raising awareness of data management issues among both the library workforce and research community, providing advice, training and education on data matters for researchers, postgraduates and undergraduates, developing both technical capacity (e.g. storage facilities) and professional capability (i.e. library competence) in data curation, and formulating or shaping policy at local (university) and national levels. In the US, practitioners who have gained experience in this area acknowledge the specialist technical skills needed, but also comment on the relevance and applicability of traditional library competence in areas such as metadata, collections, liaison, reference and instruction (Gabridge 2009; Witt 2008). Choudhury (2008, p. 217, 218) suggests that 'new roles of "data scientist" or "data humanist" ... may represent the future of subject librarianship', while arguing that 'Scientific datasets may be thought of as the "special collections" of the digital age'.

While some sources suggest the need for a new category of digital data management or data curation professionals as a defined career path, others, including many of those working in the field, see the required roles as an extension of traditional curatorial work and argue that the need instead is to train and educate professionals at different career stages and from various backgrounds to work in digital or data curation (Yakel 2007; Hank and Davidson 2009). Reports from the US, UK and Australia all point to significant skills gaps and shortages in the field (Yakel 2007; Swan and Brown 2008; Henty 2008). Most sources emphasise the importance of specialist technical skills and sufficient disciplinary knowledge, but many also highlight non-technical skills and personal qualities as equally critical, in addition to LIS expertise, including knowledge of copyright and intellectual property issues, as well as traditional activities such as selection and the reference interview, re-purposed as a 'data interview' (Henty 2008; Gabridge 2009; Garritano and Carlson 2009; Witt and Carlson 2007). Gabridge (2009, p. 18–19) summarises the multi-faceted skillset needed for the new role of 'data liaison':

> The highly self-motivated liaisons who want to work in this realm will need to have very strong analytical, project management, and problem solving skills, as well as the ability to work independently at the intersection of digital data, technology, and metadata. These core skills are the base on which training in digital preservation concepts, data modeling, data standards, policy, and data collection and management can be added to round out a data liaison's preparation.

Experience from the field thus suggests that library competencies provide a good foundation for data management, but they need to be combined with additional technical competencies.

Despite the numerous reports and case studies published recently, there is no consensus on the preferred strategy to close the data skills and knowledge gaps identified. Progress has been hindered by the range of different players potentially needing training and education, shortage of funding in the UK for curriculum development and programme participation, and uncertainty about who should take the lead in moving things forward. However, there are parallels here with information literacy, which similarly required multi-faceted provision for diverse audiences, including general education for undergraduates, advanced training for postgraduates, specialised curricula for LIS students (including differentiated pathways for mainstream and specialist career tracks) and professional development for experienced practitioners (including different lengths, levels and modes of programmes for different roles and backgrounds). A mixed economy of CPD via short courses, summer schools and extended programmes, combined with specialist credit-bearing modules offered individually and as designated pathways or programmes, complemented with the extension of information literacy education to cover data literacy could be the way forward, with LIS schools collaborating rather than competing with each other and the wider community.

Conclusion

Professional education for library work has generally moved away from vocational programmes on librarianship or library science to degrees including information in their title, provided by schools with broader portfolios covering information technology and/or business. Both educators and practitioners have raised concerns about the position of library education in large schools and the implications for curriculum development, but collocation with information systems and/or management education offers opportunities to extend module choice for library students, particularly in relation to the technical skills and understanding needed for digital library environments. Some practitioners have criticised reduced coverage of traditional topics such as cataloguing, reference work and collection management, while others want more provision for contemporary concerns such as information literacy, teaching and digital curation. Specialised courses in academic librarianship are common in the US, but offered by only a few schools in the UK, though subjects related to academic libraries may be covered in other modules. Many schools have introduced new electives on technology-related topics and a few have introduced whole programmes with a digital library focus, but commentators continue to debate the need to improve professional education in librarianship for the digital world, especially in digital libraries and data curation, which has been facilitated in the US by national funding.

References

Abbott, C., 2003. *HIMSS (Hybrid Information Management: Skills for Senior Staff): Final Project Report*, Birmingham: University of Birmingham. Available from: http://www.himss.bham.ac.uk/Documents/final/ProjReportfinal.pdf. (accessed 15 July 2010).

ACRL, 2010. 2010 top trends in academic libraries: a review of the current literature, *College and Research Libraries News*, 71 (6), 286–92.

Allen, D.K. and Wilson, T.D., 1996. Information strategies in UK higher education institutions, *International Journal of Information Management*, 16 (4), 239–51.

Allen, L., 2005. Hybrid librarians in the 21st century library: a collaborative service-staffing model. *In: 12th National Conference, Association of College and Research Libraries*, April 7–10, 2005, Minneapolis, Minnesota, Chicago, IL: American Library Association, Association of College and Research Libraries, 291–301. Available from: http://www.acrl.org/ala/mgrps/divs/acrl/events/pdf/allen05.pdf (accessed 9 July 2010).

Aproles, C., Johnson, A.M. and Farison, L., 2008. What the teachers are teaching: how MLIS programs are preparing academic librarians for instructional roles, *Journal of Education for Library and Information Science*, 49 (3), 195–209.

Bailey, E., 2010. Educating future academic librarians: an analysis of courses in academic librarianship, *Journal of Education for Library and Information Science*, 51 (1), 30–42.

Bell, S.J. and Shank, J.D., 2007. *Academic Librarianship by Design: A Blended Librarian's Guide to the Tools and Techniques*, Chicago, IL: American Library Association.

Bennett, S., 2009. Libraries and learning: a history of paradigm change, *Portal: Libraries and the Academy*, 9 (2), 181–97.

Bewick, L. and Corrall, S., 2010. Developing librarians as teachers: a study of their pedagogical knowledge, *Journal of Librarianship and Information Science*, 42 (2), 97–110.

Biddiscombe, R., 2002. Learning support professionals: the changing role of subject specialists in UK academic libraries, *Program*, 36 (4), 228–35.

Choi, Y. and Rasmussen, E., 2006. What is needed to educate future digital librarians: a study of current practice and staffing patterns in academic and research libraries, *D-Lib Magazine*, 12 (9). Available from: http://www.dlib.org/dlib/september06/choi/09choi.html (accessed 9 July 2010).

Choudhury, G.S., 2008. Case study in data curation at Johns Hopkins University, *Library Trends*, 57 (2), 211–20.

CILIP, 2004. *Body of Professional Knowledge, London: Chartered Institute of Library and Information Professionals*. Available from: http://www.cilip.org.uk/sitecollectiondocuments/PDFs/qualificationschartership/BPK.pdf. (accessed 9 July 2010).

Corrall, S. and Lester, R., 1996. Professors and professionals: on changing boundaries, in Cuthbert, R. ed. *Working in Higher Education*, pp. 84–100. Buckingham: Society for Research into Higher Education and Open University Press.

Dahlström, M. and Doracic, A., 2009. Digitization education: courses taken and lessons learned, *D-Lib Magazine*, 15 (3/4). Available from: http://www.dlib.org/dlib/march09/dahlstrom/03dahlstrom.html (accessed 9 July 2010).

Dale, P., Leharne, M., Knight, T. and Marshall, K., 2006. Professional engagement: the subject specialist in higher education, in: Dale, P. Holland, M. and Matthews, M., eds, *Subject Librarians: Engaging with the Learning and Teaching Environment.* Aldershot: Ashgate, 19–31.

Gabridge, T., 2009. The last mile: liaison roles in curating science and engineering research data, *Research Libraries Issues*, 265, 15–21. Available from: http://www.arl.org/bm~doc/rli-265-gabridge.pdf (accessed 9 July 2010).

Garritano, J.R. and Carlson, J.R., 2009. *A Subject Librarian's Guide to Collaborating on e-Science Projects, Issues in Science and Technology Librarianship*, 57. Available from: http://www.istl.org/09-spring/refereed2.html#15 (accessed 9 July 2010).

Gold, A., 2007. Cyberinfrastructure, data, and libraries, part 2: Libraries and the data challenge: roles and actions for libraries, *D-Lib Magazine*, 13 (9/10). Available from: http://www.dlib.org/dlib/september07/gold/09gold-pt2.html (accessed 9 July 2010).

Gorman, M., 2004. Whither library education?, *New Library World*, 105 (1204/1205), 376–80.

Hallam, G. and Calvert, P., 2009. Australia; LIS education, In: Abdullahi, I., ed. *Global Library and Information Science: A Textbook for Students and Educators*, IFLA Publications 136–37. Munich: KG Saur.

Hahn, K.K., 2008. *Research Library Publishing Services: New Options for University Publishing*, Washington, DC: Association of Research Libraries. Available from: http://www.arl.org/bm~doc/research-library-publishing-services.pdf (accessed 9 July 2010).

Hank, C. and Davidson, J., 2009. International data curation education action (IDEA) working group. *D-Lib Magazine*, 15(3/4). Available from: http://www.dlib.org/dlib/march09/hank/03hank.html (accessed 15 July 2010).

Hanson, T., ed. 2005. *Managing Academic Support Services in Universities: The Convergence Experience*, London: Facet.

Henty, M., 2008. *Developing the Capability and Skills to Support e-Research*, Ariadne, 55. Available from: http://www.ariadne.ac.uk/issue55/henty/. (accessed 9 July 2010).

Hey, T. and Hey J., 2006. E-science and its implications for the library community, *Library Hi Tech*, 24 (4), 515–28.

Higgins, S., 2008. The DCC curation lifecycle model, *International Journal of Digital Curation*, 3 (1), 134–40. Available from: http://www.ijdc.net/index.php/ijdc/article/view/69 (accessed 9 July 2010).

Lewis, M., 2010. Libraries and the management of research data, In: McKnight, S. ed., *Envisioning Future Academic Library Services*: Initiatives, Ideas and Challenges. London: Facet, 145–69.

Lynch, B.P., 2008. Library education: its past, its present, its future, *Library Trends*, 56 (4), 931–53.

Mbabu, L., 2009. LIS curricula introducing information literacy courses alongside instructional classes, *Journal of Education for Library and Information Science*, 50 (3), 203–210.

McKnight, S., 2010. Adding value to learning and teaching, In: McKnight, S., ed., *Envisioning Future Academic Library Services: Initiatives, Ideas and Challenges*. London: Facet, 197–215.

Middleton, M. and Hallam, G., 2001. Generic education for specialist information professionals, *Australian Law Librarian*, 9 (3), 181–94.

Owens, L. and Leonhardt, T., 2009. North America; LIS education, In: Abdullahi, I., ed. *Global Library and Information Science: A Textbook for Students and Educators*, IFLA Publications 136-137, Munich: KG Saur, 549–63.

Peacock, J., 2001. Teaching skills for teaching librarians: postcards from the edge of the educational paradigm, *Australian Academic and Research Libraries*, 32 (1), 26–42. Available from: http://alia.org.au/publishing/aarl/32.1/full.text/jpeacock.html (accessed 9 July 2010).

Petrinic, T. and Urquhart, C., 2007. The education and training needs of health librarians – the generalist versus specialist dilemma, *Health Information and Libraries Journal*, 24 (3), 167–76.

QAA, 2000. *Librarianship and Information Management, Subject Benchmark Statements*, *AR 006 4/2000*, Gloucester: Quality Assurance Agency for Higher Education. Available from: http://www.qaa.ac.uk/academicinfrastructure/benchmark/honours/librarianship.pdf (accessed 9 July 2010).

QAA, 2007. *Librarianship and Information Management, Subject Benchmark Statements, QAA 201 12/07*, Gloucester: Quality Assurance Agency for Higher Education. Available from: http://www.qaa.ac.uk/academicinfrastructure/benchmark/statements/Librarianship07.pdf (accessed 9 July 2010).

Ray, J., 2009. Sharks, digital curation, and the education of information professionals, *Museum Management and Curatorship*, 24 (94), 357–68.

Swan, A. and Brown, S., 2008. *The Skills, Role and Career Structure of Data Scientists and Curators: An Assessment of Current Practice and Future Needs*, Report to the JISC, Truro: Key Perspectives. Available from: http://www.jisc.ac.uk/publications/documents/dataskillscareersfinalreport.aspx (accessed 9 July 2010).

Varalakshmi, R.S.R., 2009. Curriculum for digital libraries: an analytical study of Indian LIS curricula, *D-Lib Magazine*, 15 (9/10). Available from: http://www.dlib.org/dlib/september09/varalakshmi/09varalakshmi.html (accessed 9 July 2010).

Wallace, D.P., 2009. The iSchools, education for librarianship, and the voice of doom and gloom, *Journal of Academic Librarianship*, 35 (5), 405–409.

Walter, S., 2006. Instructional improvement: building capacity for the professional development of librarians as teachers, *Reference and User Services Quarterly*, 45 (3), 213–18.

Walters, T.O., 2009. Data curation program development in US universities: the Georgia Institute of Technology example, *International Journal of Digital*

Curation, 3 (4), 83–92. Available from: http://www.ijdc.net/index.php/ijdc/article/viewFile/136/153 (accessed 9 July 2010).

Webb, J. and Powis, C., 2004. *Teaching Information Skills: Theory and Practice.* London: Facet.

Witt, M., 2008. Institutional repositories and research data curation in a distributed environment, *Library Trends*, 57 (2), 191–201.

Witt, M. and Carlson, J.R., 2007. Conducting a Data Interview, Libraries Research Publications. West Lafayette, *In:* Purdue University Libraries. Available from: http://docs.lib.purdue.edu/lib_research/81/ (accessed 9 July 2010).

Yakel, E., 2007. Digital curation, *OCLC Systems and Services*, 23 (4), 335–40.

Chapter 5

The Library Chameleon: Physical Space

Liz Waller

Introduction

Since the days of the Library at Alexandria, libraries have been offering information, advice and a place to study. In more recent years with the increasing move to electronic publications and the explosion of information available via the internet, various voices have announced the demise of the physical library and its relevance to the modern learning experience. In the digital environment is there still a need for a physical space in the university?

Learning Spaces: The National Context

Space utilisation and the development and use of learning spaces have been the focus for much research and discussion in the past few years. Bodies such as the UK Higher Education Space Management Group[1] and the Joint Information Systems Committee (JISC)[2] have both issued guidance on the importance of appropriate learning spaces in higher education (HE) estates provision. The Higher Education Funding Council for England (HEFCE), recognising the importance of informed space planning for the future, has sponsored through its Leadership, Governance

---

1   http://www.smg.ac.uk/.
2   www.jisc.ac.uk.

and Management fund "Learning Landscapes in Higher Education"[3], a project intended to promote collaboration between academics and estates professionals in the creation of new learning spaces.

The JISC has been at the forefront of encouraging creative thinking in learning space design; its publication *Designing Spaces for Effective Learning* (JISC 2006) suggests the mantra for space as: Flexible, Future-proofed, Bold, Creative, Supportive and Enterprising. This report is only part of the body of work funded by the JISC with later projects running under the e-Learning and Innovation Programme (now closed).

This work, alongside other initiatives such as the Designing Libraries website[4] which began as a collaboration between the University of Aberystwyth, the Museums, Libraries and Archives Council (MLA), the Chartered Institute of Library and Information Professionals (CILIP) and more recently the Society of College National and University Libraries (SCONUL), together with articles from practitioners, contributes to the growing body of work on learning space, providing guidance for architects, estates personnel, and librarians in planning and implementing new learning spaces.

Learning Spaces: The Library Context

Over the centuries our libraries have responded to political, technological and pedagogical changes in the environment to remain relevant and at the heart of the learning experience. Recent drivers for change have been: increasing student numbers, ubiquitous technology, the rise of the so-called digital native, changes to learning, teaching and assessment and of course the growth in e-information.

The past few years, prompted by these drivers, has seen the rise of the information commons and learning commons concept, both overseas and in the UK. Lippincott (2007) suggests that there is no commonly accepted definition of these terms but argues that they have in common access to content (print and electronic), access to power, hardware and software, and lastly access to assistance in the use of technology and content. These are seen to be exciting, stimulating spaces lending themselves to collaborative and even social learning (Bryant et al. 2009). At the same time however our customers still need access to what might be viewed as traditional library spaces, offering opportunities for individual learning in quiet or silent environments (Beard and Dale 2008). We also have to consider the needs of researchers working in both physical and virtual library spaces, and the services and roles required to support them in emerging environments. The Association of Research Libraries (ARL) gives a thorough insight into the facilities required by reseachers.[5]

---

3 http://learninglandscapes.blogs.lincoln.ac.uk/.
4 http://www.designinglibraries.org.uk/.
5 http://www.arl.org/rtl/space/index.shtml.

That the library remains at the heart of the academic experience even in a predominantly digital environment is evidenced by the various exciting new libraries and refurbishments which have been completed since 2000, with further developments planned for the future.

Learning Spaces: The Institutional Context – Case Studies

So how have the new libraries and refurbished libraries responded? How have they reinterpreted library space to bring it up to speed with the demands of 21st century teaching and learning, creating new and interesting offerings of learning spaces to their customers?

What has become evident through these developments is a strategic response to the specific institutional contexts. If one looks across recent developments they are not generic clones of each other; each learns from what has passed before and with stakeholder consultation develops a space response to fit their institutions' needs.

But the physical space also demands a rethink of service strategy – some institutions have also taken the opportunity to reconsider their approach to customer support and service delivery within their innovative learning spaces. There has been recognition that this has made a difference to the uptake of new provision, guiding the end user to effective use of the development.

To illustrate how libraries have developed spaces for the digital age, four libraries have been selected to serve as case studies; University of Warwick, University of Leicester, University of Nottingham and University of Edinburgh. Each offers its unique interpretation of space for learners in their specific context: at the same time common threads are evident, offering insights into trends in learning space development.

Case Study 1: University of Warwick: Learning Grid and Library Development
With thanks to Robin Green of the University of Warwick who provided the information on which this case study is based.

The original library was built in the 1960s and was considered to be one of the key buildings of the 1966 Development Plan; it had remained almost unmodified since that time. Since 2004 a series of projects, designed by architects MJP, have led to the 'reinvigoration of library services and learning environments at Warwick'.

These projects have included the Learning Grid (2004) which is a development occupying a space of about 1,350 square metres on two floors in University House. It has capacity for approximately 300 students. Managed by the library and open 24/7, the Grid provides flexible, IT-rich space supporting independent learning. A wide range of equipment is available – scanners, electronic whiteboards, wireless network, video cameras, networked PCs. Space is open plan but rooms for formal presentations are also available. Permanent staff support students alongside student advisors. Limited eating and drinking is allowed in the Grid. The Grid was used as a space exemplar by JISC in its Designing Spaces for Effective Learning publication.

In addition to the Learning Grid, Warwick has more recently redeveloped 40% of the library building, including the Teaching Grid and Research Exchange (2008). The development was funded by the University, Higher Education Funding Council for England and The Wolfson Foundation.[6] The vision for the library redevelopment was: 'To provide a stylish, iconic, inspiring, user-centric, comfortable, colourful, visually exciting, fun, attractive, welcoming, varied and flexible space that celebrates intellectual activity and learning'.

The deliverables for the project were, a more attractive entrance floor incorporating:

- a café;
- social learning space and increased floor space for users;
- a more open and legible building by removal of visual and physical barriers;
- colour coding and improved signage;
- attractive and welcoming study environments supporting different modes of teaching, learning and research;
- improved user facing support;
- managing growth in book stock;
- 200 new study spaces in a range of layouts with access to multimedia resources;
- creation of two spaces, one teaching and the other postgraduate study focused;
- an IT services help desk;
- a new 100 seat lecture theatre;
- two PC suites (each with 85 computers) and 24-hour access.

Refurbishment has extended the IT capability of the building to accommodate known and anticipated IT developments, including a PA system, wireless and Radio Frequency Identification (RFID). Within the library there is a combination of fixed IT and multimedia workspaces (plasma screens, SmartBoards, DVD TVs), round tables for group work, and soft seats fitted together to make angled sofas with integral power and data points as well as swivel single user laptop tables, plus high long tables with padded bench seats. These provide a wide range of layouts with some flexibility for users to move the various types of chairs and some tables around. The space is open plan and could be reconfigured with little expense. Though the furniture is good quality (much of it Steelcase), it has

---

6   http://www.wolfson.org.uk/.

suffered at the hands of the students – broken legs, swivel tables bent because of excessive weight on them, etc. This is all accidental damage with no evidence of deliberate vandalism. It does highlight the intensive use of the facilities and the need for robust furniture choices when refurbishing space.

To release space for the development a new off-site book store for less popular book stock (retrievable within one day) was put in place. In addition there has been use of compact mobile shelving in a library extension, which is proving to be 50% more efficient in space use than traditional shelving. The building has been zoned to create noisier, informal learning environments on the first two floors, with quiet and silent study space on the upper floors.

The Teaching Grid provides space for academics to explore new learning technologies and modes of delivering learning. It is being used for developmental workshops, course and events, and a range of teaching and learning activities. The facility has been designed to be re-purposed if the current function is not taken up by academics.

The Wolfson Research Exchange has been provided for research postgraduates with a focus on collaboration. It features one small lecture space which houses 90 delegates and is configurable to two or three rooms as required, a Creative Wall which is used as for projection (there is a matrix system which allows projection onto the wall from events held within the exchange or elsewhere in the University) and as a magnetic white board, break-out space, and desking for 60 students including an area for quiet study.

There have been changes to service strategy with the implementation of the new spaces in the library. The old-style issue desk is replaced by service pods with customers and staff co-existing rather than separated by nearly one metre of issue desk. Fixed enquiry points have gone, apart from the service pods by the entrance. Roaming advisors have been introduced in place of enquiry desks, dealing with all first line queries from IT to catalogue, and library advisors rather than professional librarians now deal with the front line interactions and referrals.

The deliberately open plan style of the social learning floors spawns high noise levels, and at certain times of day the library has become a very popular place with an emphasis on social engagement rather than social learning, so some complaints are received from users, academic staff and some library staff.

Currently there has been no formal evaluation of the new spaces. The growth in usage (footfall in the library is up by over 50%) has proved the success of the development, and informal feedback has been received through student liaison committees, student barometer results and other mechanisms. The new informal spaces have been particularly successful as they have provided a new type of space that was not available in the library before.

Changes to the service model and the roles involved have been reviewed with staff and refined over time.

> There is a real buzz in the library – it really makes me want to come here to work. It's so much more than just a library.

Case Study 2: University of Edinburgh: Library Refurbishment
With thanks to Sheila Cannell of the University of Edinburgh who provided the information on which this case study is based.

Edinburgh University Library originally opened in 1967; the current redevelopment began in 2006[7], and is scheduled for completion in 2012. The project budget is £60 million, funded through the capital acquisitions budget of the University, including the Science Research Investment Fund (SRIF), Tax Increment Financing (TIF) and fundraising. The currently partially redeveloped library is used as a venue for visitors, and is seen as an attraction encouraging investment in the University if not the library directly.

The architect for the 1967 building was Sir Basil Spence, the project architect being Andrew Merrylees. The building is now listed. The architects for the redevelopment are Lewis and Hickey, who are also responsible for interior design. The practical imperative for the redevelopment was the discovery of asbestos in the building. This discovery had arisen when the University was investigating its 1960s estate. A driver for development was the desire of the University to improve its estate, the library featuring as an investment in the student experience. It is now viewed as the primary academic building for learning. The phased approach to redevelopment is proving to be beneficial as changes can be incorporated in the light of living with the design. These changes are not cost neutral but the benefits are considered to outweigh the costs.

The project seeks to provide space which is flexible and capable of housing either books or study space in the future. A variety of different spaces are available to suit individuals or groups, with some spaces allowing users to create their own study environment. Seminar rooms, meeting areas and a café are provided; the last of these provides social space for relaxation.

The development has pervasive technology, allowing users access to both print and electronic resources, and to virtual help which sits alongside traditional face to face support mechanisms. Books which are rarely used are placed in on-site compact shelving, or in an off-site store.

A 50% increase in usage has been logged during the academic year 2008/09, although entry figures had decline in 2007/08 due to the disruption caused by the early phases of the work. Although not proven, there is a suspicion that the length of individual stays has increased. Spaces are now much more flexible and capable of adapting to new uses.

Furniture has been critical to the success of the redevelopment. Quality is very important; new furniture has been used alongside refurbished original desks and chairs. There is little power-enabled furniture as it is not felt to be robust. The furniture is designed to be moveable but there are limitations to this as furniture has to be centred around power provision from the floor boxes.

---

7   http://www.is.ed.ac.uk/mlrp/redevelopment/Vision.htm.

The building is fully wireless enabled with the additional provision of 450 fixed PCs, although it is believed that laptop use is as intensive as the use of these machines. Power is provided to the desktop in many areas, with a raised floor present everywhere with the exception of the ground floor. Floor boxes are also provided for power but are not successful due to trailing cables and tops to floor boxes being displaced. Different kinds of furniture are used to populate the different areas, and as the building incorporates social learning space, a menu of behaviours has been introduced through signage as a means to differentiate expected behaviours in the areas. With an extensive café as part of the redevelopment this helps define the boundaries for eating and drinking in the facilities.

To encourage use of the collections, and to make them easier to navigate, the collections strategy has been rethought. This has included the creation of an off-site store and the concentration of the high use book collection on the ground floor. The use of items from Special Collections is promoted, with inclusion of seminar rooms in their new suite of accommodation. Special Collections stores are delivered to British Standard BS5454 recommendations for the storage and exhibition of archival documents. Conservation and digitisation units look towards the future preservation and dissemination of collections.

RFID tagging of the high demand book collection has aided the move to increased self-service. Self-issue and self-return of stock has released the service desk to deal with more substantive user queries. Desks cover library, IT and e-learning questions and roving help is also in place.

One unique feature is the use of 'holopros'[8] in the large reception area. This uses holograph projection technology and is being used for knowledge transfer in the University. They have been used to advertise such diverse topics as special collections, parasites from the veterinary department and the Chaplaincy labyrinth.

Group pods have been one of the big success stories of the project. They are intended for use by groups of three to seven people and include a PC with provision for two to three laptops to be used along with a large screen plasma display and six sockets for headphones. Pods appear to encourage various types of learning; a lot of project work has been observed, but also peer mentoring. They have been described as 'a visualization of social and collaborative learning'.

Part way through the project the library is finding that its users need strong encouragement to use collections other than those on the ground floor. Maintenance of the building and some furniture types are an issue because of the extremely high usage. The redevelopment has already been perceived as a successful University project and there has been a significant increase in usage and positive feedback from users. The library awaits the outcome of the 2010 National Student Survey, and 'Library as Place' scores in its 2009 survey have already increased.

---

8   http://www.holopro.com.

Case Study 3: University of Nottingham Learning Hubs
With thanks to Susan Storey and Valerie Housley of the University of Nottingham who provided the information on which this case study is based.

The Hallward Library was refurbished in 2006/07 with HEFCE capital monies and Centre of Excellence in Teaching and Learning (CETL) funding from the Centre for Integrative Learning (CIL) and the Visual Learning Lab (VLL). The original building architects were Harry Faulkner Brown and the open plan layout has lent itself well to the changes of use needed since opening in 1972. Alexi Marmot Associates were interior designers for the refurbishment.

Information Services (IS) at Nottingham is committed to develop and manage its library sites to provide support for research, learning and teaching. A Library Facilities Plan was developed in 2006 in partnership with a specialist consultancy, MoveCorp. The plan included an overview of expected use of library space over the next five years in relation to physical collections, study space and other facilities and services, taking into account the changing balance between printed and electronic information provision.

The Learning Hub concept emerged out of several activities, including benchmarking with other institutions, analysis of the relevant literature, and customer consultation. The results of these activities fed into the initial Learning Hub concept designs. The concept is designed to mesh with the University's e-Learning Strategy and the latest pedagogical research, for example, coming out of the work of the Centres for Excellence in Teaching and Learning.

The development utilised those areas in Hallward Library vacated by Manuscripts and Special Collections in spring 2006. IS senior managers, and staff carrying out backroom functions, had been relocated from Hallward Library to the King's Meadow Campus and this made considerable additional space available for redevelopment for student use. The Learning Hub is on two floors.

The reconfigured accommodation (about 3,500 square metres) was designed to contain a number of key features which are detailed below. Wireless technology is available throughout the building, and laptop plug in, including power and direct access to the network, is provided. Learning and assistive technologies which include equipment and software capable of supporting audio, video and interactive working demonstrate a commitment to changing pedagogy. Spaces are designed to be flexible and include chairs, tables, partitions and in some cases IT equipment, which can be moved to allow the creation of ad hoc group working. Group study and A/V viewing and areas for more relaxed working, including comfortable furniture and café facilities, feature in the refurbishment.

Users are supported by multi-skilled staff who handle both traditional library and IT-related queries. This is part of a new service concept which takes support to where the users need it rather than expecting them to seek help at an enquiry desk. The whole area is technology-rich, including fixed equipment in the bookable rooms and five 'mini-IMAX'. These are trolleys with a Smart board over a plasma screen and a PC, designed to be moved as needed. Some rooms have video conferencing available, and one studio has ceiling cameras to record presentations. Floors have short stay PCs (most standing height, some seated) designed to be used for 15-minute slots, and these are very popular. Various rooms in the library can be booked and most are available for drop-in use when not booked.

The furniture was designed to be flexible and attractive, so it could be moved to create the space any group needed. There is a policy of not setting it back into the original layout, so the space is seen as student centred. There is selection of different seating (operator chairs, soft seating, upright chairs, pebble stools), and tables (small, high, low, large), of a significantly higher quality and price than normally used. There are power and data plug-in floor points and some provision on pillars, and the large PC tables have additional power and data provided through flip up sockets in the desks for laptop use. There is very little dedicated staff space and a reduced-size lending desk, which puts the emphasis firmly on self-service for straightforward transactions.

In 2008 the upper two floors of Hallward Library were refurbished. These are the two stockholding subject floors, and provide traditional individual study and research space, enhanced with power and data plug in at certain desks, with pods, printing, copying and scanning on each floor, subject enquiry desks, and a new research reading room, open to all. These floors are for quiet and silent study.

The large investment in RFID technology was made specifically to create self-service as the default method for loans and returns. A new role of Information Assistant was created to offer a higher level of library and IT support, roaming throughout the Learning Hub, for extended hours. Opening on a 24/7 basis was piloted for exams in 2005, and was extended in Hallward Library (the largest) to run for the latter part of the autumn term, the whole of the spring term and until the end of the summer exams, including some vacation weeks prior to exams. A web survey was carried out in December 2007 which showed that the new space was very popular and much appreciated by returning students, who could see the difference. A small number preferred traditional library space to work in and could see no benefit to the new facilities. The Centre for Integrative Learning commissioned an evaluation study late in 2009, using observation of and structured interviews with users.

The furniture bought for level one is not as easily moved as intended, but lessons were learnt from this when buying furniture for level two. Food and drink policy works well on levels one and two but the tighter restrictions on levels three and four have to be actively policed at times. Increased laptop usage does at times strain the wireless and power provision, so these have been improved. The demands made on the lending desk for laptop loan and return have increased work for staff in a way that took the library by surprise. Loan periods and procedures have been changed to help with this.

The Learning Hub and new ways of working are very successful. An already-busy library has shown an increase in use at certain times, and the space is buzzing with activity and used as intended. It is clear that students studying subjects other than those covered by Hallward Library use the space, even though Learning Hubs were placed in three other libraries at the same time. This is the largest and best equipped space, in the centre of the University Park campus. Laptops are very popular, and a mix of library laptops and students' own laptops in use in the same group is seen. The relaxed food and drink policy on levels 1 and 2 is a success for all. The furniture and fittings are on the whole still in good condition, proving that students will treat a good facility with respect.

Case Study 4: University of Leicester Redevelopment Project
With thanks to Louise Jones of the University of Leicester who provided the information on which this case study is based. The University of Leicester is one of the winners of the 2010 SCONUL Library Design Building Awards.

The library building at Leicester originally opened in 1975. The redevelopment project consisted of a new build extension and the refurbishment of the building. The work on the extension commenced in 2005 and was ready for occupation in April 2007. This was followed by the refurbishment of the old building, with the library fully completed in April 2008. The full cost of the building was £32m, £5m realised through fund-raising, and £4m from SRIF. The remainder was provided by the University. The cost per square metre of the development was £2258. The architects were Birmingham-based Associated Architects who were also responsible for the interior design.

In the mid-1970s the University had 5,000 students, but this had grown to 14,000 on campus so a need for an extension was evident. There was also a need to improve the quality of the space, and to meet the increasing demands for a high quality student experience.

The structure of the building with its concrete floors meant that there were issues around the delivery of flexible IT, a key deliverable for the library. This was addressed through the addition of a raised access floor, the resulting low ceiling heights being accepted as a compromise. The library had been unable to satisfactorily address demand for group and social space provision which had arisen.

Leicester recognised the rapid evolution of academic libraries and wished to be at the forefront of development. It required the new building to be adaptable to handle future changes such as the reorganisation of collections, alterations to the print/electronic balance of collections and the introduction of new services. The library aimed to provide a varied range of high-quality study spaces for undergraduate and postgraduate students, and academic staff, including help facilities and relaxation space. Leicester sought to provide 20 years of expansion space for their printed collections alongside a high level of network connectivity to give good access to electronic collections. Facilities for information skills teaching and seminars allowed library staff to develop user skills for the modern information environment.

The library at Leicester is at the heart of the campus and was one of the first major investments by the University in recent years. The library project was seen as raising the bar for University facilities.

The development has delivered a single seamless space as demanded by the library in its initial planning principles, and has a modern, light, welcoming ambience. User spaces have expanded to 1,500 of all types with pervasive wireless networking. The library now includes the Kirby and West Special Collections Suite for rare books and manuscripts to BS5454 standard, and incorporates additional student facilities such as the Careers Service, Student Learning Centre, AccessAbility Zone and an adjacent but separately accessed 500-seat lecture theatre with associated seminar rooms was also part of the project. Further details of provision can be found on the University of Leicester website.[9]

The development has realised a large increase of provision for fixed IT, almost double the number of workstations that were available in the previous library. To facilitate the use of the wireless provision there is power to the desktop. Desks are bespoke, traditional furniture and not easily moveable. The library has concentrated on modern, classic design for its furniture, with the use of leather for soft furnishing. Art work is also a feature in the building, again with an emphasis on quality. The Group Study rooms are provided with plasma screens, wireless internet access and a PC, and are currently the only provision of this nature on campus. Now these have proved to be a success, more of these are planned elsewhere.

A key feature of the development is the quality of the space which has been delivered; this has been viewed as sending a message about the nature of Leicester as a university. As a part of this the library is definitely viewed as a modern research library, not as a learning centre.

Leicester is not a converged service but within the library the Help Zone is staffed by library and IT staff. Joint training is in place so both sets of staff can answer basic IT and library questions. IT services have closed their external IT help desk. This is seen as answering student requirements and was planned in from the beginning of the project. The library is also looking at virtual help, piloting the use of Meebo and also investigating NorMAN.[10]

Self-service was another strategic imperative and this has been well received by the users. Opening hours have been extended to 24/7 during the summer exam period and vacation opening hours have also been extended. Self-service online payments are in place for photocopying and printing, and the library is looking at online payment of fines and room bookings. With stock RFID tagged, self-issue and return and self-pickup of holds are in place. As a result of this emphasis on self-service, staff are redeployed to offer roving help; this includes assistance with the fixed PC equipment.

Some evaluation has taken place. A satisfaction survey on the library environment ran in April/May 2009. This sought to assess satisfaction with the

9   http://www.le.ac.uk/library/about/building/index.html.

10   http://www.norman.net.uk/.

particular improvements which had been requested by users. All areas were rated 'very good' or 'good'. National Student Survey (NSS) scores for library facilities have increased by 10% to 91%, and scores from postgraduate research students have also improved. Leicester is still tweaking its facilities; for example a silent study zone in the Graduate School Reading Room has been implemented following the initial opening.

The success of the building means that occupancy is very high, which brings its own problems. Areas for further development include the IT training rooms, which are thought to be too traditional in approach. The real successes of the building are considered to be the aesthetics and the quality of the architecture which are viewed as exciting, the new self-service model, group space and the Graduate School Reading Room. Unusually for a development including a refurbishment the building is rated BREEAM[11] excellent.

Key Themes

Since 1993 and the Follett report[12], libraries have been changing and evolving to meet the needs of users who teach, learn and research in an increasingly digital environment. Strong themes emerging from the four case studies and from the wider HE environment are:

- flexibility
- collections
- access to technology
- service strategy
- variety in space provision
- furniture.

Flexibility

Currently libraries are juggling competing needs for space within their estate. Space allocation appropriate for 2010 may not be suited to 2020, 2015 or even 2012. In creating spaces we need to be aware of the speed with which developments in technology, pedagogy, economics and publishing may arise, and design in the ability to shift provision to meet the challenges that change may present. This has been specifically mentioned in the case studies. In addition a strong trend is the creation of spaces which can be reconfigured by the end user to fit their particular requirements when they visit the library. Whilst somewhat constrained by power

---

11   http://www.breeam.org/.

12   http://www.ukoln.ac.uk/services/papers/follett/report.

delivery, this type of provision is welcomed by users, and will continue to feature in new library developments.

Collections

Various reports predict an increasing move to more born digital materials, and a rapid decline in original print materials. In her presentation at the NPO conference in 2004, Helen Shenton (2004) talked about future collections storage. She featured British Library commissioned research into this area, which predicted an increase of 100% in the annual output of monographs between 2004 and 2020; a 70% increase in the output of UK serials between 2004 and 2020; a 50% increase in serials published solely in e-format by 2016; by 2020, 25% of newspaper being published solely in e-format and that by 2020 40% of UK monographs would be available in e-format only.

However in 2010 librarians are struggling to manage still expanding print collections which are hungry for space. In the HE library community many are moving to a rationalisation of collections, with lesser used materials moving to deeper storage, often away from the main library building. This is allowing librarians to devote more space which, when IT enabled, provides access to both heavier used print materials and an increasing range of e-resources, software and learning environments. The struggle to balance space for collections against other space needs is seen at two case study libraries, Warwick and Edinburgh. Long-term collection strategy is also seen in the rationale for development at Leicester.

To assist this situation various initiatives are underway in the area of collaborative collection storage. The UK Research Reserve (Shorley 2008) is creating a distributed national research collection, between the British Library and the Higher Education sector. This will remove duplicate copies of journal titles, preserving two copies of each journal title within the UKRR membership. Phase 2 of UKRR is seeking to free up 100 km of shelving in member libraries by 2013, releasing space to be used for other purposes. The White Rose consortium (Senior 2007), in addition to their work on collaborative journal storage, has also investigated a similar approach to monograph provision. Perhaps this is an inevitable area for development in the future?

Access to Technology

Following the Follett report, librarians have witnessed the change in the provision of IT and e-resources in their libraries. Our libraries being delivered now show pervasive provision of IT with attempts to ensure that the current set-up will be able to respond to future demands. Wireless access is now standard, with provision of power to the desktop. An increasing range of hardware is readily available to the users, either fixed or through laptop loan. It is inevitable that we will see an emphasis on technologies supporting the creation of multimedia, rather than just access to it, as new assessment methodologies become available to students. The provision of a wider range of technologies is leading libraries to examine their service strategies.

Service Strategy

Libraries across all sectors have been moving to increased self-service. Routine activities such as the issue and return of stock, and payment of fines, have enabled libraries to look again at their use of staff. Whilst service desks of some description are still evident, they often sit alongside roving help, delivering assistance to users across library buildings at the point of need. These changes have also seen harmonisation of IT and library help, sometimes through the same staff, sometimes with colleagues in IT services. This multi-skilling is likely to increase as the divisions between what constitutes a 'library' and 'IT query' become more blurred. Noticeable too, in the Edinburgh case study, is the inclusion of e-learning help with the service desk provision.

Variety in Space Provision

Each of the case study libraries is providing a wide variety of study spaces for their individual user populations. Each shows a mixture of silent, quiet and collaborative spaces, in open plan or provision of group rooms or pod structures which encourage group interaction. Throughout all these spaces, IT provision, whether through fixed IT or through wireless, is evident. Café provision features in our case studies, as it does in many new developments, providing refreshment and social learning space for the extended opening hours featured in the new buildings.

In each institution, consideration has taken place with regard to the different spaces within the library in the context of space provided elsewhere in the University. In some cases, such as Leicester and Warwick, specific facilities have been deliberately placed in the library. At the same time universities are looking more strategically at space outside the library and developing social learning spaces across their campuses.

Delivering the right kind of space and the right mix of spaces will be increasingly important in maintaining the relevance of the library to the academic experience. The ability to change space around, as mentioned previously, will assist with this. Various libraries which have undergone recent new builds or redevelopments have found the need to re-purpose space arises relatively quickly. The library will need to be constantly in touch with the needs of its different user groups, ensuring the best provision for all.

Furniture

New types of learning space have demanded new and innovative furniture to ensure that they are fit for purpose. There is an increased and necessary emphasis on both quality and robustness. Selection of furniture to cope with the high volume of usage is very important, and exchanging experience with colleagues through personal contacts or sites such as Designing Libraries will be useful.

Furniture is being used to define spaces, which makes necessary changes to space use simple and relatively inexpensive to implement. Also a blend of more traditional with new and experimental types of furniture is evident, the exact mix selected to fit the needs of each individual institution. In most instances power and data delivery to all areas either directly through furniture or though floor sockets or other power delivery mechanisms ensures the blended use of e and print resources in our current hybrid environment.

Evaluation

In this area the JISC funded *Study of Effective Evaluation Models and Practices for Technology Supported Physical Learning Spaces* project (JELS[13]) sought to identify and review the tools, methods and frameworks used to evaluate technology supported or enhanced physical learning spaces. It was intended that the findings of the investigation would contribute to the body of knowledge on the development of learning spaces, any frameworks and guidelines arising from the study informing all stages of development.

The study, which reported in June 2009, is a useful snapshot of the state of evaluation in the UK HE and FE sector. It highlights current frameworks and methodologies used in evaluation, though it concludes that the area is in need of further development. Currently evaluation tends to revolve around justification of expenditure on spaces and the degree to which these are valued by students. Evaluation of the impact of these spaces on learning is less developed, with a few notable exceptions such as the work of:

- the Centre for Inquiry-based Learning in the Arts and Social Sciences (CILASS);
- the Centre for Excellence in Learning and Teaching (CETL);
- the JISC funded JELS project has developed its own framework for the structure and operation of evaluation studies;
- Framework for the Evaluation of Learning Spaces (FELS). This provides: a common vocabulary to standardise evaluations, a checklist of issues to be considered by individual practitioners and evaluators and a structure to describe the nature and character of evaluations completed.

13   http://www.lsri.nottingham.ac.uk/jels/.

Various evaluation mechanisms have been used to assess the success of spaces in the case studies, notably user questionnaires and comments. The JELS project shows the way forward to a more mature evaluation framework which the sector will be well advised to draw upon as we seek to demonstrate the full value of learning spaces in the digital age.

Summary

That the library is still at the heart of the academic experience in the digital age is evidenced by the success of our case studies in their institutional environment, and these are only a small number of exciting and innovative redevelopments within the HE sector. The sector is developing its consideration of the continuing need for learning spaces in the digital age, and placing the library firmly as principal deliverers of this space.

In planning our spaces for the future we can utilise frameworks such as the JISC Infokit framework *Planning and Designing Technology – Rich Learning Spaces* which suggest the use of the following for development of a business case (JISC 2009):

- political environment
- economy and its effects
- sociological and societal influences
- technology
- legal (current and impending)
- environmental considerations
- pedagogy
- values of the organisation

Like chameleons responding to their environment, libraries have changed and evolved to ensure that they can support their different user groups in using both print and e-resources, and the accompanying technologies. This response to environmental changes and pressures will ensure the role of libraries at the heart of learning, teaching and research in HE institutions in the future.

References

Beard, J. and Dale, P., 2008. Re-designing services for Net-Gen and beyond: an holistic review of pedagogy, resource and learning space. *New Review of Academic Librarianship*, (14), 99–114.

Bryant, J., Matthews, G. and Walton, G., 2009. Academic libraries and social learning spaces: a case study of Loughborough University Library. *Journal of Librarianship and Information Science*, 41 (1), 7–18.

JISC, 2006. *Designing Spaces for Effective Learning*. Available from: http://www.jisc.ac.uk/publications/programmerelated/2006/pub_spaces.aspx (accessed 5 January 2010).

JISC, 2009. *Developing the Vision: Planning and Designing Technology – Rich Learning Spaces*. Available from: http://www.jiscinfonet.ac.uk/infokits/learning-space-design/imagination/vision/index_html (accessed 11 February 2010).

Lippincott, J.K., 2007. *Assessing Information Commons, Linking the Information Commons to Learning: How to Measure Success*. Vantage Point, EBSCO: Available from: www2.ebsco.com/enus/NewsCenter/publications/vantagepoint/Pages/vantagepoint.aspx (accessed October 12 2009).

Senior, C., 2007. Collaborative collection management of monographs: the White Rose experience. *SCONUL Focus*, 41, 34–7.

Shenton, H., 2004. *The Future Shape of Collection Storage, Where Shall we Put It? Spotlight on Collection Storage Issues*, NPO conference 2004, London, 58-63.

Shorley, D., 2008. Past its shelve by date? United Kingdom Research Reserve (UKRR): a twenty-first-century strategy to protect our research information for the future, *New Review of Academic Librarianship*, 14 (1) 115–20.

Chapter 6
Virtual Advice Services

Rachel Geeson

Introduction

Virtual advice services encompass email, FAQs, Instant Messaging (IM), chat and SMS text messaging. This chapter will concentrate mainly on instant messaging and chat services. For ease of reading the term 'chat' will be used to mean online synchronous communication either by IM or web chat products, except where a distinction needs to be drawn when comparing the subtleties of the two different types of service.

Snapshot of Current UK Activity

Virtual reference is a mainstream service in today's libraries (DeVoe 2008).

Although virtual reference in the form of chat may be mainstream in the US and Australia, chat enquiry services have been slower to evolve in the UK. This is despite the ubiquitous use of email reference services. At the time of writing, only 20 of the 133 Higher Education Institutions (HEIs) listed on the Universities

UK website[1] had a chat service visibly available on their library's web pages. Literature from UK institutions on their experiences of using IM/chat reference is scarce, with only two recent articles (Hvass and Myer 2008; Haynes 2009).

The relative 'newness' of this type of service in the UK is also demonstrated by the existence of the Virtual Enquiry Project 2008–2009, a collaboration between staff at Edinburgh Napier University and Carnegie College, partly funded by the Scottish Library and Information Council. The project 'aimed to look at the practice of virtual reference, or live chat support in the British academic library sector, and produce information for academic libraries considering starting a virtual reference service' (Virtual Enquiry Project 2009). The website offers a range of help and advice on establishing chat reference and includes case studies of some academic libraries which offer such a service.

In order to provide a snapshot of current activity among UK HEIs, a survey of 15 institutions with chat services was undertaken by the author in November 2009 and their experiences are reflected throughout the chapter. The longest running services had been instigated in 2006 (two institutions) and some services were very new, having been started in the early part of 2009 (four institutions); the rest fell somewhere in between. Eight used OCLC Questionpoint (subscription required), four used Meebo/Plugoo (free), two used LivePerson's LivePerson (subscription required) and one used Altarama's VRL Plus (subscription required).

Reasons for introducing a chat enquiry service were many and varied, although none of them unexpected. Respondents cited:

- the need to engage with students using the social media they were accustomed to using on a day to day basis;
- flexible support for distance and partner students;
- equity of service;
- providing a route into library services for individuals who may feel intimidated asking library staff;
- support for users who may find verbal communication difficult;
- an experiment in exploring the use of web 2.0 technologies;
- immediate interaction with a student (as opposed to advice via email).

One respondent summed up thus:

> The benefit that live chat can offer to off-campus students is huge. Queries that may have taken a week to resolve by multiple emails can now be answered in a few minutes and desktop sharing removes the need for long complex two way email/phone communications regarding how to navigate online resources.

---

1   http://www.universitiesuk.ac.uk.

Instant Messaging vs Chat

When choosing a chat product the issue of cost versus functionality arises. Can the cost of a (chat) subscription service be justified when free (IM) products are available which many students already use? It really depends on the amount of 'back-end' functionality required by the library and how staff want or need to be able to interact with its users.

Instant Messaging Services

Free software includes IM services such as AIM (America Online Instant Messaging), Google Talk, Yahoo! and Windows Live Messenger. These services typically offer text chat, the ability to 'file transfer' and URLs to be typed as means of directing users to other web pages. Individuals must have an account with these services to use them. In the early days of chat it was an inconvenience that users either had to create an account and download software in order to use the same system chosen by the library, or the library had to create multiple IM accounts. More recently, free chat aggregator software such as Meebo and Pidgin let users create a single 'buddy' list irrespective of which IM service they have an account with. This is a useful feature as it allows a library's customers to contact the library via IM using the service they already have an account with. Meebo and Plugoo bring together all of the major IM platforms: AIM, Google Talk, Yahoo! and Windows Live Messenger (Meebo also includes Myspace IM and Facebook chat).

In addition, Meebo and Plugoo offer the functionality of embedding a widget into a web page (in this context a small window for users to type in their query), allowing any and, crucially, anonymous visitors to initiate an IM session. Free software offers quick easy access to a library's enquiry service for users but usually provides no helpful context for staff operating the system such as a user's identity/email address or course/faculty/school. IM systems do not provide a sophisticated means of gathering statistics or recording session transcripts.

Commercial Chat Products

Software designed for use by libraries has lots of useful behind-the-scenes features such as statistics logging, a record of session transcripts and sometimes a 'news management' feature that can be used to disseminate important information to staff working on the enquiry service. Virtual enquiry service managers are able to analyse exactly who queries are coming from and discover whether certain queries reflect widespread issues or pertain just to particular groups. Queries that crop up at certain times of the year can be pre-empted by posting relevant information on the library's web pages, on the Virtual Learning Environment (VLE), blogs and all the usual outlets for student information.

Subscription services are configurable, giving an institution the freedom to add appropriate branding and gather whatever data are required from the user at the point they ask their initial question. When the service is busy messages can be displayed to students in a queue asking them if they want to continue waiting or choose another option such as searching FAQs. Staff can follow up a query if a student 'disappears' as their email address is logged by the system. Certain chat products allow satisfaction surveys to be presented to a user after a transaction. Usually neither staff operating the service nor users have to download any software in order to use the system and staff can converse with more than one student at a time.

The chat transaction itself has greater functionality and is much richer as a result. It offers the ability to use scripted replies (including an initial 'welcome to our service' type message which allows staff breathing space to take in the question), add bookmarks, push web pages to customers and 'co-browse' (i.e. screen-share). In fact commercial services lend themselves to showing a student information in context rather than giving them a quick answer, so a chat session (as opposed to IM) can veer more towards the 'instructional'. Staff are able to take advantage of so-called 'teaching moments' (Desai and Graves 2008; Devlin et al. 2008) where users are effectively taught how to find the information they are looking for. Commercial products also come with the security of technical support and are more often than not hosted on the supplier's server, negating any need for input from local IT departments. At the end of a chat session the user has the option to view/print/email the transcript for future reference, which is particularly helpful for the student if they have been guided through a complex research question.

Subscription services can offer a degree of interoperability with other university systems, e.g. email, which is advantageous if a question needs to be transferred to another member of staff. This can be done within the chat system but the email will arrive in the recipient's normal inbox. It ensures that any loose ends can be tied up if an 'out of office' reply is received by the person transferring the question, and enhances the timeliness and quality of service given to the user. A chat service offers the opportunity to have a joined up approach to virtual advice – popular chat queries can be turned into FAQs on externally facing web pages or scripted replies within the system if the query requires a complicated or in-depth answer.

On a day to day basis, the immediacy of the chat medium ensures that the library obtains feedback very quickly on electronic services (for example) that are not working, as it is much easier and quicker for the user to send a message via a highly visible widget than finding an appropriate email address to report problems to.

Staffing and Running a Chat Service

A good user experience will be the best marketing tool. (Zino 2009)

The way in which a chat service is operated and staffed and the quality of the answers given to users are not to be underestimated. As a method of quality assurance (to guarantee staff buy-in and expertise) it has been suggested that a chat service should be staffed by keen volunteers from amongst the staff (Coffman 2003), but this is a luxury many libraries could not afford. On a purely pragmatic level, who staffs the service will depend on how many hours the service needs to run and the number and grade of staff available to operate the service. It also depends on the depth of help the library wants to be able to provide and whether the chosen chat software offers a robust means of transferring questions to others if necessary.

It is likely (and this is borne out by the survey respondents) that members of staff currently working on information or enquiry desks would constitute the core team for service delivery. Whether the service is run from a public enquiry desk that also deals with face-to-face enquiries or from a separate desk 'behind the scenes' will depend on local staffing structures and the opportunities or constraints these present. It is generally recommended that chat is run from a separate desk (Hvass and Myer 2008). However even if a public service desk is too busy to operate a chat service during core hours, it may be able to deal with queries during evening opening hours for example. The library should bear in mind the public relations aspect of their service: it is better to deal with queries in a timely and efficient manner for fewer hours per day than to offer a longer service but keep customers waiting for long periods. If a customer has a negative experience they will probably not use the service again.

Survey responses indicated that services with longer opening hours were staffed at times from public enquiry desks that also dealt with face-to-face enquiries. There was a trend for services with longer opening hours to be staffed from a separate point during core hours (sometimes used to receive telephone calls as well) but reverting to cover from a public desk in the evenings and weekends. Services with shorter opening hours tended to be staffed only from separate desks 'behind the scenes'.

Service models, in the form of staffing, set-up, opening times and usage figures varied quite widely between institutions. In fact, the few things that virtually all institutions had in common and agreed on were the difficulties experienced in relation to successful operation of the service. These overwhelmingly reflected staffing issues:

- staff buy-in;
- cover for sickness;
- not having enough staff to provide longer opening times;
- confidence in using the software;
- the fear of being 'monitored'.

Types of staff operating the services varied as follows:

- professional only (five institutions);
- professionals and paraprofessionals (five institutions);
- professionals, paraprofessionals and library assistants (two institutions);
- paraprofessionals only (two institutions);
- IT helpdesk advisors (one institution).

It is important to consider whether staffing a chat enquiry service amounts to extra duties for staff or whether it sits within an established level of public service. The way a new service is sold to staff and the effect on their workload will influence motivation and buy-in. It is important to get staff to view the service as a core activity rather than an adjunct to their regular day to day work, particularly if staffed from a separate point. Staff may feel resentful if they see the service as taking them away from an already heavy workload, especially if they are unable to continue with their normal tasks and particularly if they perceive that the service is underused and/or 'gimmicky'.

As staffing is an issue, either having enough staff simply to cover 'normal' operation or when under pressure from sickness, it has to be decided whether the service is peripheral or central to the enquiry portfolio. Which services 'give' when short staffed? Virtual or face-to-face? It is worth considering that 'virtual reference users do not perceive virtual reference as a novelty or as a marginal service, but see it as a significant service option' (Granfield and Robertson 2008). It is crucial to ensure that staff are online when the service is advertised as open. If operation has to be curtailed for any reason, an explanatory note should be added to the access points of the service. It is irritating to a user if the service is advertised as open but no-one is online, and furthermore it appears unprofessional. 'How libraries will staff both in-person and virtual reference services given the economic realities in an era of shrinking budgets' (Naylor et al. 2008) may be of concern, but a chat service can be delivered flexibly from staff's own PCs rather than a dedicated 'enquiries' computer, and delivery of the service can be switched to public desks if necessary.

Training Issues

Some staff may have already used chat software socially and some will not have done. Inevitably, as staff will also have differing comfort levels with IT, group training sessions are a good way to foster an inclusive atmosphere and offer peer support to those who are less confident (and they can be fun!). They work well when staff are able to pair up, one person acting as the 'customer', and one acting as the staff 'operator'. Staff should be encouraged to practise asking and answering questions with their training partner outside of official training sessions.

Using a small number of staff as 'key' or 'expert' trainers means that extra support can be given to others as and when required. It will also help reassure staff when a service goes live if an expert trainer is able to sit with them through their first few transactions.

Staff may have concerns about their answers being recorded as part of the session transcript with the fear of being monitored or picked up on an 'incorrect' answer (a fear reflected by the survey). The fact that transcripts are recorded brings into sharper focus differing levels of expertise in answering enquiries and reflects gaps in staff knowledge. This undoubtedly also exists during face-to-face transactions, but goes largely unnoticed. It also reveals good and not-so-good customer service practices.

Taking this into account, transcripts can be used as a positive tool for further staff training (Haynes 2009). After all, it is commonplace in the commercial world to record phone calls or transcripts for training purposes, but this must be done with sensitivity. 'Incorporating trust in a working environment is a significant factor affecting buy-in for a new service. A non-threatening, non-judgemental workplace encourages staff to be more accepting of change and receptive to new services and changes in workload' (Ogbaa et al. 2008, p. 31).

The analysis of transcripts may also reveal the need for more scripted replies, especially if the topic is complicated or unusual. A chat service actually has the potential to increase the knowledge base of staff due to the scripted information available and could therefore be particularly useful for a weekend or less regular workforce.

It will help to reassure staff if there is a robust system for transferring questions to colleagues if they are unable to answer a question themselves. Staff should be empowered not to feel scared or apprehensive about trying to help a student but also recognise that a query should be passed on as and when appropriate – in the same way as a face-to-face query might be. There must also be guidance and protocols for staff on what to do if they receive offensive comments or complaints via the service.

When it comes to dealing with enquiries, exchanges via a chat service tend to be much more casual (from both parties) than if a student were asking a librarian for advice face-to-face. This is surely one of the reasons why the medium appeals to students, particularly those who might feel too intimidated or embarrassed to ask a question in person (Hvass and Myer 2008; Granfield and Robertson 2008). 'Text' speak and abbreviations are commonly used and it is ideal if the service can be personalised with the name of the librarian on duty rather than a generic 'librarian online' persona. One survey respondent described how students repeatedly addressed them with a dubiously shortened version of their first name, much to their annoyance! Presumably the latter would not happen in a face-to-face encounter; in fact both parties might not even be aware of each other's name. It can also be liberating for staff to interact with students in a very informal manner and helps to break down the perceived image of the 'stuffy and boring' librarian.

Students have expressed surprise and delight that the library is offering a means of communication that they are accustomed to in a more social context.

As described above, the use of scripted replies can help to overcome some of the staff confidence and 'monitoring' issues and are undeniably useful when used appropriately. However, staff should be encouraged not to over-rely on scripted replies and to be sure to respond to the user's exact questions rather than feeling pressured into sending out the automated response that seems to be the best match. There must be a balance between the use of scripted answers and friendly spontaneous interaction; in fact 'librarians should not hesitate to use conventions that express the feelings and emotions that they would express in a face-to-face transaction' (Breitbach and Demars 2009). The use of emoticons or text symbols (e.g. to denote a smiling face) can help with this. There is no point in having a more casual system for communication if staff on duty do not interact like human beings; Zino (2009) observes that 'the first step to improving [virtual reference] is for librarians to stop acting like computers'.

The challenges of conducting virtual reference have been documented (Luo 2007; Jane and McMillan 2003). In particular the absence of eye contact, visual clues and the difficulty of perceiving 'tone' in the written word have been noted as potential barriers to communication. However, in important respects, dealing with a virtual customer is not really very different to dealing with someone face-to-face or on the telephone. Staff still need to get to the heart of the question using reference interview techniques in the same way as if the customer was physically present. Pressure to handle a transaction quickly may result in a poor or non-existent reference interview (Breitbach and Demars 2009) which will in turn result in an unsatisfactory experience for the user.

Flexibility

Provision of a chat service offers flexibility and choice to students in the way they contact the library, but it also offers an element of flexibility to staff and staffing structures. We have seen above how this is reflected in the different ways the HEIs surveyed have chosen to staff their services.

Web-based services can be delivered and accessed from any computer with an Internet connection, thus having the ability to serve multiple user groups simultaneously. Rather than staffing enquiry points at multiple campus locations, a chat enquiry service can serve all locations from one point. Although often perceived as a service aimed predominantly at distance learners, it is interesting to note that users of a chat service may not be off-campus, but may just be on a different floor of the library, reluctant to give up the computer they are using or to interrupt their work to ask for help at a physical enquiry point.

For instance, as a result of 'public service coverage reductions' at Ohio University library, Booth (2008) describes a pilot project involving setting up a

'Skype video kiosk', i.e. a dedicated virtual reference desk, using Skype and a webcam as a means of assisting users on-campus:

> we anticipated that patrons engaged in research or unable to locate library materials would use the Internet-ready, interactive kiosk for both directional and reference assistance, and that Circulation staff ... would refer patrons to the kiosk in the event of an information need.

While this approach may be a step too far for UK institutions, within a strategic context a virtual advice service allows a library to offer an enhanced student experience and increased access to enquiry services without additional staffing, or, alternatively, to offer an equivalent level of service with fewer personnel.

An additional advantage of a completely web based system is that it can be used as part of an institution's contingency or disaster planning. One of the HEIs surveyed had recently written the operation of a chat enquiry service from staff homes into their contingency procedures in the event of university closure, and this plan was actually put into action during recent bad weather conditions in the UK. A weekend virtual advice service could also be provided from anywhere even if the library was physically closed. A chat enquiry service also offers the potential to be used by other departments in the university, e.g. careers, disability support, placement support, international office, a central enquiries team, or by converged services as a first line enquiry point. Many may already be using Skype or similar for student support. In some subscription chat products customers can be referred to different 'virtual desks' as appropriate within the system.

Usage and Publicity

One of the things libraries have been concerned or surprised about are the low usage figures of chat enquiry services (Naylor et al. 2008; Radford and Kern 2006). Radford and Kern (2006) describe the circumstances surrounding the closure of nine chat reference services in the US as long ago as 2006; the six major reasons for closure were funding problems, low volume of enquiries, low volume of enquiries from target population, staffing issues, technical problems and issues surrounding institutional culture. Indeed, some early adopters of IM and chat services in the US became disillusioned with their experiences: 'in the past few years, the tone of articles on [virtual reference] has shifted from giddily optimistic to cautiously optimistic to neutral. Much of this change has been due to the relatively small number of users' (Vilelle 2005).

However, the availability of newer free or low-cost and more flexible technology now allows libraries to position their services more effectively and take the service into the students' world. It is clear that offering help at the point of need is key (Meier 2008). Wells et al. (2003) observe:

> If patrons are attempting to use the OPAC or a database and get frustrated, they won't take the time to back out, i.e. go to a previous page, then click on the chat button and ask for help. They are more likely to settle for what they can find or just quit.

It is essential that a chat service is marketed and positioned properly. The more the service is publicised, the more it will be used, and in this respect the visibility of the chat service itself is the best publicity. Widgets (provided by IM aggregators and commercial chat products) come into their own in this context as they allow a chat 'presence' to be embedded strategically into any web pages, including VLEs.

In the HEIs surveyed, the average number of queries varied, from hardly any (4–5 queries per month) to high use (250 per week). So why did uptake differ so much? In some cases where usage was low, it was because opening times were fairly short. It could also have been the case that opening hours did not coincide with when users wanted to use the service, or it was not clear when the service was open (Radford and Kern 2006).

The relationship between service opening hours, number of chat enquiries received and entry point to the service was interesting. It might be expected that institutions with a low number of opening hours[2] would receive a low number of queries and institutions with a high number of opening hours would receive a high number of queries. However, this was not necessarily the case. The important elements in the equation appeared to be how many entry points to the service there were and perhaps even more crucially, where these were placed.

Take the example of Institution A and Institution B. Both had relatively low usage figures when the only entry point to their service was via their library home page. Institution A embedded their chat service within their VLE in September 2009 and since then, despite only being open for four hours a day Monday to Friday, received over 100 chat enquiries per week as a result.

Institution B received 263 queries during the whole of the 2008–2009 academic year but on introducing a chat widget to the library tab of their VLE in September 2009, they received 831 queries during the Autumn term alone. There is a salutary lesson here – libraries cannot take it for granted that students will use services just because they are provided – libraries must take their services into the student world and integrate with other systems they use on a daily basis.

A similar situation is evident if Institution C and Institution D are compared (both used the free software Meebo). Institution C was open Monday to Friday 09.00–22.00 with variable four hour slots on Saturdays and Sundays, making

---

2   For the purposes of this survey, a low number of opening hours per day was defined as less than 09.00–17.00, Monday–Friday, i.e. less than normal office hours. An average number of opening hours was defined as 09.00–17.00 Monday–Friday (or the equivalent eight hours per day) and a high number of opening hours was defined as more than 09.00–17.00 Monday to Friday, plus any weekend hours.

a total of 73 hours per week. They received 'over 50 [chats] per week' during October but 20 or less during quieter times, a fairly modest number taking into consideration the long opening hours. Institution D, with a service open for only 20 hours per week received 30 queries on average during that time. Institution C had the entry point to their service on the library home page only whereas Institution D had entry points to their service on the library home page, the VLE and their Facebook page.

It may seem obvious, but the more wisely chosen places libraries have an entry point to their service, the more queries will be generated. The earlier work of Wells et al. (2003, p. 135) upholds this view,

> having the [chat] button only (or primarily) on the home page does not act as … a deterrent to asking a question, but if the chat button is on other pages, people will take advantage of its availability … the more pages where chat access is provided, the more the service will be used.

If a service is visible, easily accessible and positioned in lots of prominent places, then usage will be higher than if chat is hidden under an 'Ask a Question' type link on a library's web pages.

Feedback received by institutions from users had been overwhelmingly positive. Only one institution reported that the service was not popular with their users; this HEI only received five queries per month but the service was only open for two hours a day. One other HEI had not explored feedback as they felt the software they were using was not appropriate for their requirements.

Co-browsing

All software, including free IM programs, allow URLs to be sent as part of an answer. Commercial packages also offer the ability to 'push' web pages to users, i.e. the member of staff can navigate to a web page on the right of the screen and 'push' this to the user so they can see the information. Certain commercial packages also offer the ability to 'co-browse' or 'desktop share' with users so that they can be guided through electronic resources in real time, seeing the same screens as library staff. However, co-browsing within chat software can cause problems if the web pages accessed via this route are 'secure', i.e. are licensed electronic resources such as databases, e-journals and e-books. IP recognition and other methods of authentication are not successful due to the configuration of the chat software and the fact that the secure resources are essentially being accessed via a third party server, not that of the home institution.

Some survey respondents commented that co-browsing did not work properly in their current product. A way of overcoming this is the integrated use of webinar or online meeting software within the chat product (LivePerson, which was not designed as a library-specific product, has this functionality built-in). This gives operator and user the freedom to screen-share/desktop share in its truest sense and look at subscription e-resources together unhindered. A product used by one HEI, Altarama's VRL Plus, allows the chat software to integrate with third party desktop sharing software to provide a solution to the authentication problem.

Another important issue surrounding co-browsing or desktop sharing during a chat session is ensuring (as far as practicable) that the user is a bona fide member of the institution. It is not uncommon for users to enter a chat service using their non-university ID so need to be questioned further to ascertain their student status. Other considerations include the time taken to conduct a co-browse session initiated within a chat. If the service is busy, would the operator have time to do this and still attend to other users asking questions? If desktop sharing is initiated within a chat session, what happens if another user submits a question to the service? Would a third party viewing the staff member's desktop be able to see another student's question and personal details?

It may be the case that true co-browsing or desktop sharing sessions are better conducted outside of the timetabled chat enquiry service where the member of staff can devote more time to the exchange under less pressure, and access to subscription e-resources is not restricted. However this is achieved, using chat in a more exciting and creative way should definitely be pursued. Breitbach and Demars (2009) argue that creating more interactive content for use in virtual advice sessions can enrich the user experience far more than using text alone. Videos (either created in-house or via YouTube), images and web annotation tools can be utilised to make transactions more engaging, appealing and helpful, whilst using the fuller potential of web based services; what begins as 'chat' becomes 'look', 'watch', 'listen'.

Virtual Advice by Appointment

Let me show you how it's done! (Glassman et. al. 2009)

So far chat has been discussed within the context of an ad hoc enquiry service where users contact the library with queries as they arise. However, a chat service can also be used proactively to offer virtual one-to-one (or one-to-many) advice appointments, with varying degrees of sophistication depending on the product used.

A user could be invited to connect to a chat service at a certain time to be steered through a problem by a particular member of staff, either with text chat only, co-browsing or using a telephone whilst screen sharing. In this guise a chat service does not have an impact on staffing in the same way that a timetabled public duty does; rather virtual advice sessions/drop-ins are scheduled into an individual's workload in the same way that a face-to face appointment or group teaching session might be.

If a library is using 'webinar' software such as Adobe Connect, WebEx, GoToMeeting, or Megameeting, then a very sophisticated virtual advice session can be run. This type of software allows full desktop/application sharing, online white board functionality, text chat, voice-over-IP (VOIP) and a webcam to be used. Glassman et al. (2009, p. 303) describe supporting medical students in the US via a product called 'Glance' using a 'combination of PowerPoint presentation and live demonstration.' Sessions on topics such as database searching and using bibliographic software were offered.

Few, if any, university libraries in the UK are currently using this technology to support students. Of the 15 HEIs surveyed none had offered library training via their chat service or used it with VOIP where this feature existed. However, three stated that this was the next step in enhancing their virtual advice services and that they were planning to offer appointments or scheduled sessions in the near future, either via their existing chat product or other webinar software.

The Mobile Campus and Beyond

> The mobile phone as a communication device beats all other devices in one significant way: portability. (Buczynski 2008)

The popularity of smartphones in recent years (O_2 has sold a million iPhones in the UK – Mintel 2009) means that students are increasingly accessing information and services via this route. According to Mintel (2009) those in the 15 to 34 age group, encompassing the traditional student age, are 'the most likely to purchase and trade up to more expensive phones.'

The 2010 launch of the iPad in the UK, along with the Windows 7 phone and Google's Android operating system will no doubt excite more interest in developing services compatible with smartphones and mobile devices. Libraries will need to assess their services, chat and others, for compatibility with new and emerging technologies. Free IM services are ahead of the game in this respect – there is a Meebo app for the iPhone and an interface customised for mobile web browsers used by smartphones (e.g. WindowsMobile; Symbian; Blackberry). A recent example of such work was the J!SC-funded project, 'Mobile Campus Assistant', led by the University of Bristol, which created a prototype to:

> [make] time and location sensitive information available to students via their mobiles and location-aware smart phones. For example, where is the nearest available PC? Where is the nearest wireless hotspot? What events are happening today? When is the next bus to the hall of residence? Which library is open now? (Jones 2009)

The company oMbiel is now offering this type of service commercially with its CampusM application and the tagline, 'bringing together on their mobile, all of the university services that students love using' (oMbiel 2010).

The irony will not be lost on librarians to see the shift in status of the mobile/cell phone from a device threatening the more traditional aspects of library decorum to a piece of technology essential to a student's social and academic life. Buczynski (2008) comments on the move from 'managing phone use behavior' to '[engaging] … users via … audio tours, text message reference service, text message alerts, and mobile library collection search engines.'

In Australia, the Curtin University of Technology has a pilot web presence 'Curtin Library Mobile' which aims to provide access to key library information and services. It also offers a well-established SMS reference service. SMS reference services are typically only useful for simple questions requiring short answers, as text messages are limited to 160 characters. Much less has been written about SMS reference than chat but the service provided by Curtin features in two articles (Hill et al. 2007; Profit 2008). None of the UK HEIs surveyed were using an SMS texting service for enquiries although two reported that they were considering it for the future.

Beyond the university campus and on a decidedly more ethereal plane there has even been comment on the potential of reference services within Second Life, virtual reference within a virtual world, (Gerardin et al. 2008) and so-called 'embedded librarianship', i.e. library skills instruction as part of 'distance learning courses taught within virtual environments' (Davis and Smith 2009). It remains to be seen whether such practice is 'gimmick or groundbreaking' (Buckland and Godfrey 2008).

Conclusion

It is clear that there are exciting times ahead for virtual advice services and it will be challenging for libraries to meet their customers in the worlds they want to inhabit. Virtual advice services, as part of a suite of help for students, can only enrich the student experience and enhance the perception of the academic library as an adopter of new technology and provider of services at the point of need. The growth of mobile technologies will bring this into sharper focus still, as we strive to keep up with our users' expectations of a personalised, flexible and collaborative learning experience. Some proprietary databases and e-journals already have apps designed for mobile device access and others have mobile web versions of their products. As quality information becomes easier to access on the move, students will expect greater and greater immediacy with answers to their queries. In addition, libraries will need to think hard about the way they deliver mobile-friendly information on the web and 'redesign with information structure in focus, not graphic design' (Greenall 2010). Users will not necessarily want or be able to see information within the context of a traditional website, and information/advice will need to be disaggregated into bite-sized chunks. However, it does offer libraries the opportunity to experiment with the delivery of virtual advice services in media-rich formats which are perhaps better suited to mobile devices than text-heavy content.

As we have seen from the examples of chat reference services within the UK, there is room for different and flexible approaches, and certainly no 'one size fits all'. It seems appropriate to give the last word to a survey respondent whose comment sums up the current position of many UK HEIs:

> At present we are very much 'dipping our toes in the water' but the further potential that the technology offers is very exciting – increasingly it becomes apparent that live chat will be a vital tool for us to fulfil our aim of providing equitable support to customers no matter where they are.

The author would like to thank staff from the following institutions for their input to the survey:

> Anglia Ruskin University
> Bournemouth University
> Heriot-Watt University
> King's College London
> Lancaster University
> Staffordshire University
> Teesside University
> University of Aberdeen
> University of Birmingham
> University of East London
> University of Edinburgh
> University of Liverpool
> University of St. Andrews
> University of Sunderland
> University of Wolverhampton

References

Booth, C., 2008. Developing Skype-based reference services. *Internet Reference Services Quarterly*, 13 (2–3), 147–65.

Breitbach, W. and Demars, J.M., 2009. Enhancing virtual reference: techniques and technologies to engage users and enrich interaction. *Internet Reference Services Quarterly*, 14 (3–4), 82–91.

Buckland, A. and Godfrey, K., 2008. *Gimmick or Groundbreaking? Canadian Academic Libraries Using Chat Reference in Multi-user Virtual Environments.* In: World Library and Information Congress: 74th IFLA General Conference and Council, 10–14 August, 2008, Quebec, Canada. Available from: www. ifla.org/IV/ifla74/papers/158-Buckland_Godfrey-en.pdf (accessed 21 March 2010).

Buczynski, J.A., 2008. Libraries begin to engage their menacing mobile phone hordes without shhhhh! *Internet Reference Services Quarterly*, 13 (2–3), 261–69.

Coffman, S., 2003. *Going Live: Starting and Running a Virtual Reference Service*. Chicago: American Library Association.

Davis, M.G. and Smith, C.E., 2009. Virtually embedded: library instruction within Second Life. *Journal of Library and Information Services in Distance Learning*, 3 (3/4), 120–37.

Devlin, F., Currie, L. and Stratton, J., 2008. Successful approaches to teaching through chat. *New Library World*, 109 (5/6), 223–34.

Desai, C.M. and Graves, S.J., 2008. Cyberspace or face-to-face: the teachable moment and changing reference mediums. *Reference and User Services Quarterly*, 48(1), 242–54.

DeVoe, K.M., 2008. Chat widgets: placing your virtual reference services at your user's point(s) of need. *The Reference Librarian*, 47 (3), 99–101.

Gerardin, J., Yamamoto, M. and Gordon, K., 2008. Fresh perspectives on reference work in Second Life. *Reference and User Services Quarterly*, 47 (4), 324–30.

Glassman, N.R., Habousha, R.G., Minuti, A., Schwartz, R., and Sorensen, K. 2009. Let me show you how it's done! Desktop sharing for distance learning from the D. Samuel Gottesman Library. *Medical Reference Services Quarterly*, 28 (4), 297–308.

Granfield, D. and Robertson, M., 2008. Preference for reference: new options and choices for academic library users. *Reference and User Services Quarterly*, 48 (1), 44–53.

Greenall, R.T., 2010. Mobiles in libraries. *Online*, Mar/Apr, 16–19.

Haynes, W., 2009. ASSISTing you online: creating positive student experiences at the University of Wolverhampton. *SCONUL Focus*, 46, 86–90.

Hvass, A. and Myer, S., 2008. Can I help you? Implementing an IM service. *The Electronic Library*, 26 (4), 530–44.

Hill, J.B., Hill, C.M. and Sherman, D., 2007. Text messaging in an academic library: integrating SMS into digital reference. *The Reference Librarian*, 47 (1), 17–29.

Jane, C. and McMillan, D., 2003. Online in real time? Deciding whether to offer a real-time virtual reference service. *The Electronic Library*, 21 (3), 240–46.

Jones, M., 2009. *Mobile Campus Assistant: Final Progress Report*. Bristol: University of Bristol. Available from: http://mobilecampus.ilrt.bris.ac.uk/final-progress-report (accessed 21 March 2010).

Luo, L., 2007. Chat reference competencies: identification from a literature review and librarian interviews. *Reference Services Review*, 35 (2), 195–209.

Meier, J.J., 2008. Chat widgets on the library website: help at the point of need. Computers in Libraries, 28 (6), 10–48.

Mintel, 2009. *Telecoms*. London: Mintel. Available from: http://academic.mintel. com (accessed 21 March 2010).

Mintel, 2010. *Smartphone Wars: Attack of the Bravo*. London: Mintel. Available from: http://academic.mintel.com (accessed 21 March 2010).

Naylor, S., Stoffel, B. and Van Der Laan, S., 2008. Why isn't our chat reference used more? Finding of focus group discussions with undergraduate students. *Reference and User Services Quarterly*, 47(4), 342–54.

Ogbaa, C., Fisher, L.F. and Ancelet, L., 2008. Implementing VR on the fly: staff motivation and buy-in. In: Lankes, R.D., Nicholson, S., Radford, M.L., Silverstein, J., Westbrook, L. and Nast, P., eds. *Virtual Reference Service: From Competencies to Assessment*. New York: Facet, 27–33.

oMbiel. 2010. *Campus MTM Bringing Together on their Mobile, all of the University Services that Students Love Using*. Birmingham: oMbiel. Available from: http://www.ombiel.com (accessed 21 March 2010).

Profit, S.K., 2008. Text messaging at reference: a preliminary survey. *The Reference Librarian*, 49 (2), 129–34.

Radford, M.L. and Kern, M.K., 2006. A multiple-case study investigation of the discontinuation of nine chat reference services. *Library and Information Science Research*, 28, 521–47.

Vilelle, L., 2005. Marketing virtual reference: what academic libraries have done. *College and Undergraduate Libraries*, 12 (1/2) 65–79.

Virtual Enquiry Project, 2009. *The Virtual Enquiry Project*. Available from http:// www.virtualenquiry.net (accessed 16 November 2009).

Wells, C.A., Wallace, D.P. and Van Fleet, C., 2003. Location, location, location: the importance of placement of the chat request button. *Reference and User Services Quarterly*, 43 (2), 133–7

Zino, E., 2009. Let's fix virtual reference. *Library Journal*, February, 94.

Chapter 7

The Reading E-volution

Jill Beard and Penny Dale

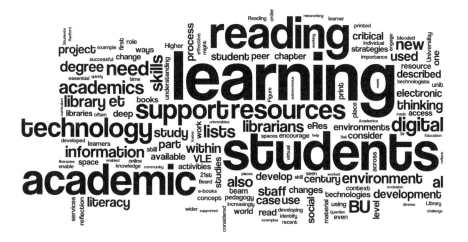

> We see nothing of these slow changes in progress …
>
> Charles Darwin: *On The Origin of Species* 1859

Introduction

Writing these words in the middle of the 19th century, Darwin described evolution as a slow and gradual process. In contrast the reading e-volution at the beginning of the 21st century has happened quickly. This is evolution that is only too visible. However it is nonetheless a true evolution, as the changes fomented are permanent and irreversible. The speed at which learning environments are moving from the 19th century to the 21st century can be measured in years and months, even weeks and days. This chapter will attempt to describe some the changes and challenges for librarians, learning technologists, academics and others as they seek new ways, and reinvent old ways, of supporting students in new environments.

Technology in Higher Education

The Department for Business, Innovation and Skills 2009 report *Higher Ambitions: The Future of Universities in a Knowledge Economy*, described the challenge of driving-up excellence in higher education (HE) within a climate of funding constraints and the '... need to focus resources where they can have the greatest return ...'. *Higher Ambitions* noted that collaboration and the use of technology is central to learning, echoing Bradwell (2009) who wrote in *The Edgeless University* 'technology can help universities move from where they are now to where they need to be'. He further describes 'the university becoming defined by its function – provider and facilitator of learning and research – not its form' (Bradwell 2009).

This chapter will consider how collaborations between librarians, academics and learning technologists make a difference to the student experience, delivering blended learning to enable students to develop academic and digital literacies as they read for a degree in an environment where print is just one of the resources available to them. They will still need to deliver the sought-for academic excellence, making effective and efficient use of resources. They will also need to foster collaboration and reflection, arguably even more important using digital resources where provenance and authority is often less clear than in purely print environments. In 2007 Ipsos MORI (p. 15) described technology fading into the foreground; we think that this phrase describes succinctly the wireless and increasingly mobile world in which academic communities are working. The question is, can the academic library support their community with this rapid change and meet the challenges outlined by *The Guardian* in 2008 under the banner 'Libraries Unleashed'? Libraries have to adapt and change to reflect the requirements of blended learning and what the student does (Biggs 2007), and what this means for universities.

New Ways of Working

Much has been said about the way students of different generations and backgrounds interact with technology. Prensky (2001) and Oblinger and Oblinger (2005) were pivotal with their discussions of digital natives, digital immigrants and Net-Gen students when describing the changes and challenges for education. It would be relevant to ask, for example, how students' social networking might be mirrored to enhance academic skill development through peer learning schemes.

Library and information staff who have worked in HE libraries during the last few decades will struggle to reconcile the expectation that university libraries are places of silence and order with the realities of their institutions, where much has already changed in the learning landscape; a change that will accelerate during the second decade of the 21st century as technology and economics impact on the pedagogy. As we pointed out in 2008 when describing the situation at Bournemouth University (BU): 'The importance of aligning pedagogy with technology, resource and space has driven all the recent developments' (Beard and Dale 2008).

However there is still tension between the perceived rationality of the library and the social construction of knowledge. This tension was articulated by Radford

(1998). He described the perception of a library as 'a place where each item within it has a fixed place and stands in an *a priori* relationship with every other item'.

In the same paper Radford refers to Umberto Eco's murder mystery novel *The Name of the Rose*:

> Eco's library is a labyrinth contained within a fortress, replete with booby-trapped rooms and secret passages. The organization of texts within the library/labyrinth is known only to the librarian.

The concept of a library as an impenetrable, and sometimes perilous, place is widespread in the literature of the 20th – early 21st centuries. From the world of fantasy, Terry Pratchett's library at the Unseen University and the dangerous books in the Restricted Section at J.K. Rowling's Hogwarts School are just two examples from contemporary fiction.

The other reality that HE libraries still have to consider is continuing demand for the very order and rationality that Radford (1998) challenges. Whilst printed books remain part of the currency of learning they have to be kept, found, borrowed and returned. Individuals still require places for silent study, with printed material and/or increasingly with technology. To accommodate these diverse and diversifying needs, library space has to be flexible.

Buildings must be able to accommodate both social and individual learning from undergraduate to Doctorate level whilst incorporating the technologies that are transforming how learning takes place. The possibilities of virtual learning environments, the ability to deliver library resources integrated within the unit of study, and the willingness of students to engage with blended environments (Ball et al. 2007) have only begun to be explored.

The Possibilities of Technology

The possibilities of new technologies, the availability of resources online and new ways of learning and using acquired knowledge herald seismic changes in HE libraries (*Guardian* 2008). Their demise is not inevitable, but there is no room for complacency. The history of reading is full of examples of services being provided in the absence of buildings recognisable as a library. For example, the circulating libraries of the early to mid-20th century thrived in the UK from newsagents, corner shops and Boots Chemists until public libraries fulfilled the need for recreational reading. In the 18th century coffee houses provided cultural and social space; in some ways they were the forerunners of the learning environments in contemporary universities.

Students today use information differently from their predecessors (Dale 2006, p. 27). They are the first generation to have grown up surrounded by digital technology, whose first port of call for information is, more often than not, Google.

The challenge is to provide support for all students whatever their background, all of whom will increasingly work in virtual and real spaces.

The CIBER (2008) briefing paper on the information behaviour of the researcher of the future confirms trends outlined in recent studies and highlights the OCLC global survey (2006) concluding that the Google generation stereotype may be broadly true. However their review articulates concerns that rapid and easy access to information may be to the detriment of developing the academic skills of creative and independent thinking.

Academics are also expressing concerns about the urgent need to develop academic skills in the Google-dominated world. Notably Brabazon (2007, p. 39) encourages librarians and teachers to:

> overtly – rather than implicitly – support new modes of reading, writing and communicating, integrating discovery, searches, navigation and the appropriateness of diverse resources.

The relationships between learners, their background, the resources and their media as well as the places in and from which students learn are all changing. Those spaces whether virtual or physical need to demonstrate significant agility (Heppell et al. 2004) to meet the needs and expectations of diverse student cohorts. By 2015 they will include for example those for whom e-books were a standard part of their secondary curriculum, as well as returning students who first graduated when e-books were only a small part of their resource access and at a time when academic literacy skills would perhaps have been at their lowest ebb.

Technology, Pedagogy and Learning Space

The importance of aligning pedagogy with technology, resource and space has driven all the recent developments at BU. There has been equal importance associated with the transformational technology of the virtual learning environment (VLE) (Ball et al. 2007) and the reshaping of the learning space (Beard and Ball 2008). Morineau et al. (2005) explored the effectiveness of memory recall in relation both to the locations in which electronic books are accessed and the hardware used. They considered the need to create not only optimum on-screen reading but also appropriate environments. By creating the right ambience and facilities with the expressed mix of silent, group and technologically-rich spaces (Walton 2006) students might better develop those academic, critical and reflective skills which can then be described as enabling students to read for their degrees and beyond.

A report (Winter et al. 2010) of a study of postgraduates' effective use of e-learning published in 2010 concluded that effective e-learners share many of the characteristics of effective learners in general. The students in the study were able to use technology to meet their learning needs, but the need varied from learner to learner. One of the recommendations concurs with our research into one element of successful reading for a degree in the digital world, namely the development of critical thinking when evaluating internet resources. The JISC Learning Literacies (LliDA) Project (Beetham et al. 2009) reviewed a wide range of activities in an attempt to establish the kinds of capabilities valued, taught for and assessed. The ways in which capabilities are supported and the values placed on staff and student are described as 'literacies of the digital' (Beetham et al. 2009). The next part of this chapter will develop this theme, focussing on academic literacy and in particular reading in the digital context.

Reading for a Degree

Do students still "read" for a degree? As digital resources proliferate and access to multi-media becomes universal, students are relying less on print resources. The shift to electronic resources is both rapid and incremental, and as print declines, making even more information available and accessible through electronic routes, we need to ask to what extent learning in a largely digital environment can be considered as "reading". This chapter will also consider changes in learning styles

Figure 7.1   Social study space in The Sir Michael Cobham Library
© **Bournemouth University 2008**

necessitated by the shift to e, and consider what skills and literacies students need in order to be successful learners in a digital, and post-digital, world.

The Higher Education Academy funded *Innovative e-Learning with e-Resources (eRes)* Project in 2007–8 was an accelerator for this process at Bournemouth University. The next part of this chapter will consider the three aims of this project, and how they have contributed to the subsequent development of the learning environment at BU and indeed the wider academic community.

The Pedagogical Framework

eRes looked at how academics were re-considering their teaching in the context of an increasingly digital environment. This was achieved by gathering examples from across BU of pedagogical frameworks that brought together learning activities and academically led quality e-resources within the unit of study. Some 13 case studies were documented. Full details of these case studies along with the accompanying briefing papers are available from the BU website.[1]

Academic staff involved in the case studies observed that engagement with e-resources contributed to the acquisition and retention of information and deep learning, concurring with Laurillard (2002) and Moon (2007, p. 114). Large groups of students benefited from this approach as did students studying topics that have proved difficult to engage with (Dale and Cheshir 2009). Academics were asked if they felt that the Web 2.0 technologies they were using enhanced students' ability to think critically and engage with deep learning. They were also asked if they felt that the new technologies promoted reading. The responses were encouraging. One academic who developed a completely online degree commented 'because if we're saying that reading for a degree is important, we have to stop putting the reading in a box'.

Another academic teaching a traditional subject used a discussion forum to encourage reflection and deep learning in a large cohort. When asked if she felt that the technology encouraged further reading her reply was unequivocal 'Oh, yes, definitely. And that was the whole idea really of the reflection, to actually go out and use some of their own resources'.

This was typical of the case studies that described activities designed to facilitate reading and reflection. Different tools available on the VLE were used to do this including blogs and wikis, discussion boards and social bookmarking.

Reading Strategies

A search of the literature has shown that there has been little written to date on reading strategies and academic skills development in a digital environment. In

---

1   www.bournemouth.ac.uk/library.

2003, librarians at the University of the West of England (UWE) coined the term 'reading strategies' to draw attention to the fact that reading lists are only part of a wider 'reading strategy' that should consider not only what students read but how they will get access to their reading material. The results of the work at UWE have led to what can be described as a hybrid solution, identifying and providing electronic material to supplement and complement print resources (Chelin 2005). This work did not address how reading, critical thinking and learning might take place in this digital world. Work at Edge Hill College (Martin and Stokes 2006; Stokes and Martin 2008) describes reading lists as Cinderella rather than superstar despite their time under the spotlight, and notes concerns from both academics and librarians that strategies need to develop autonomous learners and avoid spoon-feeding.

Reading lists have long been used by academics to guide their students through literature seen as essential to their studies. Conversely they have often been used by students as a sort of talisman, to prove to themselves and their tutors that they have 'read for a degree'. So for both academics and students, reading lists have been passive. As Stokes and Martin (2008) observe 'it is thus timely to develop a richer understanding of reading lists'.

At BU this process was already underway. Before the introduction of the university-wide VLE, reading lists at BU were poorly appreciated and sadly underused. In a survey of two academic schools in 2005 (Beard et al. 2007) less than 30% of students were aware of their course reading lists on the library catalogue. Following the introduction of the VLE in 2006 reading lists were embedded in every unit, and in a BU internal evaluation of the VLE in 2007, after only one year, 43% of students were using the online reading lists. These lists are no longer seen as closed and static but are being developed by academic unit leaders in partnership with the subject librarians to include not only books and journals but also links to e-books, e-journals and websites. Social bookmarking is being used to enable academics to share with librarians ideas for new resource inclusion. The Copyright Licensing Agency (CLA) Trial Licence for Photocopying and Scanning signed by BU in 2006 enabled sections of books and journals published in the UK to be scanned and made available at unit level. Over 500 items were linked in the first year of use. This quickly increased to over 750 items across the core curriculum. From August 2008 the licence also included US publishers (subject to exclusions). This e-availability enabled the integration of the separate short loan collection, with its limitation of one item to one user, into the main bookstock enabling students to access essential resources anytime and anywhere.

Focus groups held at Easter 2008 at BU with taught students from across all schools and levels, explored what students expected of the library in the future. Students made positive comments about the inclusion of key chapters within their VLE units. The students also articulated the need for different styles of information literacy support, especially to enable successful use of e-books (Constable 2008).

The new approach to reading lists at BU spearheaded the drive to develop new tools for information literacy within the VLE; developing from being passive lists, used as crutches by both students and academics, into an active and dynamic resource. They are part of a directional package on a route to resource discovery. It is anticipated that during the second decade of the 21st century technology will enable academics to lead the creation and delivery of reading lists, which will be embedded in the VLE with dynamic links directly to the content. Students are able to use social bookmarking and social networking tools to share and comment on the resources and record their reflections. The role of learning technologists in this context is to introduce the technology, while academics who are developing the skills of list creation are supported by librarians.

Staff Development and Support

The third strand of eRes considered the support that academic staff need in order to engage with technology and encourage reading in an electronic environment. For this section we are indebted to the work of our colleague Linda Byles.[2]

The HE sector has seen a variety of staff development approaches to foster pedagogic change in relation to e-learning (Clegg et al. 2000; Taylor 2003; Wilson and Stacey 2004). The eRes project considered how different staff development strategies could be supported through the creation of a multidisciplinary support team. eRes sought to assist academics to implement innovative pedagogical practices that brought together learning activities and e-resources. This process was a collaborative venture involving a staff developer, learning technologists and librarians. The skills and expertise of the team ranged across knowledge of pedagogy, technology, information resources, and organisational structures. There was recognition here that curriculum development did not rest with one individual but was a shared responsibility (Taylor 2003).

The Team Approach

The eRes project team employed a case conference approach to review the progress of the projects and case studies. Each case study was allocated a broker from the project team. The role of the broker was to support each academic with their case study and facilitate access to relevant services and support, both within Academic Services and the wider university community. The broker was normally the individual who had first contact with the academic, but this could change where the emphasis of the case study fell into another sphere. For example, one academic started off working with a librarian to identify library resources then moved on to work with a learning technologist to explore the potential of wikis.

This degree of flexibility in the services was significant, fostering a recognition amongst academics that academic support and related services often overlap. It

---

2   http://www.bournemouth.ac.uk/eds/eres/documents/eResstaffdevelopmentbriefing paper.pdf.

Figure 7.2   Technobooth in The Sir Michael Cobham Library
© **Bournemouth University 2008**

also enabled team members to move out of their traditionally defined roles to a wider support function. Two years on from the project the concept of working with blended learning is an established part of the institutional PGCert programme (Beard et al. 2009). The importance of peer support whilst collaborating and sharing resources when using technology was observed as students used the social learning spaces in The Sir Michael Cobham Library at BU to plan, research and write group assignments.

Working with Academics

The level of involvement with the team varied according to the project being worked on and the competencies of the individual academic. This was an iterative process however, which saw both the expansion of projects as new insights emerged and the contraction of goals as constraints outside the projects impinged on developments. The context in which academic staff worked was seen as paramount in supporting them to achieve their goals. All faced the challenge of balancing work commitments and implementing change. Support was directed to help staff come to an understanding of how they could manage this process and identify what they could and could not achieve.

The development of self efficacy for academic staff emerged as a primary goal of the project. Strategies to promote this included networking, peer support, involvement in dissemination activities both internally and externally, and a debrief session at the end of the project.

Critical Thinking and Academic Literacy

Successful critical thinking, learning outcomes and pedagogy are all central to the concept of reading for a degree. Critical thinking is an' elusive concept' (Moon 2007, p. 19) which can provide some context for developing a definition of successful reading, describing activities required to read for a degree. To become autonomous learners, students need to be motivated and acquire the skill of 'deep learning' as described by Marton et al. (1984). Marton et al. also identify a separate skill of 'strategic learning' focussed on achieving the highest possible grade or mark. To link the internal dialogues necessary for deep or strategic learning, Laurillard (2002) has taken the concept of the conversational framework and developed it to include the conversation between learner and teacher. Scheja (2006) describes the notion of 'delayed understanding' which captures the complications of a study situation where perceived lack of time to reflect on learning material obstructs students' understanding of course material. Scheja observes that time to reflect on previous experiences is an essential component in the understanding of learning materials. The Quality Assurance Agency for Higher Education (2000) used National Level Descriptors to describe the characteristics, achievements and attributes of learning at each level, from Level C at undergraduate level to Level D at doctorate level. There would appear to be a clear link between most, if not all, of the attributes of critical thinking, deep or strategic learning and becoming an autonomous learner, and what is expected of students reading for a degree.

Successful e-reading strategies encourage deep learning, contribute to critical thinking and encourage autonomy. The interactive nature of the learning process in the electronic environment demands a broad view of academic literacy. Web 2.0 technologies necessitate a re-evaluation of how students acquire and develop academic literacy skills. Kope (2006) listed a number of learning skills and strategies that she groups under the term 'academic literacy'. These range from critical thinking and advanced reading skills to learning with and from technology. Critical thinking is an essential skill in the print environment but is arguably even more vital in the digital learning environment. The plethora of electronic resources available demands a level of discernment and evaluation on the part of students that earlier generations learning from books and a small selection of printed journals did not have to consider.

The interactive nature of the learning process in the electronic environment is discussed by Crook (2005) who observes that 'The growth of new information and communication technologies (ICT) demands a broader view of academic literacy' and he refers to Ware and Warschauer (2005) who identify four ways by which ICT re-mediates the tradition of printed language. Across HE a considerable amount of effort is put into helping students acquire academic literacy. We suggest that peer support could be used to foster this interactivity and enhance information seeking skills.

Peer Support

How much student peer support might add to the development of academic literacy is a question unanswered as this chapter was written. As academic skills support materials are routinely made available to students online within communities that encourage communication, and as peer support schemes to support academic learning grow, it is not impossible to imagine that the answer 'I ask my peers' when given to the question 'where do you go for help?' will be a cause for celebration. The e-volution will be complete. Librarians, learning technologists and academics will provide the structures and inspiration whilst the students will collaborate and contribute to knowledge by demonstrating critical thinking and reflection as they 'read for a degree'.

Conclusion

We have identified three major themes emerging from this chapter. Firstly, partnerships are clearly vital, not only between HE librarians and other student support professionals, but also with academics, librarians in other sectors and, most importantly, students themselves. The success of the eRes project at BU was both immediate and long-lasting, giving impetus to new working relationships and student support services. A second theme is the role of the student, who is after all the primary stakeholder in their learning, and we look forward to a debate about the possibilities and role of peer assisted support. The third theme is the overarching role of technology. New applications are developed on an (almost) day to day basis and an explosion in the number of hand held devices has already begun. Some of these applications disappear as quickly as they appeared; librarians and others must strike a careful balance between moving with technology and making costly and/or embarrassing mistakes. This takes us back to partnership and the value of colleagues across and beyond the HE sector. Perhaps even more importantly it is about listening to our users, our students, who are leading this e-volution.

References

Ball, D., Beard, J. and Newland, B., 2007. E-books and virtual learning environments: responses to transformational technology. *The Acquisitions Librarian*, 19 (3–4), 165–82.

Beard, J., Dale, P. and Hutchins, J., 2007. The impact of e-resources at Bournemouth University 2004/6, *Performance Measurement and Metrics*, 8 (1), 7–17.

Beard, J. and Ball, D., 2008. Reshaping the future. *LIBER Quarterly: The Journal of European Research Libraries*, 18 (2).

Beard, J. and Dale, P., 2008. Re-designing services for the Net-Gen and beyond: a holistic review of pedagogy, resource and learning space. *New Review of Academic Librarianship*, 14 (1/2), 99–114.

Beard, J., Byles, L. and Newland, B., 2009. Technology rich learning spaces – opportunities and risks. In: *The Fourth Symposium on Social Learning Space: Learning Outside the Square*, 6 April 2009. Oxford Brookes (Unpublished).

Beetham, H., McGill, L. and Littlejohn, S., 2009. *Thriving in the 21st Century: Learning Literacies for the Digital Age (LLida Project)*. Available from: http://www.jisc.ac.uk/media/documents/projects/LLidareportjune2009.pdf (accessed 20 May 2010).

Biggs, J., 2007. *Teaching for Quality Learning at University: What The Student Does*. 3rd ed. Maidenhead: Open University Press.

Brabazon, T., 2007. *The University of Google: Education in the (Post) Information Age*. Aldershot: Ashgate.

Bradwell, P., 2009. *The Edgeless University: Why Higher Education Must Embrace Technology*. Available from: http://www.demos.co.uk/files/Edgeless_University_-_web.pdf (accessed 12 May 2010).

Chelin, J., 2005. Five hundred into 4 won't go – how to solve the problem of reading list expectations. *Sconul Focus*. 36, 49–51.

CIBER, 2008. *Information Behaviour of the Researcher of the Future*. UCL. Available from: http://www.ucl.ac.uk/slais/research/ciber/downloads/ (Accessed 29 January 2010).

Clegg, S., Konrad, J. and Tan J., 2000. Preparing academic staff to use ICTs in support of student learning. *The International Journal for Academic Development* 5(2), 138–48.

Constable, L., 2008. *The Library Information Needs of Bournemouth University students: A report for Bournemouth University Academic Services. Bournemouth University*. Available from: http://www.bournemouth.ac.uk/asfeedback/docs/BU taught students report April 08.pdf (accessed 29 January 2010).

Crook, C., 2005. Addressing research at the intersection of academic literacies and new technology. *International Journal of Educational Research* 43, 509–18.

Dale, P., 2006. Professional engagement – the subject specialist in higher education. In: Dale, P., Holland, M. and Matthews, M., eds. *Subject Librarians: Engaging with the Learning and Teaching Environment*. Aldershot: Ashgate.

Dale, P. and Cheshir, K., 2009. Collaboration between Librarians and Learning Technologists to enhance the learning of health sciences students. *New Review of Academic Librarianship*, 15 (2), 206–18.

Dale, P., Holland, M. and Matthews, M., eds, 2006. *Subject Librarians: Engaging with the Learning and Teaching Environment*. Aldershot: Ashgate.

Guardian, 2008. Libraries unleashed. 30 April 2008.

Heppell, S., Chapman, C., Millwood, R., Constable, M. and Furness, J., 2004. *Building Learning Futures. A Research Project at Ultralab within the CABE/*

RIBA "Building Futures" Programme. Available from: http://rubble.heppell. net/cabe/final_report.pdf (accessed 13 March 2010).

Ipsos MORI, 2007. *Student Expectations Study: Key Findings from Online Research Discussion Evenings held in June 2007 for the Joint Information Systems Committee*. Available from: http://www.jisc.ac.uk/media/documents/ publications/studentexpectations.pdf (accessed 26 March 2010).

Kope, M., 2006. Understanding e-Literacy. In Martin, A. and Madigan, D., eds, *Digital Literacies for Learning*. London: Facet.

Laurillard, D., 2002. *Rethinking Teaching for the Knowledge Society*. Educause Review. 37 (1), 18–25.

Martin, A. and Madigan, D., eds, 2006. *Digital Literacies for Learning*. London: Facet.

Martin, L. and Stokes, P., 2006. Reading lists under the spotlight: Cinderella or superstar? *Sconul Focus*. 37, 33–6.

Marton, F. Hounsell, D. and Entwistle, N., eds, 1984. *The Experience of Learning*. Scottish Academic Press: Edinburgh.

Moon, J., 2007. *Critical Thinking; An Exploration of Theory and Practice*. London: Routledge.

Morineau, T., Blanche, C., Tobin, L. and Guéguen, N., 2005. The emergence of the contextual role of the e-book in cognitive processes through an ecological and functional analysis. *International Journal of Human – Computer Studies*. 61 (3), 329–48.

Oblinger, D. and Oblinger, J., eds, 2005. *Educating the Net Generation*. Boulder CO: Educause.

OCLC, 2006. *College Students' Perceptions of Libraries and Information Resources: A Report to the OCLC Membership*. Dublin: OCLC.

Prensky, M., 2001. Digital natives, digital immigrants. *On the Horizon*, 9 (5), 1–6.

Quality Assurance Agency for Higher Education, 2000. *Handbook for Academic Review*. QAA.

Radford, G., 1998. Flaubert, Foucault, and the bibliothèque fantastique: toward a postmodern epistemology for library science, *Library Trends*, 46 (4), 616–34.

Scheja, M., 2006. Delayed understanding and staying in phase: students' perceptions of their study situation. *Higher Education*, 52 (3), 421–45.

Stokes, P. and Martin, L., 2008. Reading lists: a study of tutor and student perceptions, expectations and realities. *Studies in Higher Education*, 33 (2), 113–25.

Taylor, J., 2003. Managing staff development for online education: a situated learning model. *Journal of Higher Education Policy and Management*, 25(1) 75–87.

Walton, G., 2006. Learners' demands and expectations for space in a university library: outcomes from a survey at Loughborough University. *New Review of Academic Librarianship*, 12 (2), 133–49.

Ware, P. and Warschauer, M., 2005. Hybrid literacy texts and practices in technology-intensive environments. *International Journal of Educational Research*, 43, 432–45.

Wilson, G. and Stacey, E., 2004. Online interaction impacts on learning; teaching the teachers to teach online. *Australasian Journal of Educational Technology*, 20 (1), 33–48.

Winter, J., Cotton, D., Gavin, J. and Yorke, J., 2010. Effective e-learning? Multi-tasking, distractions and boundary management by graduate students in an online environment. *ALT-J Research in Learning Technology*, 18(1) March 71–83.

Chapter 8
Institutional Repositories – Now and Next

Alma Swan

In the competitive environment of a global higher education market, Open Access repositories provide a platform on which a university can showcase its research. Open Access helps prospective students make a judgment on which university to choose, shares blue-skies research with the widest possible audience and supports outreach activity to open up higher education to new communities.

Dr Paul Ayris, Director of Libraries, University College London

Introduction

Institutional repositories are becoming essential tools for universities. How could they be otherwise, when they provide the solution to a number of issues critical to the future functioning of these institutions?

First, they provide the means to disseminate the outputs from universities cheaply, effectively and efficiently. Through this dissemination they buy visibility and presence for the university. Where the outputs of an institution once only reached a small proportion of the potential world audience through subscription journals, they can now be disseminated to all interested parties via the Web from the network of university repositories that is forming across the globe.

Second, as a result of this worldwide visibility, repositories provide universities with new impact. Research can only make an impact if other people can see its results and build on them. The corollary of these things is that a repository also provides a very effective marketing tool for a university, showcasing to the world and especially to potential researchers and students the research that the university carries out.

There are advantages within the institution, too. If the whole research output is collected in the repository, then it becomes part of the management information system of the university. Managers can see what is being produced, by whom, when, and where outputs are being formally published. Such analysis, especially if carried out in a comparative context, can inform future planning activities and budget allocation decisions of research managers. In countries where there are national research assessment processes, repositories will be forming the base layer – the collecting point for outputs and the locus for reporting processes.

So far, this is a list of important but rather prosaic parts of the vision for repositories, focusing on institutional advantages and benefits. There is a much broader vision to explore as well. Repositories will form the data layer of the future – the layer where research articles, datasets and other digital items that support research will be located. This system will support the e-research (or e-science) agenda, facilitating the sharing of research data and their curation and preservation. Services, too, will work on this data layer, aggregating content in different ways, analysing content, disseminating it in targeted ways, providing in-out communication channels, and enabling researchers with the means to organise and display their own content in new ways.

This may all sound ideal but there is a long way to go before the vision can be realised. This chapter will therefore also reflect on progress so far in technical, cultural and policy areas. It will discuss the barriers that have already been surmounted and those that threaten future progress. Lessons already learned will be drawn upon to help develop a discussion of what needs to be done in these three areas – technological development, cultural change and policymaking – and where responsibilities lie for action and leadership if the vision is to be realised.

The Rise and Rise of Institutional Repositories

It is not even a full decade ago that the first repository, built by and for the School of Electronics and Computer Science (ECS) at the University of Southampton[1], was launched to the world, employing the original – and at the time newly-developed – repository software, EPrints.[2] Established to showcase the School's research

---

1   http://eprints.ecs.soton.ac.uk/.

2   http://www.eprints.org.

programme and to support its strengthening Open Access agenda, the repository was rapidly underpinned by a mandatory policy implemented by the then Head of School, Professor Wendy Hall; the policy's aim was to fill the repository with the target content.

Now, eight years on at the start of 2010, that repository contains approaching 5,000 journal articles, over 7,000 conference papers (this is a School in a discipline where peer-reviewed conference papers are a predominant form of output), nearly 300 books, more than twice that many book sections (chapters), 60 technical reports and nearly 250 theses. It also houses nearly 1,000 other items such as conference posters, briefing papers, teaching materials and so on. Usage levels are huge, with downloads averaging 30,000 per month: this is usage primarily by people who do not have access to these items through subscribed-for channels – that is, new, additional usage on top of the usage from publisher websites that serve subscribers.

The ECS repository is not alone. It shares a brotherhood with some 1,600 other repositories,[3,4] 80% of which are institutional, including – naturally – an institutional-wide sibling at Southampton University. Growth in numbers of repositories has been remarkable (more than one per working day established over the past three years) though unsurprising, given the benefits they bring to universities.

The Roles and Benefits of a Repository

A university repository should fulfil a number of roles within the institution, but that is not to say that it should be all things to all men and women. The real success stories are repositories that have been established with clarity of purpose and implemented with that purpose strongly in focus. The repository can do the following for an institution:

- open up and offer the outputs of the institution or community to the world
- maximise the visibility of outputs, thus providing the greatest possible chance of enhanced impact as a result
- showcase and sell the institution to interested constituencies – prospective staff, prospective students and other stakeholders
- support the data-rich research process
- collect and curate digital outputs (or inputs, in the case of special collections)
- provide a workspace for work-in-progress, and for collaborative or large-scale projects

---

3   http://roar.eprints.org/.
4   http://www.opendoar.org/index.html.

- facilitate and further the development and sharing of digital teaching materials and aids
- support and sustain student endeavours, including providing access to theses and dissertations and providing a location for the development of e-portfolios
- manage and measure research and teaching activities.

What are Repositories Doing Now?

A Research Assessment Tool

The last point in the list above is one of the strongest drivers for repositories in the UK now, as preparations begin in earnest for the new national research assessment exercise, the Research Excellence Framework (REF), to be carried out for the first time in this new form in 2013. Institutions participating in this will need to have in place a system for providing, electronically, a record of all their research outputs: the repository is prime candidate for this role.

As well as this, research funders are now beginning to plan for better monitoring and evaluation of the research they support in the future. The UK's seven Research Councils between them annually fund research worth £3 billion. Their ultimate aim is to do two main things: demonstrate tangible results for society from the research they fund; and encourage wealth creation and an improvement in the quality of life. The Research Councils, through their umbrella body, Research Councils UK (RCUK), plan to collect the outputs of the research they fund in Britain and analyse the outcomes of that research in various ways. RCUK will do this using the network of university repositories, harvesting from those repositories the outputs from Research Council-funded work into a database which will form the basis for analysis: where a university does not have a repository the onus will be on the institution to ensure that RCUK is in possession of the outputs it needs by alternative (and resource-intensive) means. By the time this system is in place it is unlikely that any research-based universities in the UK will not have a working repository but, should there be any stragglers, these new requirements should act as a final catalyst.

In addition to demands from third parties, universities themselves are now beginning to see the repository as part of their management information system. Certainly, the REF has increased their awareness of the potential here, but it is not the whole story. In the days of print-on-paper, universities never collected and utilised the products of their research and teaching efforts. Now, in the digital age, doing such a thing becomes not only possible but also relatively simple, given some careful thought and planning.

Open Access

This is not the only driver for repositories, though. The repository provides the means for researchers and their institutions to comply with research funders' requirements to make funded work Open Access. And, beyond research funders, the well-documented enhancement of visibility and impact for an institution's research from Open Access (Swan 2010) is anyway a compelling reason for having a repository that exposes the institution's outputs to the world.

Currently, repositories are feeling their way with respect to a number of issues that act as barriers for this Open Access agenda. The low level of spontaneous deposition of outputs by researchers is the most pressing. The newest data on this still point to a general base level of around 15% (Gargouri et al. 2010). It has long been argued that institutions should formalise mandatory policies on Open Access to produce the required levels of content in repositories and this argument seems finally to be heeded. The evidence that such policies are successful in doing this has been documented by Sale (2006) and Gargouri and colleagues (2010).

Although the earliest examples of mandatory policies came from within the university sector – the School of Electronics and Computer Science in Southampton University was the first, in January 2002, and the first institution-wide mandate was implemented at Queensland University of Technology in early 2004 – it was research funders that really set the ball rolling, as the graph in Figure 8.1 indicates. That figure also demonstrates what has happened in the last few years, though:

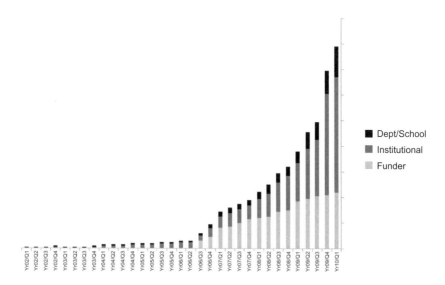

Figure 8.1   **The growth of mandatory Open Access policies from research funding agencies, research-based institutions and departments/ schools/faculties in institutions**

it has been institutions that have made the running, and will continue to do so as the institutional benefits of Open Access to the research literature become ever clearer.[5]

Even when mandatory, Open Access policies can be worded in misguided ways that do not result in the collection of maximal amounts of content. The main case is where they allow authors to opt out of depositing their articles if publisher policies seem to indicate that this is not permitted, or insist on deposit 'only when copyright conditions allow'. There are variations on this theme, all of which have the effect of permitting exceptions and thus impairing the repository's role as collector of the complete digital output of the institution. Careful attention to wording a policy can overcome all these issues.[6]

The Repository as a Showcase to the World

While the primary aim of Open Access is to enable all members of the research community to have free and unhindered access to the literature they might need to use, an institutional repository can reach further than this.

First, it makes its content available to the professional and practitioner communities – the legal and medical professions outside of academia, architect practices, engineering companies, consultancies and small- or medium-sized enterprises (SMEs). These are not well-served by university libraries, despite the need of these communities for access to academic literature and the fact that they contribute through their taxes to paying both for the research to be carried out and for university libraries to purchase subscription access. Although there may be arrangements made to use library hard-copy collections, these people are mostly locked out of digital collections by licensing agreements with publishers and can only hurdle such barriers by payment of a one-off fee each time they wish to consult a document. That the decision to pay up has to be made on the basis of seeing only the abstract, which may be rudimentary or unhelpful on occasions, adds to the problems of these constituencies.

A university repository full of research literature, along with grey literature, datasets and theses, is a treasure chest for these disenfranchised would-be users operating outside academia's gates. Evidence of how the business community can benefit has been produced by Swan (2008), who investigated the need of SMEs for grey literature from universities and found that these companies 'would welcome the chance to use reports, survey results, theses and datasets that universities could

---

5   The list of Open Access policies is maintained on the ROARMAP (Register of Open Access Repository Material Archiving Policies) website: http://www.eprints.org/openaccess/policysignup/ and the graph shown in Figure 8.1 is kept up to date and displayed on the Enabling Open Scholarship site: http://www.openscholarship.org/jcms/c_6226/open-access-policies-for-universities-and-research-institutions?hlText=policies.

6   Guidance on this is provided by Enabling Open Scholarship: http://www.openscholarship.org/jcms/c_6217/formulating-an-institutional-open-access-policy.

provide' although the provision and visibility of such literature is very poor. Ware (2009) confirmed the lack of access to the published literature (not grey literature) for SMEs, finding that 73% of UK-based SMEs and 53% of large companies (along with 27% of university researchers) have difficulty accessing journal articles they need. Interestingly, these companies are finding their way to the Open Access literature though: Ware reports that 71% of SMEs use Open Access journals and 42% use institutional repositories.

Data such as these tell the story in one way: testimonials tell it in another. One of the oldest repositories in the world, that at Queensland University of Technology in Brisbane, Australia, has collected many thousands of full-text articles since the mandate was implemented at the beginning of 2004. As it approached the fifth birthday of the mandate the deputy vice-chancellor responsible for the policy, Tom Cochrane, asked for a simple survey of authors to be carried out to find out what outcomes they had experienced as a result of putting their work into the repository. A few examples illustrate just some of the benefits authors enjoy.

Outreach to those who have no subscription access:

> There is no doubt in my mind that ePrints [QUT's repository] will have improved things – especially in developing countries such as Malaysia ... many more access my papers who wouldn't have thought of contacting me personally in the 'old' days. While this may ... increase ... citations, the most important thing ... is that at least these people can find out more about what others have done ...
>
> Professor Martin Skitmore, Urban Design

Outreach to students:

> One thing it has done is make students aware of what I'm doing outside the classroom. This is important because both undergrad and postgrad students often don't understand what we do beside teach them.
>
> Dr Belinda Luke, Accountancy

Outreach to the industrial and commercial sector:

> Just last week, the General Manager of Sustainable Development from an Australian rural industry called me – based on reading one of my research papers in ePrints. He loved what he read – which he thought was the most clear approach he'd seen on quantifying social impact – and we are now in discussion about how we can help them measure their industry's social impacts.
>
> Dr Evonne Miller, Design

Getting the Repository Layer Right

As universities and research institutes establish their repositories, advances are being made on many fronts to ensure that these repositories are truly interoperable. These advances are in both cultural and technological areas. It is worth a short discussion of these at this point because achieving workable outcomes for these things will build the best technological foundation for the new repository functionalities and services of the future.

Culturally, assuming that the progress now being seen on the introduction of Open Access policies continues, perhaps the most pressing concern is the matter of rights and licensing. The issue of rights – where the rights to research outputs reside, what use can be made of repository material, and by whom – is a tricky one. Currently, most authors continue with the traditional practice of signing the publisher's copyright transfer agreement (CTA) – usually done, these days, by clicking through an electronic version. In doing this, they are relinquishing to the publisher all the rights that publisher decides to acquire, despite the fact that not all of these are needed by the publisher to enable it to publish the work. In assigning all rights to the publisher, authors may then be jeopardising the opportunity to disseminate their work through other channels and be preventing others re-using their work in legitimate ways that can bring greater visibility and impact for that work.

The bundle of rights that most copyright agreements embrace can, very effectively, be split into constituent parts, some of which can be assigned to the publisher to enable that publisher to publish the work. Others can be retained by the author – or even, in some instances, the author's employer or funder – to enable the author to disseminate the work in other ways and to permit certain kinds of re-use.

Authors now have a number of ways to avoid assigning all rights to publishers and retaining the rights they need to ensure their work is not disadvantaged by sub-optimal dissemination. The use of 'author addenda', modifying statements that can be appended to standard publisher CTAs[7], is one way. The development of Creative Commons licences[8] has helped enormously and most repositories have a service that enables the author to assign the most appropriate of these to the work at the deposit stage. The issue can also be resolved at policy level by the establishment of a prior, non-exclusive licence for the institution or funder to disseminate the work in appropriate ways, so that whatever agreement the author subsequently signs with the publisher, this right pre-exists and persists.

---

7   For examples and guidance on the use of author addenda see Enabling Open Scholarship: http://www.openscholarship.org/jcms/c_6218/author-addenda-and-licences?h lText=author+addenda or the Open Access Scholarly Information Sourcebook: http://www. openoasis.org/index.php?option=com_content&view=article&id=152&Itemid=311.

8   http://www.creativecommons.org.

Technologically, the repository layer is underpinned by some internationally-agreed standards. Chief among them is the basic metadata standard that facilitates the harvesting of metadata from repositories, OAI-PMH (Open Archives Initiative Protocol for Metadata Harvesting). So long as repositories comply with this low-barrier standard, third parties can harvest the metadata of their content to create new web services. For example, a service might harvest the metadata for all items connected with Romance languages and use those metadata to produce a collection of research articles as part of a new digital resource for researchers in that field, pointing users back to the full-text articles in the home repositories.

So far, so good. Elaborations have been developed on the basic OAI-PMH protocol but it remains the foundation for interoperation between Open Access repositories and will likely remain so. There are more complex technical issues to surmount, though. So much is happening that it is difficult to identify the most critical areas, but two prime contenders at the moment appear to be identification and the deposit process. These were distilled from the wide-ranging list of interoperability issues and discussed by experts from across the world prior to an international workshop in 2009. At the ensuing workshop, these two topics were examined in detail and plans drawn up for collaborative work to tackle them. That programme, the Interoperable Repository Infrastructure Project (RepInf 2009), was conceived, and is now coordinated as an ongoing initiative, by the UK's Joint Information Systems Committee (JISC).

The identification problem involves the unambiguous means of identifying things. Most importantly, in this context, that means:

- identifying individual people (where more than one person may share the same given and family names);
- identifying where the same individual may publish using their names in a variety of formats;
- identifying where the same individual may publish using different names at different stages of their life, such as before and after marriage;
- identifying individual institutions e.g. authors in an institution may publish using the whole institution name and street address, or the name and street address of their centre or faculty, or just the street address;
- identifying individual items e.g. an item in a repository somewhere (and that item may also be associated with other files, such as a research article with accompanying video file or book chapter deposited along with accompanying photographs, and may be in more than one repository).

The challenge is to develop systems that work on a global scale, are failsafe – for reliability must be absolute if, say, authors are to be judged on their publishing record, or institutions are to be ranked on their outputs – and are simple to put into operation around the world. The eventual system must be agreed internationally and must take into account what has gone before, too. Already, some national systems for uniquely identifying authors exist and a new, global system must be demonstrably sufficiently better to warrant the switch from these existing systems, or must be designed to integrate them into the new whole.

Deposit of material into repositories may seem a simple matter but, as the repository network and associated cultural change develop, the need is growing for processes that aid this activity. Repository technologists envisage systems that enable repositories to 'talk' to one another, identify what items might be copied from one to another and permit items to be deposited once and end up in multiple collections, for example. As policies from funders and institutions unfold, sometimes placing authors under obligation to deposit the same item in more than one digital collection, tools that facilitate this latter process will become increasingly necessary.

A considerable amount of work is already underway on such issues and more will follow. The tool called SWORD (Simple Web service Offering Repository Deposit[9]) is one example of a pilot service. SWORD is a lightweight protocol for depositing content from one location to another (e.g. between repositories). Another example of an application in this area, this time an ongoing project, is TIPR (Towards Interoperable Preservation Repositories[10]), which is testing the exchange of information between repositories, building on previous technical work.

This is just a brief round-up of some of things being tackled to enable the repository network to function. It by no means tells the whole story. Other major areas of work can only be mentioned here but the list includes preservation, automatic metadata creation, authentication of depositors, quality control and 'trustedness' of repositories, and usage reporting. The Interoperable Repository Infrastructure Project has a wiki where past and present work on infrastructure areas is listed and described (RepInf 2009).

What Will Repositories Do Next?

Two phenomena will be particularly strong influencers on how repositories develop in future. One is the nature of scholarly enquiry itself and the other is the use of computational technologies on the research corpus. As well as these two foundational drivers, another development area will be especially intense – that of repository services. I shall start with this: it is an area rich with ideas, with technical innovation and with promise.

As soon as repositories began to increase in number, the need for service development became plain. Among early examples of services were resource discovery tools (e.g. OAIster[11], originally developed at the University of Michigan and now part of OCLC's portfolio of services for libraries), permission guides

---

9   http://www.swordapp.org/.
10   http://wiki.fcla.edu:8000/TIPR.
11   http://www.oclc.org/oaister/.

(e.g. SHERPA's RoMEO[12] service), repository listing services (e.g. ROAR and OpenDOAR) and repository-hosting services (e.g. EPrints Services[13]).

As time went on, other ideas came to fruition. Pilot services that have turned into sustained resources are SHERPA/JULIET[14], which documents research funders' Open Access policies, and services providing usage reporting (such as Google Analytics[15], AWstats[16] and Interoperable Repository Statistics[17]).

In other areas, services were developed to pilot stage but awaited a greater openly accessible body of research literature on which to work to their maximum potential. Citation analysis services are an example of this. Some discipline-specific tools are able to operate to great effect on large subject-related collections of Open Access material, such as CitEc[18], which analyses citations in the RePEc digital library[19] and Citebase[20], which works on the high-energy physics literature in the Open Access arXiv repository[21]. A citation analysis service for the whole Open Access literature remains as yet unrealised, however, though a major project has now begun under the umbrella of the Interoperable Repositories Infrastructure initiative to build such a service. If successful, this project could prove to be one of the applications that elicits a big cultural shift as far as repositories are concerned. Researchers have long lived with a reward system where citations are a major currency, especially in the natural and social sciences: a service that measures and analyses citations from and to repository content as well as formally published work will be an influential development, driving more interest in repositories from researchers.

Now to the scholarly enquiry process. There is no significant field of research that is not already rich in digital data. Many are more than this; they are data-intensive. It is not only the experimental sciences that now produce and manipulate huge volumes of data as part of the research process, though certainly the data outputs of some fields in these disciplines can be exceptionally large. Social sciences and humanities enquiry also generate data in volumes and complexities that give as much pause for thought. How are these data being looked after? How available are they to others who could use them? The argument for Open Access to the literature applies equally well to data. Who is responsible for long-term care and storage? Who should be responsible for long-term care and storage? Can I, or you, easily find a dataset that we need to use? Indeed, can we find out that it exists

---

12   http://www.sherpa.ac.uk/romeo/.
13   http://www.eprints.org/services/.
14   http://www.sherpa.ac.uk/juliet/index.php.
15   http://www.google.com/analytics/.
16   http://awstats.sourceforge.net/.
17   http://irs.eprints.org/.
18   http://citec.repec.org/.
19   http://repec.org/.
20   http://www.citebase.org/.
21   http://www.arxiv.org.

at all and, if we can, and if we can access it, can we use it, or is it in a format we cannot utilise? If we can access it, may we? And will it cost us money?

There are no answers to this body of questions in the round, at least not yet. There are whole answers to some parts, and some part-answers to the whole, but we are nowhere near resolving all the issues. It will be a long time before we are, but at least these things are under intense study and discussion and some progress is being made.

What has this to do with repositories? The answer is that there is undoubtedly a role here for repositories in the future. Some disciplines or fields benefit from centralised, professionally-managed databanks that provide curatorial and preservation services for research data. Examples are GenBank[22] in the biosciences and the UK Data Archive[23] for social sciences. But such services are available only to certain disciplines and even where they exist they cannot accept every dataset produced by researchers. They are excellent facilities for caring for larger datasets – so called 'big data' – but 'small and medium data' have no such home. It is these data products from research that will need to be looked after in the research institutions themselves and of course the institution's repository is the natural candidate for the role.

The problem is that data are so variable. Astronomy data look nothing like the data from a nationwide survey of the UK public's habits, and neither bears any resemblance to a gene sequence. On top of this un-alikeness in general, datasets come in a wide variety of formats, sizes and complexities. They may grow over time, be modified or updated, be annotated or be migrated to different formats. All this presents a considerable challenge to repository management (Lynch 2008).

So much of a challenge, in fact, that a new career path is opening up now – data librarianship. Most advanced in the US, Canada, Australia and the UK, this concept represents librarians specialised in data handling and management. New training opportunities are opening up to equip these people with the set of skills needed to take repositories into this new role as the locus for the custodianship of institutional research data. Clearly, data librarians cannot be intimately familiar with all types of research data, but these professionals will have an understanding of the provenance of research data, how they were created, how they can be manipulated and what must be done to store and preserve them properly. As well as this, they will be experts in, and advise researchers on, data policies and requirements from research funders and from institutions, and will make sure that there is provision of facilities to enable researchers to comply with such requirements. It is probable that this sort of expertise and associated repository development will not be something every institution can support. We may be looking at a future where consortial solutions are the best option for at least some of the data management process, but in all institutions where research is carried out there will need to be systems in place to ensure the proper care and management of data.

---

22   http://www.ncbi.nlm.nih.gov/.
23   http://www.data-archive.ac.uk/.

Computer technologies that work on the research literature to create new knowledge have aroused huge interest over recent years, with good reason. These are the so-called text-mining or data-mining technologies. They can, in a nutshell, identify entities (things), facts and actions in textual documents and put them together from multiple (millions, if necessary) disparate sources to create new knowledge. To these programs, a textual document is just a collection of digital data and, in effect, they can analyse these data, extract hypotheses, make correlations and distil new answers from old information.

This area of endeavour represents a major shift in our development, just as the evolution of language and the engineering of the printing press were. We are entering an age where the research literature is no longer just for humans to read, but is read by machines and manipulated in meaningful ways. Already, these types of technology are developing fast in those disciplines where the literature and other outputs from research are relatively structured and where vocabularies and ontologies and thesaurus-type work is the furthest on – disciplines such as biomedicine, computational chemistry and computer science. Advances like these in other disciplines will surely quickly follow; see, for example, Crane (2006) who discusses the potential for using such advanced technologies on the book-based literature.

The kind of potential from this type of technology is easy to appreciate, though we cannot yet imagine much of its scale. How repositories relate to it also seems obvious: they will provide the Open Access literature on which these technologies work. The repository network will become a giant database of research that can be searched not just by keywords in a title or elsewhere in the metadata of an item, but on the basis of meaning – semantics. The Semantic Web does indeed, after a slow start, appear to be materialising as the standards and conventions needed to underpin it emerge (Shadbolt et al. 2006).

Is that enough, then? Can we relax, watch repositories fill with articles and datasets and let semantic technologies begin their work? Of course, because life is never that simple, the answer is no. Much has still to be put in place. There are a number of problem areas but I shall pick just three big ones to focus on here.

First, there is authoring practice. The technologies I described briefly above work best if the raw material is presented to them in particular formats; indeed they need them to be. Of preference, they like the material to be fully 'marked up'. This means that textual documents should be produced in a form that tags or labels certain things in the text. Authors are not expected to learn to write in any particular mark-up language, but they will need to be encouraged to use newer authoring tools (such as the latest versions of word processing softwares, for example) that automatically give the document an underlying marked-up structure. In some fields, specialised mark-up languages have been developed (e.g. CML, Chemical Mark-up Language) which have been designed to improve the efficacy of semantic tools. We can expect more developments like this and, concomitantly, expect the need to educate and support authors in some ways. Most semantic mark-up research aims to produce post-writing mark-up systems: for example, the National Text-Mining

Centre is working on systems that will mark up biomedical articles once they have been supplied by their authors for inclusion in the UK PubMed Central database[24]. But in fields without such tools, author-produced XML documents are likely to be a minimum requirement and authors will need to understand why they should provide their outputs in this, rather than PDF, format.

Second, we return to the business of ownership and licensing. The most common practice at present is for authors to relinquish all copyrights to publishers. Some publishers permit authors to make the peer-reviewed work Open Access in repositories, but not all do. And of those that do, the language of the permission usually limits the author to using only their institutional repository for this, not a third-party one. Naturally, publishers rather fear the possibility of material in which they feel they have a stake appearing all over the Web.

For the purpose of human reading, this state of affairs is perfectly adequate, but it is should be clear that it will not be at all adequate if we wish to move to a future that includes computation on the literature. Open Access is not enough: these tools will need to harvest articles and copy them to new locations, creating thereby new collections of selected parts of the worldwide literature. Does this contravene the most usual types of current publisher policies? Yes, in many cases.

Moreover, the simple act of computation may also contravene some kinds of publisher permissions since many explicitly do not permit re-use in this way, even if the articles are paid for through subscription. And harvesting large bodies of the literature from publisher websites, even where access has been paid-for, also contravenes most common licensing rules.

The third matter is the issue of ownership and attribution. This may turn out to be intractable for some time. The practice in scholarly communication is always to attribute material to a previous author or creator wherever appropriate. Receiving attribution is a valued part of the scholarly reward system. If the new semantic technologies are going to 'read', process, select from and mash up material from hundreds, thousands or more articles to produce something new and useful, attribution becomes more than difficult: even if the will is there to try to acknowledge the creator of every tiny bit of data used in a new creation, in a practical sense it will become impossible to trace this accurately and satisfactorily.

Both the research and the repository communities will need to grapple with this in coming years. Already, the Creative Commons organisation has released a new licence, called CC0 (CC Zero[25]). This is a licence that authors or creators can attach to their work upon publication that in effect says that they are donating the work to the commons and need no future attribution. The idea behind this is to reduce the need for 'attribution stacking', where even a few levels of re-use of research data (and that includes textual material) brings nightmarish complexities in terms of attribution. Authors who assign a CC0 licence to their work will be

24   http://ukpmc.ac.uk/classic/.
25   http://creativecommons.org/publicdomain/zero/1.0/.

facilitating simple, permission-free, problem-free re-use of their results, to the good of future research.

Having made the investment in establishing a repository, university managers are looking for ways to maximise the return on that investment. There is plenty of scope! Undoubtedly, repositories are an essential foundation block in the future research process, but there is much thinking and much to do before they realise their full potential. Critically, this cannot happen without international consensus on direction and goals. That consensus must be reached by collaborative intent on the part of all stakeholders – research funders, institutional managers, research libraries, researchers and the public that can use and benefit from the products of research. Not a small challenge, but an entirely achievable aim.

References

Crane, G., 2006. What do you do with a million books? *D-Lib Magazine*, 12 (3), March 2006.

Gargouri, Y., Hajjem, C., Lariviere. V., Gingras, Y., Brody, T., Carr, L. and Harnad, S., 2010. *Self-Selected or Mandated,* Open Access Increases Citation Impact for Higher Quality Research. PLoS ONE (in press). Available from: http://eprints.ecs.soton.ac.uk/18493/ (accessed 20 May 2010).

Lynch, C., 2008. Big data: How do your data grow? *Nature,* 455, 28–29 (4 September 2008) doi:10.1038/455028a. Published online 3 September 2008. Available from: http://www.nature.com/nature/journal/v455/n7209/full/455028a.html (accessed 20 May 2010).

RepInf., 2009. *The International Repositories Infrastructure Project.* Available from: http://repinf.pbworks.com/ (accessed 20 May 2010).

Sale, A.H.J., 2006. Comparison of IR content policies in Australia. *First Monday,* 11 (4). Available from: http://eprints.utas.edu.au/264/ (accessed 20 May 2010).

Shadbolt, N., Berners-Lee, T. and Hall, W., 2006. The Semantic Web Revisited. *IEEE Intelligent Systems,* 21 (3), 96–101. Available from: http://eprints.ecs.soton.ac.uk/12614/ (accessed 20 May 2010).

Swan, A., 2008. *Study on the Availability of UK Academic 'Grey Literature' to UK SMEs: Report to the JISC Scholarly Communications Group.* JISC. Available from: http://eprints.ecs.soton.ac.uk/17667/ (accessed 20 May 2010).

Swan, A., 2010. *The Open Access Citation Advantage: Studies and Results to date. Technical Report.* Available from: http://eprints.ecs.soton.ac.uk/18516/ (accessed 20 May 2010).

Ware, M., 2009. *Access by UK Small and Medium-sized Enterprises to Professional and Academic Literature.* Bristol: Publishing Research Consortium. Available from: http://www.publishingresearch.net/documents/SMEAccessResearchReport.pdf (accessed 20 May 2010).

Chapter 9

Making the Repository Count:
Lessons from Successful Implementation

Matt Holland and Tim Denning

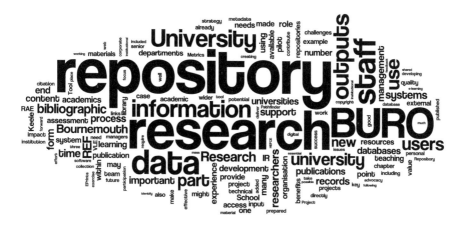

Introduction

We accept that institutional repositories (IR) are a good thing for universities. They solve the problem of knowing what research is being published. They contribute to the free and wider dissemination of knowledge, enhance the visibility of research outputs and speed up its use. Despite all these positive outcomes, implementing a repository remains a challenge. This chapter uses "real world" experience to identify what some of the challenges are and to suggest strategies that might be adopted to overcome them. The chapter focuses on three areas: how the IR fits with the university organisation, how to promote the use of the IR to end users and contributors, and how to secure long-term benefits for the broadest range of stakeholders. It does not deal with technical and copyright issues, which are covered in the chapter by Alma Swan, *Institutional Repositories – Now and Next*. Two short case studies are incorporated in the discussion, including a description of the implementation of Bournemouth University Research Online (BURO). Reflections on these three areas form a major element of the text that follows.

How the Institutional Repository Fits with the University Organisation

Making the Case for the IR and the Library in Research Information Management [RIM]

Research outputs are part of the product of a university, its staff and research centres. The success of the institution is to an extent judged by the volume and quality of research outputs. Academics and research administrators at all levels are actively involved in promoting research as part of the university corporate communications strategy. One consequence of this is that everyone involved needs access to information about research outputs. This includes web designers creating staff profiles and web pages, senior managers preparing reports for committees and boards, academics preparing bids for funding, marketing professionals showcasing research, and research administrators preparing for research evaluation. Communicating the centrality of bibliographic information to the management of the research information process is a key task to ensure the success of the repository.

To illustrate this point it is instructive to look at the experience of the pilot exercise to collect and analyse data for the Research Excellence Framework (REF) the replacement for the Research Assessment Exercise (RAE). Twenty-two universities were chosen to take part in the exercise and to collect data to test the collection methodology and bibliometric measures that may form part of the REF evaluation (HEFCE 2009). Looking specifically at the process of collecting data for submission to the Higher Education Funding Council for England (HEFCE) there is a clear lesson that universities should 'press forward with ongoing efforts to strengthen their central Research Information Management (RIM) systems and capture a majority of all research outputs.' (Technopolis 2009b, p. 2). The report goes on to analyse the specific implications for research information management systems, which include:

- Have a publications database that links to other university systems such as HR (staff) and finance (contracts, research income)

- Move towards a system where all research outputs are captured and catalogued. (Technopolis 2009b, p. 4)

In reporting on the possible impact of the REF on staff, the experience of the 22 participants was that:

> In all cases, the library is expected to play a fuller role in the future, with an increased workload associated with maintaining more comprehensive and up to date repositories and bibliographic databases. (Technopolis 2009b, p. 4)

The Role of IT Departments

The IT department is a key player in the developing use of repository data. Bibliographic data form part of the information that flows through the networks and applications that IT departments maintain and deliver. There is an opportunity to contribute more and better bibliographic data to enhance the overall quality of information available to the university and to enhance bibliographic data by linking with other information in the system. A university may also maintain a number of systems that either harvest or use bibliographic data related to research outputs, for example a closed system that supports research information management or a repository for public use and human resource systems. The experience of the JISC REF pilot studies is that very few universities have all three systems, some have no effective system or are developing one, and few are integrated.

In designing systems to capture and use bibliographic data the 'input once, use many times' principle is important. Academic, researchers and their support teams will not support repeated requests to input or provide the same data for different purposes. Good technical solutions that enable data to be shared between systems are an important underpinning. From the Bournemouth case study the problem was resolved by designating the repository as the main data source, raising the profile of the repository with academics and gaining their support. The message that went out to academics was that the repository was the only place they needed to contribute publication information. In practice the integration of systems has some way to go but the objective of one source of data has been clearly signalled to the IT department for future developments.

The Role of HR Departments

HR departments have a number of points of contact with bibliographic data and possibly require a repository solution or at least research information management. The pilot REF required that institutions identify certain criteria, for example early career researchers, when researchers joined or left the university and where they originated from or departed to. Synchronising these data with publication history raised significant concerns. Looking to the future the benefits of being able to identify, for example, whether research outputs were produced within a period of employment at a given institution, or to which institution the credit should accrue in research assessment will be important. Technological solutions save the many person hours it might take to do this manually and enable repeated questions to be addressed to the data, if for example universities wanted to run simulations of research assessment internally.

The second issue for HR is the point in time at which bibliographic data are supplied to the repository. The logical point is at appointment of new staff. Challenges remain in supplying data in electronic form that can also be quickly ingested into a repository or research information system. The optimum format would be a complete list in a popular bibliographic format or exported from a personal bibliographic database such as EndNote. The wide experience of academics and researchers of managing their own personal bibliography suggests this will be a challenge for many. A requirement that new appointees bring with them a personal electronic database of publications might at this point in time seem excessive, however, within the United Kingdom higher education sector the time and effort saved by this simple requirement would be significant.

The Value of the Repository for Corporate Communications

Communicating research outputs to a wider audience can be a key role for the repository. This goes beyond arguments from the perspective of Open Access and the wider and free dissemination of research. The repository can be available to media outlets as well as the higher education community. Press releases and news outputs on websites can include links to research outputs as part of a package. Searches of repositories form part of creating an academic biography. News outlets may trawl repositories looking for interesting research.

The repository itself tells a story, how big it is, how well used it is, how many people access it and where it appears in world or national rankings. Fortune favours the brave in these areas but they make for good internal communications, and with the help of professional communicators, can make good external publicity.

The Role of the Repository in Learning and Teaching

The example of Keele University demonstrates a repository that is dedicated to learning materials. It plays a key role in revealing hidden resources to colleagues for reuse and supporting the learning and teaching infrastructure. There is a case study of the IR at Keele University later in this chapter. Self-archiving using the repository, including unpublished papers, keynote speeches, conference papers or grey literature makes available to students resources that might otherwise be difficult to find or not be available at all. Repositories can also provide part of the answer to the question, "who is teaching me and what are their research interests?" by grouping research outputs easily by author, research group and faculty. The repository is a resource that can deliver content into virtual learning environments and can make an obvious connection for students between teaching and research.

The Role of the Repository to Research Management

The precursor to any research assessment exercise is the strategy universities adopt in their presentation of data. Part of the benchmarking of researchers and research centres is creating a picture of an institution's research and where possible, modelling likely outcomes in any assessment exercise. This is harder with qualitative assessment but in the new REF process some form of quantitative assessment of research outputs using bibliographic or citation analysis is planned. The challenge here is that there needs to be some reference to external citation databases – ISI Web of Science and Scopus – which will offer universities information from their databases in the form of bibliographic data and citation analysis.

Although the research assessment may drive a process of assessing or measuring research productivity and impact, universities may see value in running metrics, measures of what is happening in terms of research across the data to provide a picture of where we are now, as part of a management information desktop. Examples of simple questions that could be asked could include 'Which academics and which departments are most productive?' 'Are outputs being published in high impact journals?' 'Which journals are publishing our outputs and applying a measure to the quality of outputs?' There are challenges in the sensible use of these data, the use to which data are put, and the limits that apply need to be clearly communicated to users.

Repository managers have to make choices about the direction and content policies of their databases. In making these choices one lesson is clear, that universities need a complete and accurate record of research outputs going forward. Libraries will have a role in providing or supporting this. Repositories may be part or all the answer to this challenge. Making an assessment of who needs these data and how they are harvested points to who IR managers should be talking to and what services they might offer.

How to Sell the IR to End Users

Starting perhaps at the end of the process, the aim should be to create autonomous end users. Users who will contribute (or cause their research outputs to be added) to the repository, or check the validity of records sourced from other databases and be prepared to review and edit their own records.

Gaining support for repositories at a senior level is essential. As has been discussed earlier in this chapter a repository can answer pressing needs for the university as an organisation. Communicating with faculties and relevant professional services within the university and being able to evidence support from senior managers can move the repository from a 'nice to have' to an 'essential to have' tool. In presenting the repository to users, being able to say this is seen to be important moves the discussion of why it is needed to "how can we take part".

Whatever form the repository takes in any institution, it is important to have a product that can be demonstrated to end users as purposeful and worthwhile. This will be informed by the strategy for the repository. At Bournemouth University (BU) where the repository was the designated source for university research outputs, the aim was to gain a critical mass of records, with some full text, to prove the concept that a single project, BURO, could replace several smaller, localised and less effective bibliographic databases. Considerable investment was made in staff time to harvest or ingest records, edit and check them, before the repository was rolled out to academics and researchers. Not only was it possible to demonstrate the added value of well designed repository software but in most cases to show staff records for their own work already included in the repository.

Librarians need to be change agents (Holland 2000), drawing on many years of experience in information skills and demonstrating the value of databases or the latest electronic resource in selling the repository to end users. The following will be helpful promotional tools:

- a webpage that is dedicated to the IR that can sell to end users, and host training materials, instructions and policies in one location
- clearly thought through presentations to give to senior academics and researchers, that can sell the value of the repository
- hands-on workshops on how to use the repository
- clearly thought through arguments for the value of the repository to end users
- embedded links to the repository in the university intranet and extranet
- consistent dissemination of information about the repository through the established channels of communication.

Users will value flexibility. Keeping the users' needs central to the task of selling the repository and being prepared to go the extra mile wins champions in academic departments, and develops islands of experience for other staff to draw on. Consider trying:

- working with individual staff who show an interest to input their complete bibliography
- offering to input records on behalf of staff to 'manage the gap' between developing expertise within their departments in using the repository and the roll out of the repository
- partnering with academic departments and other parts of the organisation to deliver sessions into workshop series, meetings and roadshows
- being prepared to give extra 'temporary' access to expert users to help shape their own inputs
- being open to feedback and prepared to configure elements of the repository – for example the subject structure – to the needs of departments
- creating a forum to communicate with end users, a blog or wiki, that talks directly to users about the challenges and success of the repository and the issues it raises.

Universities may mandate participation in the repository, however, at the centre of the idea of an autonomous user – a willing participant in the project – is the belief that it is a useful exercise for them. Being prepared to sell the benefits to the individual is important and there are good arguments to use depending on the individual circumstances of the organisation. Broadly they are:

- that the repository increases the visibility of research
- it can provide an easier and quick measure of research impact: the number of downloads; in certain disciplines a measure of impact can be hard to achieve where journals or forms of publication are not well represented in citation databases
- the repository is one route to evidence mandated Open Access publication to research funders
- the future trend is for universities to mandate or require recording outputs in some form of central database. There is no reason to delay participation – you will have to engage at some point
- it is a single point to feed information into university systems, and information can be drawn from the repository instead of requests for information made to individual researchers
- the repository is a tool to manage publications: exporting to reference management software or directly to documents, reports and research proposals, and a persistent URL to link to publications
- repositories provide a robust system for self archiving including different versions of the same document
- repositories provide access to groups who might not otherwise have access, for example prospective students and those studying in developing countries.

Securing Long-term Benefits

As organisations that produce research, universities have perhaps surprisingly not been traditionally effective at recording research outputs from their own staff and researchers. This is the lesson from the Research Excellence Framework pilot (although there are gradations of success with some very effective systems in place). While there are many users and uses for these data, the 'collect once use many times' principle means that the repository will either be the core of any system or a consumer of outputs from another publication system or Current Research Information System (CRIS).

The potential for the repository is to move from a 'nice to have' tool managed by the library to the centre of the research information management infrastructure. Clearly the growing importance of bibliographic data of this type places the library in a key position to contribute to this strategically important area of activity. Securing long term benefits requires an understanding of how this information flows within any institution and a willingness to engage with potential users. The different experience of Bournemouth and Keele demonstrates a capacity for the repository to evolve through the many contacts made within the organisation. Although this chapter has not covered technical aspects of the repository, the necessary engagement with external data providers cannot be ignored. Collaboration with external organisations such as HEFCE and commercial organisations who may, for example, offer consultancy services on the back of these data to the university cannot be ignored.

Case Study 1: Bournemouth University Research Online (BURO)
With thanks to Emma Crowley, Institutional Repository Manager at Bournemouth University.

Milestones
2007 The IR was handed over to the library from the corporate centre. A publicly available version was released in a 'soft launch' in May; during the year legacy databases were ingested and checked. The Metrics Tool was commissioned and implemented. Data quality checks and editing were begun.

2008 The migration to v3.04 of EPrints[1] began, with a focus on one School to achieve a complete record of publications. The RAE data were uploaded in March and the Metrics Tool rolled out at the same time. The following month BURO was promoted and made available to all Schools. Towards the end of the year data for the HEFCE REF pilot were uploaded manually and reviewed.

2009 April 2009 saw the introduction of 'Browse Author' functionality and REF focussed advocacy sessions began with the Library and the Centre for Research and Enterprise collaborating. The 'Self Edit' tool was introduced in the following month, along with new functionality suggested by feedback from academics. From June the advocacy role was subsumed into the Subject Librarians' role, taking the form of workshops and one-to-one sessions with academic and research staff. In December PhD e-theses from BU were added to the database.

2010 A new IR editorial team was created and subsumed into core library activities, along with a mock REF and the creation of a new Publications Policy.

What next? Possible integration with CRIS.

Background

Bournemouth University Library took over management and development of the institutional repository, known as Bournemouth University Research Online

---

1 http://www.eprints.org/.

(BURO), from the corporate centre in January 2007. EPrints manage and host the repository on behalf of Bournemouth University.

At that time Bournemouth University was in the process of launching a new corporate strategy, one part of which was a focus on enhancing research capacity. The strategy raised a number of practical questions. What research is already published by university researchers and staff? How is information about new publications collated? How is that information presented to internal and external audiences to promote research activity? The implementation of BURO was intended to resolve these questions. As well as the new strategy there were three concurrent strands of activity that were important to the development of BURO: a more co-ordinated approach to research information management, preparation for the 2008 RAE and participation in the pilot for the REF.

Implementation

The first task was to integrate legacy databases from four university schools. The contents of these databases were imported into the BURO 'review area' by EPrints and checked by professionally qualified librarians at Bournemouth before being deposited into the 'live' BURO archive.

The aim was for BURO to achieve a critical mass of records to make it useful and attractive to staff and researchers and to reflect the research output of the University to 2007. Bibliographic records were imported without full text, although links were included to external sources using the Digital Object Identifier (DOI). The inclusion criteria, based on guidelines approved at Board level, were interpreted broadly, keeping in mind the need to know what has been published. It became apparent that the volume of data had to be contained. A 'cut-off point' of 2001 was established, based on the time frame for the 2008 RAE. Research outputs published prior to 2001 were not excluded, although records would not be input centrally by the library. EPrints encouraged the university to think about other forms of publication, to reflect the international standing of Bournemouth Media School and their multimedia outputs, and create input forms for images, exhibitions, multimedia and moving image.

Development

The University Librarian and the BURO Project Manager gave a series of presentations to School Research Committees, explaining the purpose of BURO, demonstrating the software and encouraging participation. Full support for BURO at the highest level of the University gave added impetus to this initiative.

The 2008 RAE was a key influence on BURO. BURO was not used to collect data for the RAE 2008 as an existing process was already in place. However, discussions over the contribution of BURO with the team responsible for the RAE were very productive, in part because of the shared experience of the challenges in collecting bibliographic data. The RAE dataset was imported into BURO and it was agreed at that stage to use BURO as the core for future research assessment data collection activities. Bournemouth University became part of the JISC REF pilot of 22 institutions to test the new REF process and as a consequence BURO was chosen as one of five case studies looking specifically at data collection issues (Bolton 2009).

Throughout this period a concerted effort was made to input centrally as many records as could be feasibly identified from research active staff. This period of mediated deposit involved appeals to staff to submit CVs via e-mail, culling personal web pages for publication lists. The message to staff at that point was if you send it we will input it.

Preparing for participation in the REF pilot meant that the BURO Team were asked to focus specifically on one School. During the first three months of 2008, working closely with School administrators, BURO was used to capture the entire output of the School. This was broadly successful. The School were very committed to BURO; they understood the benefits and were able to communicate that message to staff.

BURO did experience some problems with data quality, specifically in staff profiles, which were created on BURO for each staff member, containing information about schools and research centres. During the implementation of BURO the university introduced a new Research Centre structure which had to be retrospectively added to staff profiles, as were minor changes to the University organisation. The costs of addressing these changes were signalled to the University Executive who allocated funds to pay for staff time to edit BURO. When BURO was officially rolled out to all staff and schools in April 2008 it contained a critical mass of 3,000-plus records.

In response to feedback from the School, two small but important technological enhancements were instigated. Firstly, a self-editing tool was introduced within each item to allow academics who had not initially deposited an item to create and amend (or add full text to) a copy of the original. Secondly, an 'Author Browse' page enabled researchers to more easily locate their publications; to compare themselves with colleagues; and to re-use the persistent web-link for their outputs in their email signatures, as a further means of promoting personal research excellence.

Advocacy

BURO has been an essential part of a wider change agenda aimed at embedding research into the core activities of Bournemouth University (Crowley et al. 2009). Academics are now largely autonomous users of BURO, depositing items in the repository as part of their personal research processes. Crucial to this change agenda and to BURO's success has been carefully coordinated advocacy and prompt response to user feedback, which encourages academic engagement. The Library collaborates closely with Staff Development and the Centre for Research and Enterprise, providing guidance, briefing sessions and hands-on workshops, many targeted towards preparation for the REF and the potential citation benefits of BURO. The Subject Librarians are the main contacts for training; providing one-to-one guidance and copyright reassurance in each School, and new staff are introduced to BURO at induction. We intend to implement an institutional publications policy, which will mandate inclusion of all academic outputs in BURO, but it is winning the hearts and minds of researchers that is crucial, and judging by the speed at which it is growing this has largely been achieved.

Metrics Tool

Early on in the development of BURO its potential to provide information about current research activity was realised by the University Executive, who raised the possibility of producing a number of metrics based on publication outputs. These included the journals in which staff published listed by number of publications and by impact factor, lists of publications by organisational unit and author. These have been used in various reports required by University boards and committees. A Metrics Tool was commissioned by the University from EPrints, who devised a series of reports using a specification, which could be run against BURO.

Overall the Metrics Tool has had a positive effect on the development of BURO. It provided a significant focus on data quality, integrated BURO into the University information management structure and provided a driver to move BURO forward and direct effort and resources to where they were most effective.

Public Relations Benefits

BURO is a public relations success, with accomplishments regularly incorporated in the Vice Chancellor's newsletters. Internally it provides useful information to managers and has raised the confidence of senior managers within the University. The focus on achieving a critical mass made BURO the natural source for information on research, and access to BURO was integrated into the University web presence using the tag *Our Research*. Researchers' publications in BURO will soon also be directly linked to staff web profile pages. BURO is included in a number of Open Access repository search tools, such as OAIster[2], and the Intute[3] Repository search, which together with its access via prominent search engines such as Google, will further heighten retrieval of the content. Academics feel empowered by the number of 'hits' BURO receives. At the time of writing BURO

---

2   http://www.oclc.org/oaister/.
3   http://www.intute.ac.uk/.

has grown to in excess of 10,000 records, meaning that it is among the largest in the UK. It has attracted positive publicity inside and outside the University for this achievement, making it into the top 200 of the World Ranking Web of Institutional Repositories.

Future Challenges

The foremost ongoing BURO advocacy issue is to improve digital preservation by increasing the number of Open Access deposits. Looking ahead, possible future enhancements include the integration of citation data from ISI Web of Science or Scopus, development of the BURO Metrics Tool to improve internal and external reporting, and the insertion of a REF plugin. At present, similarly to other UK institutions, we are also investigating CRIS products such as Symplectic Elements and Avedas' CONVERIS. Adoption will require considerable technical planning to enable a multitude of existing institutional systems, including BURO, to interface effectively. Most importantly workflows need to be agreed to ensure that the positivity accrued through BURO advocacy is maintained.

Case Study 2: Keele University Content Repository

Material for this case study draws on a report prepared for the UK Higher Education Academy (HEA) as part of a Pathfinder Project[4] completed in 2008.

In the Beginning...

This case study provides an overview of developments at Keele University over a four-year period that starts in 2005 when the student population was growing rapidly and work had begun on a new 'University Strategic Plan'. This made explicit for the first time a commitment to:

- support e-learning to assist flexible styles of teaching and on and off-campus learning
- enhance the student learning environment by further development of e-learning opportunities

This new plan provided the impetus for a successful bid in 2006 to take part in Phase 1 of the HEA Benchmarking Project, a process which, we believed, would provide a clear picture of the current state of play regarding e-learning at Keele and provide the basis for further work. Much had already been achieved at this

---

4   http://www.heacademy.ac.uk/assets/York/documents/ourwork/learningandtech/completed/pathfinder/Journey_Reports/Keele.pdf.

stage with the recent appointments of e-Learning Fellows for each faculty, a staff development officer with specific responsibility for e-learning support, additional technical support in Information Services and an extended remit for the existing staff development team.

As part of the project a new, loosely grouped, team was formed which crossed some of the vertical organisational structure in the university and brought together academic and support staff, members of the IT services team, librarians and the newly appointed 'evangelists' in the form of e-Learning Fellows. The team, known informally as the Elf Group, became the focal point for moving forward the concerns uncovered by the Benchmarking process to a second project to develop a content repository as an important part of the university infrastructure for supporting teaching and learning. The result was a successful bid to the HEA Pathfinder Programme.

Our formally agreed Pathfinder Project deliverables included:

- A well-understood and specified mechanism for using a repository for storing digital 'content' independent of a specific delivery tool e.g. virtual learning environment (VLE) or 'Learning' Server.
- Clear, documented work-flow frameworks for creating, sharing, tagging and using digital content in all its forms. These will be made available for use both within and beyond Keele.
- Procedures for generating data regarding the use of digital assets relevant to strategic and operational planning, and the creation of the datasets required by external agencies such as the Copyright Licensing Agency (CLA).
- One or more Staff Development Modules created using materials held on the repository as exemplars of 'good practice' which can be shared across university faculties and between institutions.
- An exemplar collection of resources, including documents and a variety of digitised multimedia assets with metadata tags, made available in the repository for staff use in a range of teaching, learning and research activities.

We had started by considered a range of national initiatives associated with the development and use of digital content and in particular the use of shared repository systems such as Jorum[5]. The JISC website and wider searches across the internet revealed an almost bewildering collection of material offering advice on all aspects of repository design, development, roll out and support. It also provoked a good deal of anxiety amongst team members unfamiliar with the mysteries of metadata, workflows and XML but this wore off as we realised that much of this could be scaled down to match our particular needs.

---

5   http://www.jorum.ac.uk/.

What did the Project Achieve?

Whilst the Keele Pathfinder Project developed directly from the earlier Benchmarking work and drew on the expertise of the established Benchmarking team there were two further essential elements needed before work could start in earnest.

The first of these was relatively easily achieved. After evaluating a number of repository packages we identified the Intralibrary product from Intrallect[6] as the best fit with our intended approach and found them willing partners in an exploration of the use of their repository system as a basis for managing materials scanned under the CLA licence. This would also be an opportunity to consider the best way to exploit their recently developed Powerlink which provided convenient and controlled access to resources in the repository from a VLE of the type already in place at Keele.

The second element was the appointment of a member of staff who could contribute time and expertise to the project. This would be someone with an established knowledge of CLA licence arrangements and librarianship qualifications that would enable them to take the lead in developing strategies for metadata tagging objects held in a content repository. Here the project was further enhanced by the availability of a librarian already in post with extensive IT and metadata skills and by the opportunity to use Pathfinder funding to bring into post a digitisation and copyright officer, bringing forward an appointment already planned for the following year.

Installing and commissioning the repository software, integrating this with our VLE and enrolling staff users proved generally unproblematic, and it soon became clear that the tough challenges were not essentially technical but conceptual. From the outset the repository proved a reliable and stable environment for storing and managing the use of materials scanned under the CLA licence. The links with the VLE were easy to implement and the reporting features incorporated in the repository software evolved in line with our needs as new versions emerged.

The close collaboration between academics and IT, support and library staff resulted in huge improvements to the interface between the VLE and the repository. However this apparent progress on the technical front concealed, to some extent, the much more intractable hearts and minds issues. Enticing hard-pressed academic staff to place resources normally 'hidden' inside their online teaching modules into a potentially more open repository where they could make them available to others is not without its own challenges. The actual 'process' must be easy, certainly as easy as putting material directly into the VLE, but more importantly, access to the resources by others has to be organised so that staff retain a degree of authority over who might see and use their material. This is, of course, notwithstanding any assertion of Intellectual Property Rights (IPR) which the institution might make. Our work confirmed that workflows can be minimised

---

6   http://www.intrallect.com/.

for those materials that will not require extensive metadata because of their limited applicability, whilst additional tagging can be added post publication as and when required for resources with wider usefulness.

This work has continued, with opportunities to explore more intuitive ways of searching the repository for material and then providing links to selected items in the VLE. Most recently we have started to develop easier ways for staff to deposit material directly from their desktop using a simple drag and drop process coupled with the use of workflow templates to add defined metadata automatically, and to put content into specified collections.

However, much remains to be done. The creation of a content repository draws attention to issues associated with IPR including copyright, ownership and the moral rights of authors. Resources can require much closer scrutiny to ensure that there has been no infringement of the copyright of others during their creation. A move towards a more open approach to educational resources may need to go hand in hand with some form of quality assurance as teaching and learning materials are disseminated more widely. The protection of a Creative Commons Licence, perhaps with requirements for attribution and control over derivatives, could be automatically asserted when materials are downloaded.

Conclusion

This chapter and the two case studies identify specific and practical lessons. There are broader lessons to be learned that underpin successful projects.

- Link projects with the delivery of broader strategic and policy objectives. Demonstrating that projects can deliver practical outcomes that serve the wider organisation enhances the impact of projects and gains support at a senior level.
- Collaboration across the organisation breaks down barriers and ensures that projects consider the real challenges for users and the needs that they would like the project to address.
- Demonstrating working or pilot versions is the most effective way to convince potential users and contributors of a project's value. Look at what we have done, not look at what we say we will do.
- Making projects efficient for end users is important, which means working hard to reduce the burden in time and effort of participating.
- People, not technology, are important in projects that aim to harvest and deliver content. This means investing time and effort in communicating, persuading and listening to potential users.

References

Bolton, S., 2009. *The ICT Implications Arising from the Research Excellence Framework Bibliometrics Pilot.* JISCinfonet. Available from: http://ie-repository.jisc.ac.uk/338/ (accessed 13 March 2010).

Crowley, E.J., Northam, J., Petford, N. and Johnstone, P., 2009. *BURO: A Bespoke Repository for the UK Research Excellence Framework and Beyond.* In: ARMS 2009 – 11th annual conference of the Australasian Research Management Society, 16–18 September 2009, Christchurch Convention Centre, Christchurch, New Zealand. Available from: http://eprints.bournemouth.ac.uk/11216/ (accessed 20 May 2010).

HEFCE, 2009. *Report on the Pilot Exercise to Develop Bibliometric Indicators For the Research Excellence Framework.* Issues Paper 2009/39. Available from: http://www.hefce.ac.uk/pubs/hefce/2009/09_39/ (accessed 13 March 2010).

Holland, M., 2000. The change agent. In: Reid, B.J. and Foster, W., eds. *Achieving Cultural Change in Networked Libraries.* Aldershot: Gower, 105–107.

Technopolis, 2009a. *Identification and Dissemination of Lessons Learned by Institutions Participating in the Research Excellence Framework (REF) Bibliometrics Pilot. Results of the Round One Consultation – May 2009.* Available from: http://www.hefce.ac.uk/Pubs/RDreports/2009/rd09_09/ (accessed 13 March 2010).

Technopolis, 2009b. *Identification and Dissemination of Lessons Learned by Institutions Participating in the Research Excellence Framework (REF) Bibliometrics Pilot. Results of the Round Two Consultation – September 2009.* Available from: http://www.hefce.ac.uk/pubs/rdreports/2009/rd18_09/ (accessed 13 March 2010).

Chapter 10

Building Useful Virtual Research Environments: The Need for User-led Design

Melissa Terras, Claire Warwick and Claire Ross

Introduction

Recent developments in online resources have led to the establishment of Virtual Research Environments (VREs): suites of applications, services, and resources which aim to enhance the research process by aiding scholars to carry out a range of complex research activities. The definition and concept of what constitutes a VRE continues to evolve, as developers attempt to create flexible and adaptable frameworks of resources to support both large and small scale research across a variety of disciplines. VREs are often integrated with Digital Libraries and Virtual Learning Environments (VLEs), to allow users to analyse and manipulate existing digital research data.

The construction of a VRE is a lengthy and costly process. Given their experimental nature, it can be difficult to define user requirements, and to create tools which are actually required, or useful to the communities they are supposed to support. Therefore to ensure the success of VREs, it is essential that developers liaise closely with the user community they are providing services for. This chapter will discuss the potentials inherent in VRE technology, whilst addressing the relationship that such environments have to their users. A case study involving the Joint Information Systems Committee (JISC) funded Virtual Research Environment for Archaeology (VERA) project will be presented to demonstrate that close integration with the relevant community is crucial if a VRE is to provide computational tools that reflect research practice.

As with the development of any computational system which is created to aid existing processes, the integration of user feedback into the VERA development process was key to its success. This chapter will focus on the integration of user led design and evaluation in the VERA project, demonstrating the complex nature of creating VREs. Although this chapter will concentrate on tools created for the archaeological community, issues of user led design, user feedback, and user needs analysis are applicable to the development of VREs for any discipline. These steps should ensure that the limited resources available for creating online digital environments to aid research processes are used effectively. VREs (and other digital resources such as Digital Libraries and VLEs) will only be a successful approach to facilitating scholarly activity if they are developed with consideration for their potential communities. This chapter aims to stress the necessity of including users into a systems design process, whilst highlighting opportunities that exist for librarians to become more involved in the creation, management and curation of VREs and their related research data.

Virtual Learning and Virtual Research Environments

Towards the close of the 20th century, software systems designed to support teaching and learning emerged within the Higher Education community. Many institutions began to investigate the provision of an array of online tools that, although originally created for distance education, increasingly supplemented traditional classroom activities. Systems for online communication with students, course administration, provision of lecture notes and reading lists, collection and return of coursework, assessment, generation of student feedback, and the creation and maintenance of class content became commonplace (JISC 2002). Featuring emergent Internet technologies such as blogs, wikis, and online forums, these Virtual Learning Environments (VLEs), as they commonly became referred to (although a standard definition is still elusive) became commonplace across university campuses. Many of these VLE technologies (for example, Moodle, Sakai, or Blackboard) linked to institutional resources, such as the university library, becoming part of the teaching and learning framework. By 2005, 95% of Higher Education Institutions within the UK had invested in some type of VLE technology, 50% of which linked to the library catalogue in some way (Jenkins et al. 2005).

Universities are not only seats of teaching and learning, however, as a large part of academic activity is focussed on research, and the systematic investigation of all aspects of science and culture. The rise of Internet technologies, and the development of related online databases and tools, are changing academic approaches to research:

A revolution is taking place in research. It is fuelled by the ever-increasing sophistication of the e-information universe and by rapidly advancing ICT capabilities. This new generation of research, e-research, is epitomized by its collaborative, multi-disciplinary nature, the increasingly huge volumes of data it processes and generates, and the advanced infrastructure that enables the sharing of vast amounts of computer power and storage. (Wusteman 2008, p. 40)

This has inevitably led to proposals and attempts to create technologies which would specifically facilitate the research, as well as the learning, process:

... the new [technological] developments are making the process of carrying out research more complex and demanding. The aim of a Virtual Research Environment (VRE) is to help researchers manage this complexity by providing an infrastructure specifically designed to support the activities carried out within research teams, on both small and large scales. (JCSR VRE Working Group 2004, p. 1)

A VRE shares more in common with a Managed Learning Environment, that sum of services and systems which together support the learning and teaching processes within an institution. The VRE, for its part, is the result of joining together new and existing components to support as much of the research process as appropriate for any given activity or role. (Fraser 2005)

Although the term VRE is yet to reach a 'mainstream academic community' (Dunn 2009), it has been adopted to cover a range of technologies, and can be both fluid and vague:

As the name virtual research environment implies, the aim is not to build single, monolithic systems, but rather socio-technical configurations of different tools that can be assembled to suit the researchers' needs without much effort, working within organisation, community, and wider societal contexts. (Voss and Proctor 2009, p. 183)

VREs aim to support collaboration, encourage multidisciplinary research, allow the use (and reuse) of data, and facilitate the research environment. They aim to provide an integrated environment that supports the work of research communities. It is worth noting that often:

Digital libraries lie in the heart of these technologies, acting as an information grid that consists of a collection of resources for learning and teaching, data repositories for research purposes, or as archives of diverse cultural heritage materials. (Sim et al. 2006)

It is therefore important that those involved in Digital Libraries are aware of the growing interest in VREs within the university sector, and address what this means for both the user wishing to undertake research as part of a VRE, and the information professional providing digital information to populate such environments, or encourage their use and uptake.

Much talk regarding VREs is at a relatively high level: VREs do not have as defined a set of tasks, or resources, as their VLE counterparts. Whilst VLEs are often identifiably similar, VREs can differ widely in their requirements depending on which research task they are supporting, and therefore each VRE can be highly individual, depending on bespoke technology (Van Till 2009). Furthermore, much technical work has to be undertaken on drawing together heterogeneous data sources, and allowing access to datasets that were never designed to work in parallel together. There are procedural, technical and even philosophical challenges which need to be addressed together to allow the creation of a VRE:

> In parallel to the piloting, investigation and scoping of VREs there is convergence on multiple fronts whether it is the evolution to an all-encompassing e-framework, agreed portlet standards, integration between institutional portals, VLEs and emerging VREs, or more generally the gradual acceptance of open standards, open source software and open access. (Fraser 2005)

A report by the UK JISC was commissioned in 2004 to create a roadmap for the development of VREs across the Higher Education sector (JCSR 2004). This called for the development of technical frameworks to facilitate VRE technologies, whilst liaising with the related research communities to build research environments which met users' research needs. Later that year, JISC established a Virtual Research Environments Programme[1] which aimed to investigate, build, and deploy VREs, whilst assessing their benefits and shortcomings, identifying the need for the development of new tools, and improving and extending the usefulness of VRE tools for UK researchers. 14 VRE projects were initially funded across both the arts and humanities[2] to explore the definition of and technological solutions for VREs in research in the UK. In 2007, four pilot projects were funded to implement VREs in Phase 2 of the JISC programme[3]. In 2009, ten VRE projects

---

1 http://www.jisc.ac.uk/whatwedo/programmes/vre1.

2 These include (amongst others): Building a Virtual Research Environment for the Humanities (BVREH) (http://www.jisc.ac.uk/whatwedo/programmes/vre1/bvreh.aspx), CORE: Collaborative Orthopaedic Research Environment (http://www.jisc.ac.uk/whatwedo/programmes/vre1/core.aspx), ISME: Integration and Steering of Multi-site Experiments to Assemble Engineering Body Scans (http://www.jisc.ac.uk/whatwedo/programmes/vre1/isme.aspx), and Silchester Roman Town: A Virtual Research Environment for Archaeology (http://www.silchester.reading.ac.uk/index.html).

3 http://www.jisc.ac.uk/whatwedo/programmes/vre2.aspx.

were funded to focus on tools, frameworks and interoperability.[4] It is hoped that this strategic investment will stimulate a change in research practices through the development of VRE solutions, which could be extended and exploited across the Higher Education community.

Users of VREs

Although there are great technological challenges in designing standards and frameworks to allow the creation of VRE technologies (covered more fully in Allan 2009), of primary interest to those providing service level assistance to VREs are the needs of those undertaking the research, and potentially using VREs to further their own study.

The extent to which a VRE can be used by specific users to achieve specified goals with effectiveness, efficiency and satisfaction is largely driven by the requirements of the user. Hence user requirements study plays an important role (Sim et al. 2006).

Given the experimental nature of VREs, it can be difficult to define user requirements, and to create tools which are actually needed, or usable by the communities they are supposed to support. To do so requires close integration with the user community in question, and it is here that the focus of VREs changes from high level pronouncements of what the technology should do, to detailed requirements analysis of what a user community actually needs in order to carry out research:

> The development and presentation of a VRE must be embedded and owned by the communities served and cannot realistically be developed for the research communities by others in isolation. Since the intention is to improve the research process and not simply to pilot technologies for their own sake, the research must drive the requirements. Undertaking a 'day in the life of your research' can be instructive and, if nothing else, will generally hammer home the point that the majority of the research community operate in a world which mixes the digital with the tangible, machines with people. In effect, the development of VREs should encourage research communities to be inward looking, reflecting on the types of research questions, the means to address them, and the acceptable ways of disseminating the answers. Understanding and articulating the research methods and culture of any given research area is key to developing a VRE. (Fraser 2005)

The interdisciplinary nature of the research, and the computational nature of the online tools themselves, mean that user needs have to be articulated to computer scientists designing the systems:

---

4   http://www.jisc.ac.uk/whatwedo/programmes/vre.aspx.

VREs have the potential to be profoundly multidisciplinary, both in their use and in their development. For the most part, it is expected that computer science will act in partnership with other disciplines to lay the foundations, integrating methods and knowledge from the relevant subject areas. Humanities scholars, for example, cannot necessarily be expected to apply tools and processes (initially developed for the e-science community) effectively to their own subjects. Better to articulate the challenges and methods and sit down with the computer scientists. This is not an alien idea for many in the humanities – there is a long history of such partnerships. Indeed, while the humanities and social sciences may not have the scale of data to contend with, they certainly have the variety and complexity of data to continue to provide interesting problems for computer science and engineering. (Fraser 2005)

However

Despite an increasing interest in VRE ... there is a lack of understanding of the extent of adoption, factors that influence their adoption, how they are used, and the implications for scholarly communications (Voss and Proctor 2009, p. 181).

It is up to each individual project to engage with users successfully, and to integrate the potential that VRE technologies display with existing working practices. The following section will use as a case study a project funded under the JISC VRE Phase Two Programme, which provided backing to produce pilot VREs. The VERA project aimed to produce a fully-fledged VRE for the archaeological community. By addressing user needs, enhancing the means of efficiently documenting archaeological excavation and its associated finds, and creating a suitable Web portal that provided enhanced tools for the user community, VERA aimed to develop utilities that encapsulate the working practices of current research archaeologists unfamiliar with VREs, enhancing their research activities, and facilitating the creation of new knowledge from the available data. To do so, it was necessary to engage fully with the research community, understanding their needs, requirements, and wants.

Our research on the VERA project adopted the method of user centred design, in which the needs and activities of users are studied so that they can inform the process of designing new information systems and their interfaces[5]. Such user centred methods have been applied to numerous studies of information seeking and use, and such studies emphasise the need to understand what users are doing in the course of their usual work, so as to design information systems and interfaces that are best suited for them (Shneiderman and Plaisant 2009). This is what Attfield et al. (2003) have called 'use-in-context'. Their study considered the processes by which students seek information and write assignments, but similar approaches

---

5   Usability Professionals' Association http://www.usabilityprofessionals.org/usability_resources/about_usability/what_is_ucd.html.

have been used by the same research group to study various different users of information such as NHS patients (Attfield et al. 2006) and lawyers (Makri et al. 2008) to understand how the use of information and technology is integrated into their everyday activities.

The use in context approach is particularly helpful, as it recognises that what users do when they work with information or use technology must be affected by the social setting in which this takes place, and does not simply concern itself with studying a user's immediate task, such as doing a web search on a particular topic. Kuhlthau's (2004) highly influential study of American high school students was one of the first to adopt this kind of method.[6] She observed the students looking for information to help them with real tasks which were part of their studies, and used this to construct a model of the information seeking process, which has influenced most recent work on how people find the information that they need in many different contexts.

More classical Human Computer Interaction methods have tended to require users to undertake predetermined tasks in a usability laboratory. This approach is still widely used to test the functionality of information systems and can help to uncover specific problems to be rectified (Ingwersen and Järvelin 2005, chapter 3). However, real interaction with information seldom happens in controlled circumstances in a laboratory, and so the use in context approach emphasises the need to understand the real circumstances in which information is needed or technology is used so that problems that exist in the real world will not be missed. Kari and Savolainen (2001) argue that we must situate information work in its broadest possible context, even recognising that spiritual beliefs may have an impact on information seeking and use.

This holistic method is closely related to Information Ecology (Davenport, 1997; Nardi and O'Day 1999). This is an approach that takes into account the whole culture of a workplace or setting, including physical features such as noise and lighting, as well as recognising that emotional and affective considerations are as important to the way people make decisions about what technology to use as reason and cognition. Davenport for example cites an example of early daisy-wheel printers which could not be used an open plan office, despite being in working order, because the noise they made was unbearably loud. Our previous studies of humanities scholars have also shown that researchers may choose to use a particular environment such as a library or archive depending on how they feel about the friendliness of the staff, the level of light, or the cramped physical conditions, as much as their knowledge of its information resources (Rimmer et al. 2008).

When studying the users of VREs then it can be argued that use in context is an ideal method, because by the very nature of the VRE itself we must expect its use to be embedded in the everyday research tasks of the user. Thus to produce a VRE

---

6   This study was originally carried out in 1993, but the reference we have used is to the second edition of the book in which her results were published.

that is most useful in the desired context we must understand the circumstances in which it will function. For the VERA project we therefore decided that, when studying the very complex environment of an archaeological excavation employing numerous staff, the use in context approach would be best suited as a way of capturing the variety of work being carried out and its relationship to the use of information technology.

The VERA Project

The Virtual Research Environment for Archaeology (VERA[7]) project investigated the use of information technology by archaeologists in the context of field excavations and associated research. The VERA project was based around an established excavation of part of the large Roman town at Silchester[8], which aims to trace the site's development from its origins before the Roman Conquest to its abandonment in the 5th century AD (Clarke et al. 2007). This large-scale, long-term excavation is run by the University of Reading's Department of Archaeology[9], and is used as a compulsory, hands-on training component of their undergraduate archaeology degree.

The rich and complex finds from the excavation have been logged, for the past decade, in the Integrated Archaeological Data Base (IADB[10]), an online database system for managing all aspects of recording, analysis, archiving and online publication of archaeological excavations. Students at the field school learn both about practice based archaeology, and how information technology can aid archaeologists with their complex recording requirements. Roman Silchester therefore provides usability experts with a site to investigate the use of advanced Information Technology in an archaeological context, and to study how such a rich database and complex research task can contribute to the design of VREs.

The goal of archaeological computing is to create a situation where 'the information flows seamlessly from excavation, through post-excavation to publication and archive' (Lock 2003, p. 265), and as a result VRE technology is very attractive for archaeologists aiming to record and detail their working practices. Archaeology has a long history of using computers to aid in the logging and analysis of related data, but the use of IT to aid field archaeology is in its relative infancy due to the physical characteristics of archaeological sites, and the difficulties of using IT in the outdoor environment (Warwick et al. 2009). The VERA project, funded by the JISC Virtual Research Environments Programme (Phase 2) and running from April 2007 until October 2009, was undertaken by researchers at the School of Library, Archive and Information Studies (now the Department

---

7   http://vera.rdg.ac.uk/.
8   http://www.silchester.rdg.ac.uk/.
9   http://www.reading.ac.uk/Archaeology/.
10   http://www.iadb.org.uk/index.htm.

of Information Studies[11]), University College London, in collaboration with the School of Systems Engineering[12], the Department of Archaeology, University of Reading, and York Archaeological Trust.[13] The project investigated the tasks carried out within archaeological excavations – focussing on the Silchester dig as a case study – to ascertain how and where technology can be used to facilitate information flow within a dig, and to inform the designers of computational tools such as the IADB how the interface and environment may be adapted to allow integrated use of the tools in the trench itself (Fisher et al. 2010).

VERA also aimed to develop a VRE in which archaeologists may integrate not only the collection, recording and interpretation of data, but can also publish results and make them available to the wider archaeological community. For example, a recent article about Silchester was able to use a snapshot of the IADB to allow readers to search the data upon which the article's conclusions were based (Clarke et al. 2007). A fully functional VRE should allow archaeologists to make their own linkages between different types of data, thereby allowing users to perform their own interpretation of data excavated on site.

One of the most fundamental concerns during the VERA project was the issue of usability and appropriate design of advanced IT. Numerous studies have demonstrated that the successful uptake of IT depends heavily on understanding users and that if new systems do not fit into existing procedures and routines, uptake of the new technology will be poor:

> Publication after publication reaches the same conclusion: that technology is important but insufficient on its own for the success of ICT-enabled projects. Again and again technology projects fall down not because the hardware is unstable, but because different systems' architectures have been poorly scoped and designed. Without good change management and careful thought given to the people using the systems as well as the technology itself, ICT-enabled projects are unlikely to be successful … (Jones and Williams 2005, p. 9).

Work on the VERA project was not only the back-end construction of a robust database that met emerging standards for portals (allowing the reusability of data, see Baker et al. 2008) but the integration of technologists with the archaeological user community to ascertain their requirements, from dig to database, and beyond. Previous attempts at using IT to aid the excavations at Silchester had met with poor reception from the archaeologists digging on the site, due to neglect of their needs and existing patterns of work. It was important that we understood where technologies could aid the current system, rather than forcing unnecessary change upon established working practices.

---

11 http://www.infostudies.ucl.ac.uk/.
12 http://www.reading.ac.uk/sse/.
13 http://www.yorkarchaeology.co.uk/.

VERA and its User Community

To integrate ourselves within the community at Silchester, we carried out a series of diary studies (Warwick et al. 2009), looking at the work patterns of different archaeological roles and the way that they are supported by both digital and analogue technologies. A dedicated researcher joined the archaeological dig at Silchester, integrating herself within the community, and ascertaining how the data cycle – from excavating an object, to recording it, to digitising it, to using the resulting database, functioned. In-depth interviews were carried out with all major stakeholders in the project, covering every possible user of the system, from managers to student diggers. A section of the site was used in 2007 to test new working practices, using new digital pens to record archaeological data in the trench which could then be uploaded immediately to the database, and these technologies were rolled out across the site in 2008 and 2009, following their successful integration into existing practices. For post-excavation analysis, user workshops were undertaken where we tested the existing IADB system, to discover where any issues emerged about its functionality, and demonstrated new iterations of the VRE in development. Interviews were also undertaken with those routinely using the IADB for archaeological research.

This integration with the user community was key to developing the existing IADB further. Without gaining the trust of the academic constituency, it would not have been possible to articulate specifications to the VRE developers. Without adequate training or explanation, tools and technologies tested within the trench would have had a hostile reception. Listening to user needs, encouraging user uptake, providing feedback, and a rewards mechanism (explaining exactly how we were trying to help, rather than hinder, the archaeological process) encouraged archaeologists at the dig, from the highest management levels to student diggers, to interact with us, and let us know both positive and negative aspects of the integration of technology into their working practices.

The VERA system which emerged from this process was an extension and rewriting of the existing IADB, with improved usability, and further facilities to allow publication, visualisation, and interpretation of archaeological information. Technical specifications have been upgraded, allowing the IADB to function on secure servers at the University of Reading, under standardised portal frameworks which will allow it to be extended and reused (Grove 2007; Baker et al. 2008). Additionally, the standards based approach to the project has allowed interoperability between several databases, including one held by the Building a Virtual Research Environment for the Humanities project at the University of Oxford[14] which holds images of ancient documents, which can now be searched through the IADB and linked to related archaeological evidence. Cross-database searching, and the linking of external research sources, is a next phase in the construction of VREs.

---

14   http://bvreh.humanities.ox.ac.uk/.

Ironically, the IADB does not appear to be very different to the regular user than it was before, aside from the increased functionality. The existing system was well used, and had evolved to fulfil many aspects of research in archaeology: the VERA project took this successful model, standardised the technology behind it to ensure sustainability, longevity, and usability, and provided additional functionality (Rains 2008). The IADB that was redeveloped as part of the VERA project is currently being used at a variety of archaeological sites across the UK and Europe[15]. A working demonstrator of the IADB that was completed as part of the VERA project is available on the IADB website.[16]

The biggest change at Silchester from the VERA project was the integration of new technologies within the dig itself: digital pens and global positioning systems that were integrated into the archaeological practice, thus speeding up recording times, as they allowed seamless transfer of new data into the existing database. Previously, records had been made on paper, and an assistant was employed over the winter months to transcribe paper records into the database. Additionally, this increase in speed of recording and logging has facilitated research by allowing access to archaeological data in real time. This demonstrates that VRE technology can exist beyond the computer interface, as recording methods and practices can change to facilitate data creation and data entry.

The construction of the VERA system demonstrated issues related to the integration of new technologies into established archaeological processes. Concerns regarding the robustness of the digital pens in the archaeological environment were quickly overcome, but issues with establishing the digital pens (and their related context sheets) as part of the recording process at Silchester centred around the fact that the new technologies did not mirror the existing system, and this had to be addressed with the user community. It was noted that there needs to be more teaching for staff so that they are more confident about supervising technology on site, and that there should perhaps be compulsory teaching for students.

The VERA project demonstrated the importance of factoring in user needs when integrating digital technologies into existing archaeological practice. Unless the voices of those working with the system are acknowledged, any new implementation of technology will not fit into existing working patterns, and so stand little chance of being adopted. Additionally, unless VREs replicate the existing methods they are designed to replace (or enhance), such as digital forms mirroring the established context forms to record the physical archaeological data at Silchester, they are doomed to failure. Using IT in the trench is not as prone to failure as might be expected given the extreme nature of weather conditions often encountered: but may be prone to failure through not taking into account the needs, practices, and habits of those for whom it is designed to help (Fisher et al. 2010).

---

15 See http://www.iadb.co.uk/for a list of projects currently using the IADB system.
16 http://www.iadb.org.uk/.

Involving Users in VRE Design

As the VERA project demonstrates, creating an integrated VRE system fundamentally relies on the creation of a community of service providers, tool builders and researchers working together to develop specific support for research tasks. This has to work alongside the development of the technical and organisational platform for integrating these tools into an overall research process: users are not terribly interested in the 'behind the scenes' nature of VREs, they just want them to aid them in their research.

De Roure and Goble (2009) describe the user-driven design principles underpinning the development of another of the JISC funded VRE demonstrator project, MyExperiment.[17] Based at the Universities of Southampton and Manchester, MyExperiment is a collaborative scientific environment where researchers can safely publish their workflows, share them with groups and find the workflows of others, enabling researchers to distribute, reuse and repurpose methodologies and so reduce and avoid reinvention of working processes. Thousands of scientific researchers are using this VRE to aid them in their work, whilst building up a community of practice. The success of MyExperiment also lies with the user-focussed approach to design this particular VRE, with all six of their design principles reflecting aspects of the relationship between researchers and developers:

- **Fit in, do not force change**: provide interfaces that connect easily to what people are already using rather than forcing them to make changes in their existing work environment.
- **Jam today and more jam tomorrow**: match the effort required for uptake with an equivalent gain, giving users immediate benefits for little investment.
- **Just in time and just enough**: do not try to develop something perfect but deliver something quickly, then improve.
- **Act locally, think globally**: start working with people you know, who are typical examples of a class of users you want to target, and keep the system flexible enough to allow customisation so that different needs can be accommodated.
- **Let users add value**: users who are engaged are likely to contribute to development in one way or another; they may extend the system, connect it to other systems or just submit a bug report.
- **Design for network effects**: keep in mind that behind each pioneer are a large number of people who will eventually take up usage, using the system in routine ways once the benefits have become sufficiently clear.

---

17   http://www.myexperiment.org/.

These six principles of development are complemented by six proposed principles of user engagement:

- **Keep your friends close**: use local contacts, early adopters and advocates to keep an ongoing dialogue open; focus on the day-to-day users but keep the senior patrons involved to utilise their weight in the community.
- **Embed**: embedding developers with users and users with developers for sufficiently long periods of time is much more effective than any other requirements elicitation technique.
- **Look at the bigger picture**: keep in mind that people use software as part of a wider context and that it needs to fit this context rather some ideal world vision of how things ought to be.
- **Favours will be in your favour**: build trust relationships through favours (such as writing custom code for early adopters) and a willingness to compromise.
- **Know your users**: maintain a good awareness of different groups of users and their different needs and troubles.
- **Expect and anticipate change**: requirements are a moving target, especially in research, where success does not lead to routine usage but to new requirements. (De Roure and Goble 2009, quoted and paraphrased in Voss and Proctor 2009, p. 185–86).

These principles, similar to the approach which we aimed to use within the VERA project, demonstrate that a pragmatic approach to managing the user-designer relationship can be successful, but it is acknowledged that the complex relationship between technology suppliers, service providers, intermediaries, and primary and secondary end users within VRE development requires careful monitoring. It is only by developing successful systems that address the particular needs of specific user groups that VRE technology will become routinely embedded in our research tasks: as we understand more about user requirements, the chances of wasting the financial and temporal investment required to build a VRE are lessened.

VREs and the Librarian

While the VERA system did not liaise directly with traditional online library systems, it should be obvious that the use of such VREs creates issues which relate closely to those raised within the Digital Library community. VREs – particularly those which depend on cross-database searching – are dependent on structured, available information. Issues of knowledge representation come into play, as do the bugbears of sustainability, data longevity, and data standards. Providers of VREs need to be trained in data curation skills, and institutional commitments must be made to provide data repository services. VREs are an emergent technology, and it can be argued that many of their implementations would stand more chance of success and longevity if the technologists involved would acquaint themselves with the vast literature and expertise on related issues within the Digital Library world:

> If VREs are to fulfil their potential as useful and usable artefacts, librarians need to have a central role in their development and application. Whether librarians are facilitated to make this contribution depends, in part, on whether they are proactive in and advocating for their potential roles… Librarians… need to be able to recognise a VRE when they see one because they should be drivers of the technology. And it is clear that librarians are increasingly identifying the VRE as an important concept that they need to investigate. Now is the ideal time for librarians to explore the potential of VREs because, at this stage of their development, there is still time to influence their eventual form. (Wusteman 2009, p. 169–73)

Yet 'Research on how these concepts and technologies, and associated practices, impact or may impact LIS research, education, and practice is lacking' (Sonnenwald et al. 2009, p. 200). University libraries have, for the most part, developed a symbiotic relationship with VLEs, as they have become part of the higher education framework. However, in a recent study, although most librarians view the future of the profession as being in the teaching of information literacy and the custody and management of digital resources, few librarians viewed the integration of VREs within library systems as core to their discipline (Brown and Swan 2007).

Although the VERA project has now ended, the IADB is now part of a JISC VRE Phase 3 Programme funded project, LinkSphere[18] (running from April 2009 – March 2011), which aims to create a unified system that provides a single virtual interface for searching across all the digital repositories and collections of the University of Reading. It can be seen that the IADB, and the work of VERA, therefore become part of the university information infrastructure, joining with other disparate academic sources in a VRE, to provide wider access to existing data. User testing and user centred development of this umbrella system is required to ensure that it matches the needs of those who will require access to information for research. As well as undertaking user studies, our team now involves a professional librarian, providing expertise and guidance on issues such as metadata, digital curation, data storage, and information access. The role of the librarian in the development of VREs is becoming more central, and more necessary.

---

18   http://www.linksphere.org/.

Conclusion

This chapter has aimed to introduce the concept of VREs, and demonstrate their relationship to existing Digital Library frameworks, whilst providing an overview of the need for user-led design when undertaking VRE development. VREs are an emergent technology, and there is much to be learnt regarding how we can create efficient, usable (and reusable) interfaces that assist complex research tasks, and access to disparate data structures. 'A successful VRE should be virtually transparent to the user: researchers do not want to use a VRE; they want to do research' (Wusteman 2008, p. 69). The best way to ensure the usefulness of VREs is to integrate closely with their research constituency. However, the longevity and sustainability of VRE technologies is dependent on many skills already possessed by the library community. Closer integration of users, creators, developers, and information specialists will ensure that sparse resources are not wasted, and the development of VREs that seamlessly blend with existing research practices and information structures.

References

Allan, R., 2009. *Virtual Research Environments: From Portals to Science Gateways*. Oxford: Chandos Publishing.

Attfield, S., Blandford, A. and Dowell, J., 2003. Information seeking in the context of writing: a design psychology interpretation of the 'problematic situation'. *Journal of Documentation*, 2003, 59 (4), 430–53.

Attfield, S., Adams, A. and Blandford, A., 2006. Patient information needs: pre and post consultation. *Health Informatics Journal*, 12 (2), 165–77.

Baker, M., Grove, M., Fulford, M., O'Riordan, E., Warwick, C., Terras, M., Fisher, C. and Rains, M., 2008. *VERA: Virtual Environment for Research in Archaeology*. 4th International Conference on e-Social Science, Manchester, June 18th–20th, 2008.

Brown, S. and Swan, A., 2007. *Researchers' Use of Academic Libraries and their Services: A Report Commissioned by the Research Information Network and the Consortium of Research Libraries*. Available from: http://www.rin. ac.uk/system/files/attachments/sarah/Researchers-libraries-services-report.pdf (accessed 6 April 2010).

Clarke, A., Fulford, M., Rains, M. and Tootell, K., 2007. Silchester Roman Town Insula IX: The Development of an Urban Property C. Ad 40-50-C. Ad 250. *Internet Archaeology*. Available from: http://intarch.ac.uk/journal/issue21/ silchester_index.html (accessed 6 April 2010).

Davenport, T.H., 1997. *Information Ecology*. Oxford: Oxford University Press.

De Roure, D. and Goble, C., 2009. Software design empowering scientists, *IEEE Software*, January/February, 88–95.

Dunn, S., 2009. Dealing with the complexity deluge: VREs in the arts and humanities. *Library Hi Tech*, 27 (2).

Fisher, C., Terras, M. and Warwick, C., 2010. *Integrating New Technologies into Established Systems: A Case Study from Roman Silchester: Proceedings of the 37th Annual Computer Applications and Quantitative Methods in Archaeology Conference in Williamsburg, Virginia*, March 2009. Available from: http://www.caa2009.org/articles/Fisher_Contribution191_c%20%281%29.pdf (accessed 6 April 2010).

Fraser, M., 2005. Virtual research environments: overview and activity. *Ariadne*, 44, July 2005. Available from: http://www.ariadne.ac.uk/issue44/fraser/ (accessed 6 April 2010).

Grove, M., 2007. *A Standards Compliant Approach to Virtual Research*. VERA blog post. Available from: http://vera.rdg.ac.uk/portal.php (accessed 6 April 2010.

Ingwersen, P. and Järvelin, K., 2005. *The Turn: Integration of Information Seeking and Retrieval in Context*. Berlin: Springer.

JCSR VRE Working Group, 2004. *Roadmap for a UK Virtual Research Environment*: Report of the JCSR VRE Working Group. JISC Committee for the Support of Research. Available from: http://www.jisc.ac.uk/uploaded_documents/VRE%20roadmap%20v4.pdf (accessed 6 April 2010).

Jenkins, M., Browne, T., and Walker, R., 2005. *VLE Surveys: A Longitudinal Perspective Between March 2001, March 2003 and March 2005 for Higher Education in the United Kingdom*. University and Colleges Information Systems Association. Available from: http://eric.ex.ac.uk/exeter/bitstream/10036/13333/6/vle-survey-longitudinal-revision2.pdf (accessed 6 April 2010).

JISC, 2002. *Briefing Paper: MLEs and VLEs Explained*. Briefing Paper Number 1 Joint Information Systems Committee. Available from: http://www.jisc.ac.uk/uploaded_documents/bp1.pdf (accessed 6 April 2010).

Jones, A. and Williams, L., 2005. *How ICT?: Managing at the Frontline*. London: Work Foundation.

Kari, J. and Savolainen, R., 2001. *Web Searching in the Context of Information Seeking in Everyday Life: The Cases of Civic and Spiritual Action*. A research proposal. Available from: http://www.uta.fi/~csjakar/kari-savolainen.pdf (accessed 6 April 2010).

Kuhlthau, C., 2004. *Seeking Meaning: A Process Approach to Library and Information Services*. 2nd ed. Westport, CT: Libraries Unlimited, Inc.

Lock, G., 2003. *Using Computers in Archaeology*. London: Routledge.

Makri, S., Blandford, A. and Cox, A., 2008. Investigating the information-seeking behaviour of academic lawyers: From Ellis's model to design. *Information Processing and Management*, 44 (2), 613–34.

Nardi, B. and O'Day, V., 1999. *Information Ecology: Using Technology with Heart*. Cambridge: MIT Press.

Rains, M., 2008. Silchester – a virtual research environment for archaeology. In: Posluschny, A., Lambers, K. and Herzog, I., eds. *Layers of Perception. Proceedings of the 35th International Conference on Computer Applications and Quantitative Methods in Archaeology* (CAA) Berlin, April 2–6 2007. Bonn.

Rimmer, J., Warwick, C., Blandford, A., Gow, J. and Buchanan, G., 2008. An examination of the physical and digital qualities of humanities research. *Information Processing and Management*, 44 (3), 1374–92.

Shneiderman, B. and Plaisant, C., 2009. *Designing the User Interface: Strategies for Effective Human-Computer Interaction*. 5th edition. London: Addison-Wesley.

Sim, Y.W., Wang, L.G. and Wills, G., 2006. *User Requirement Study for a Virtual Research Environment*. JISC Development Programmes Technical Report, Number EXSTR-IAM05-003. Available from: http://eprints.ecs.soton. ac.uk/10969/1/ecstr_iam05_003.pdf (accessed 6 April 2010).

Sonnenwald, D.H., Lassi, M., Olson, N. and Ponti, M., 2009. Exploring new ways of working using virtual research environments in library and information science. *Library Hi Tech*, 27 (2), 191–204.

Voss, A. and Proctor, R., 2009. Virtual research environments in scholary work and communications. *Library Tech* 27 (2), 174–90.

Van Till, H., 2009. *Contribution from Audience, Building a Virtual Humanities Collaboratory*. 6–7 January 2009. CRASSH. Cambridge: Cambridge University.

Warwick, C., Fisher, C., Terras, M., Baker, M., Clarke, A., Fulford, M., Grove, M., O'Riordan, E. and Rains, M., 2009. iTrench: A Study of user reactions to the use of information technology in field archaeology. *Literary and Linguistic Computing*, 24 (2), 211–24.

Wusteman, J., 2008. Editorial: Virtual research environments: what is the librarian's role? *Journal of Librarianship and Information Science*, 40 (2) 67–70.

Wusteman, J., 2009. Editorial. Virtual research environments, issues and opportunities for librarians. *Library Hi Tech*, 27, (2), 169–73.

Chapter 11

The HE in FE Digital Dilemma

Jane Russ

Introduction

The concept of studying a Higher Education programme at a Further Education Institution (FEI) in the UK is not new. In partnership with Higher Education Institutions (HEIs), FEIs have been delivering Foundation Degrees, the most recent manifestation of HE in FE, for nearly ten years. Many colleges are now delivering top-up programmes for their Foundation Degrees with considerable success. At Kingston Maurward College, for example, it is now possible in some disciplines for students to start College on a day release or a diploma programme at 14 and continue to study at the College until they graduate with a BSc Honours Degree. Many of these Foundation Degree and Honours graduates go on to find highly specialised professional careers or move on elsewhere to undertake postgraduate studies.

In the early days of Foundation Degrees, there was much discussion both about the practicalities of delivery, such as ensuring access to resources, and also the more esoteric aspects of delivery, such as the student perception of identity with the partner HEI. Libraries and Learning Resources Centres (LRCs) have always played a key role in these discussions.

This chapter will review briefly how many of the initial concerns relating to delivering resources in the HE and FE environment have been tackled and, for the most part, overcome. It will go on to explore the opportunities and challenges faced by the emerging use of virtual learning environments (VLEs).

Development of HE Library Support in the FE Environment

It is generally acknowledged that digital technologies play a key role in delivering HE in FEI resources. FE LRCs are unable to provide the wide range of materials provided in HEI libraries due to costs, lower student numbers, the cross-College diversity of student needs and accommodation. Traditionally FEIs tend not to have the research ethos that HEIs enjoy because of the different nature of their business. This has made it more difficult to justify expenditure on extensive academic collections.

In response to this, some HEIs have created book loan systems (Warner 2005) where books can be posted out or delivered to FEIs either on request by a student or in bulk to support a particular unit. This system works well but has its limitations. For example, students may have to wait for books, there is potentially a significant cost involved and the books available from the HEI library may not meet the needs of the student studying at a partner college in terms of subject coverage.

Arguably more successful has been the use of remotely accessible online resources in the form of a digital library (Ryland 2006). Where the HEI has purchased wisely, these provide wider subject coverage and break down the geographical barriers of partnership provision. Other advantages include freedom from the constraints of LRC opening hours and a format that appeals to many, but by no means all, of the students who choose to study in an FEI. VLEs provide the form of flexibility that Challis (2005) describes as essential in meeting the needs of the learners, not just those of the institution.

One student from the University of Derby described how 'e-learning fitted her lifestyle and her attitude to learning' and had helped to build her confidence (Smoothy 2006).

In response to the issue of identity, many colleges have set up a separate HE centre where students can access resources without the college having to establish a separate library which for many, especially those with small libraries, would not be feasible.

Disadvantages include password overload, training students in the use of online resources who may not be particularly confident with using computers as a resource medium (Ryland 2006), negotiating licences to cover HE in FE students (Warner 2005) and the lack of availability of some core texts in appropriate formats. Considerable progress has been made in the last few years in terms of availability of e-books but they have not completely taken over from the printed text, especially in specialist subject areas such as agriculture and animal care. Difficulties relating to the quality of computer provision in some FEIs which may have caused access problems in the early years of HE in FE have now been largely overcome as FEIs invest in improved IT infrastructures.

The Virtual Learning Environment

The Joint Information Systems Committee (JISC) describes the VLE as an 'electronic system that can provide on-line interactions of various kinds that can take place between learners and tutors, including on-line learning' (JISC 2003).

The development of VLEs across both HE and FE sectors has had a significant impact on teaching and learning, not least for libraries and LRCs. Integration of the digital library into the VLE has been widely adopted and library staff are also taking advantage of additional VLE functionality to enhance their provision (Virkus et al. 2009). For both students and staff, the VLE is a valuable tool that opens up exciting new learning opportunities and can be particularly beneficial for students and staff in the HE in FE environment. It also presents a number of challenges, and HEIs and FEIs have started to work together to overcome these and to exploit VLE technologies to ensure that they fulfil their maximum potential.

One of the fundamental issues currently under discussion is the simple question of which VLE to adopt. Most FEIs and HEIs have their own VLEs and often they are on entirely different platforms so that the look, feel and capabilities of the VLEs are different as well as the content. Learning and teaching in the HE in FE environment has traditionally been delivered in a fragmented way (Golding Lloyd and Griffiths 2008) and the VLE has the potential either to cause further fragmentation as a result of this dilemma, or to create greater cohesion if employed effectively.

Student Perspectives

Benefits

For a student studying for a degree in an FEI, the VLE can provide benefits that far outweigh the potential difficulties. It is important to consider the three fundamental ways in which these students differ from their peers studying in HEIs. The first is the environment in which they are studying, as FEIs are generally very different from HEIs and they are often geographically quite remote from their HEI.

The second is the nature of the programmes which tend to have a strong vocational and practical slant which complements the theoretical and academic learning. The final difference is the nature of students themselves. The rationale behind Foundation Degrees is to attract widening participation students who may not otherwise consider studying for a degree. It is difficult – and not particularly constructive – to generalise about these students who are likely to bring a wide range of experiences, backgrounds, ages and attitudes to the programme and consequently a wide range of needs. The VLE has the potential to help cater for these needs.

Some of the ways that online resources break down the barriers for students who are geographically remote from their HEI have already been discussed. They enable students to access an appropriate level and range of resources that cannot be provided by the limited resources of an FEI. They can transcend the barriers imposed by LRC opening times, especially for those who both work and study and can be accessed in the relative calm and quiet of an HE Centre.

The VLE continues to provide these benefits but also offers additional advantages. A VLE can provide virtual access to a library expert, either from the HEI or the FEI and a platform for library blogs, Twitter, wikis, podcasts and virtual tours. Many students are not only located at a distance from their HEI but also have work and/or family commitments that mean that there are times when they are unable to come into college. This is particularly problematic for part-time students who may experience a very intensive teaching day when they are on-campus (Warner 2005) and students on blended or distance learning programmes will have even less time to seek the support they need in the LRC.

These students can benefit from virtual inductions or training sessions which can be set up by either the HEI or FEI librarians using software such as Camtasia. Some widening participation students who may lack confidence in their academic ability may be reluctant to seek support in person as they see it as an admission of academic failure (Barber et al. 2006) and again VLE training and support materials may help to overcome this barrier. Students can even be given self-diagnostic quizzes to help them to ascertain their existing skill levels.

Other students can use these training materials to reinforce learning at a later date. This is particularly true where library skills sessions are held early in the academic year before many assignments are due and a refresher is needed later in the term. A partial solution employed by most FEI libraries is to link the training sessions to a specific assignment which puts the learning into context, giving students a greater understanding of its relevance. However, there is always a danger that there will be a long period where students do not need to use online resources to a significant level and reinforcement is required.

The use of blogs, tweeting and wikis can support this process by providing students with updates of library activities and resources throughout the academic year. They can be used to promote resources, drop-in sessions or services. Done well, they will engage the students and maintain interest in resources. If they are not done well, they will either be ignored or damage the credibility of the LRC – students are not interested in what the LRC staff had for breakfast.

The use of wikis and discussion groups can serve to provide some of the more enthusiastic students with the opportunity to discuss and share information about resources with their peers. This can be used most successfully when carried out in collaboration with teaching staff to support a group project. The resulting product can then be used to inform other students.

The practical and vocational nature of Foundation Degrees is also well-suited to the VLE. The interactive potential of VLEs matches well with the teaching styles used in vocational learning. Most VLEs have the capacity to produce highly visual resources which may include video, sound or interactive assessment tools.

In many subject areas, some learning takes place out in the field or in the workplace and the VLE can penetrate these areas in ways that traditional resources cannot.

A significant recent change in the focus of Foundation Degree strategy has been to move towards work-based learning programmes where demand is industry led. Two such programmes have recently started at Kingston Maurward, a blended learning programme in Tourism Park Management and a distance learning programme in Retail Horticulture Management.

The Foundation Degree in Tourism Park Management was developed in close collaboration with the industry body, Caravan Industry Training (CITO). The model of delivery is partly delivered by distance learning and is partly based on the study school model. Study schools are held throughout the year at approved caravan sites. In this instance, a member of the LRC can travel to the first summer school to deliver an introductory session to the students but, beyond that, the VLE is the primary source of resources. Sites are generally chosen where access to the Internet is good and computer facilities or wireless networks are available.

The capability of the VLE to meet the varying needs of widening participation students is perhaps its most powerful attribute. Traditionally, concerns have been raised about these students' lack of competency with computers due primarily to lack of past experience (Dearnley et al. 2006) but also to factors such as socioeconomic differences where some students may have had better access to computer technology than others. These concerns have started to diminish as more and more people are using computers on a daily basis. Where they still exist, many colleges have introduced training programmes or summer schools to help students to develop their skills.

Once a level of competency has been attained, students can start to take advantage of the benefits offered by the VLE. Widening participation students as a group need a wide variety of different delivery methods to suit their differing needs and learning styles. Mature students, in particular, approach learning differently from younger students (Golding Lloyd and Griffiths 2008). It is likely that the use of traditional methods of teaching alone will be inadequate to engage and create an effective learning environment for these students. Indeed, for many of them, it will be this lack of engagement with traditional teaching methods that has prevented them from pursuing more conventional routes into higher education.

The nature of VLEs encourages different and creative approaches to delivering materials, allowing for greater flexibility, social participation in the form of discussion groups and easy access to a significant amount of information about the course, the college and support services such as libraries, finance and welfare. Similarly, the VLE's capacity for personalisation is particularly useful for students in the FE environment who may need a higher level and more flexible approach to support than other students.

A recent study (Heaton-Shrestha et al. 2009) looked at the impact of VLEs on student retention in HE which focussed on six key areas – performance; engagement with the course; enhancing social integration; control and ownership; confidence and motivation and study styles. The results show that student experience of the

VLE was particularly positive in some areas that have strong applicability for the HE in FE student.

For example, the VLE's capacity to create a community, provide flexible learning opportunities and to raise confidence levels are all factors with special significance for HE in FE students with widening participation backgrounds. The most positive responses in the study were in relation to control and ownership where students felt that they had greater access to information about their course and a greater choice of 'how, when and where to learn and study'. For students studying in FE colleges, many of whom have family and work commitments or are studying remotely, this is a significant feature.

VLEs give all students the opportunity to take greater ownership of their studies which seems to appeal especially to students who are independent and have already spent time in the workforce. For example, students on an Animal Behaviour programme at Kingston Maurward College were encouraged to set up a wiki where they could contribute the findings of their own research towards a joint project. In some institutions, question and answer banks for assessment are built up on suggestions from students. Libraries can use this concept of ownership, for example by encouraging students to contribute to literature reviews or discussions on individual resources.

Disability

It may be argued that Foundation Degrees are particularly attractive to students with disabilities, especially hidden disabilities such as dyslexia or autism. The Special Educational Needs and Disability Act (SENDA) of 2001 requires all students 'to have equal opportunity in accessing information and resources whether printed or electronic' (Gerrard 2007).

The inclusive nature of the VLE can provide some students with disabilities with greater opportunities for participation and integration. For example, visually impaired students can adapt online materials to suit their needs without the need for intervention on the tutor's part. The result is material presented in a format that is tailored to meet their requirements and to minimise the negative psychological impacts that come with having to depend on someone else to do something for them. Similarly, at Kingston Maurward College, we have a student who finds it difficult to communicate with other people because of a disability. The use of an interactive online communication tool allows her to participate in discussions from which she would otherwise be excluded.

For students with dyslexia, the VLE allows students to go back to notes at a later date so that they do not have to try to get everything down in a session but can focus on the work in hand. It also means that they do not feel singled out when, for example, they receive their handouts on a different coloured paper. However, contributing to discussion boards can be a negative experience for students who find written expression difficult, especially where their use is linked to an assessment (Gerrard 2007). Not even the flexibility of the VLE can provide a one size fits all solution, and the needs of the individual must be taken into account, but it is useful to remember when designing online resources that good design for disabled people is good design for all (Cooper 2006).

The use of audio as an assistive technology for students with dyslexia or visual impairment can also provide a preferred method of delivery for other students. Special resources in digital formats can be purchased in advance for these students and the VLE also allows for feedback to be delivered in different formats, such as speech based text.

A wide range of assistive technologies can be used in conjunction with the VLE to help students with disabilities to tailor resources to meet their specific individual needs.

Disadvantages

Potential disadvantages of using VLEs to deliver and support learning to HE in FE students have been mentioned above in relation to the use of online resources in general. A significant number of mature students are embarking on programmes with limited IT skills and/or confidence. This can create an even more significant barrier where VLEs are involved with their wide range of different applications. For students who have limited experience of or confidence in using VLEs, learning to use the additional functionalities that are available, such as discussion groups, takes time. As many of these students also have family and/or work commitments, they may not have the time to learn which adds further to the pressures of study (Dearnley et al. 2006).

From a library perspective, suitable resources may not be available digitally, especially to support some of the specialised, vocational disciplines studied for foundation degrees. Golding Lloyd and Griffiths (2008) identify mature learners as needing a higher level of support than traditional learners. This may be a result of lack of experience, lack of confidence in the academic environment (Barber et al. 2006) or student expectations of the amount of preparation that they need to do to undertake academic research failing to meet reality (Warner 2005). The VLE has the capability to provide this support through its communication functions, but both HE and FE library staff need to be confident in their ability to provide appropriate support and to be clear about their respective roles in providing the support. In the FE environment, students are usually able to develop strong working relationships with library staff (Golding Lloyd and Griffiths 2008) which is invaluable in terms of support.

Library staff (Dearnley et al. 2006) need to be aware that students will not necessarily seek support in the way that they would wish. Some students will seek support from tutors, partners or even children before approaching library staff which means that support needs to be promoted strongly and resources need to be as intuitive as possible.

Which VLE?

As HEIs and FEIs continue to address these issues, a new dilemma emerges in terms of deciding whether it is better for students to use the HEI VLE or the FEI VLE or both.

From a practical perspective, students will want to have access to information about the resources and services that are available to them regardless of the location. For example, students are likely to want to access the FE library catalogue which tells them about print resources to which they have immediate access. Some specialist resources may only be available from the FEI VLE, but the HEI is likely to provide a far wider range of high cost databases of resources.

For example, Animal Behaviour and Welfare students studying at Kingston Maurward College have access to essential specialist journals, such as *Animal* and *Animal Welfare*, from the College VLE which are not available from our partner HEI. However, our partner HEI provides access to databases such as *Science Direct* and *Academic Search* which provide the breadth of resource that HE students need.

Students will need access to local college information such as library opening hours, social activities and support services but may also need this information about the HEI if they are close enough to visit. Similarly, students may need to submit information via both VLEs – for example, they may be required to provide car registration details through the College VLE for parking permits but submit their responses to the student satisfaction survey through the HEI VLE. It is apparent, therefore, that many students need access to the information and resources that are available from both VLEs. Not only is this inconvenient for the user, but it can be confusing, especially in terms of resources, as a student may not be aware of the relative merits of each.

Licences become a barrier again here as resources purchased by one institution cannot simply be loaded onto another institution's VLE without restricting access to a small number of eligible students. Methods of funding resources vary among partnerships but often there is an expectation that the FEI will purchase resources that are specific to their programmes.

Password management becomes even more complex in the VLE environment where students find themselves needing multiple passwords to access the whole spectrum of resources available to them. The introduction of Shibboleth and Open Athens alleviates this in part but, in the current transitional period, a mixed economy exists in some partnerships.

Identity also re-emerges as an issue in terms of which institution the student associates themselves with. This will often depend on circumstances and will vary from institution to institution and from cohort to cohort – sometimes between individuals. In the early days of Foundation Degrees, many students wanted to align themselves with the HEI which was in part a desire to be associated with the appropriate level of their studies (i.e. higher rather than further education) and to poor management of expectations. Students were led to believe that they could expect the same experience – including access to HE level facilities, such as library resources – as they would if they were studying at an HEI.

In reality, the HE in FE experience is very different from the HEI experience but it should still be equitable (Ryland and Ball 2005). For example, a student studying in an FEI may have fewer print resources available to them but they can expect higher levels of support in helping them to exploit the online resources. Strategies to resolve this issue have been resolved in larger colleges by setting up separate HE centres (Golding Lloyd and Griffiths 2008; Bathmaker and Thomas 2009) and many smaller colleges have been able to set up some sort of HE facility, such as an HE study room. Students now seem to identify themselves happily with both institutions in colleges where boundaries between HE and FE remain blurred and a single institutional 'habitus' or culture exists in the college (Bathmaker and Thomas 2009). These students see themselves as members of the college who are special because of their links to the HEI. This happy medium has come under scrutiny again as the VLE dilemma emerges.

Studies carried out at Kingston Maurward indicate that the debate this time, from a student perspective, revolves around familiarity rather than allegiance or status of one institution over the other. In the past, HEIs have been the leaders in most areas of ICT development probably because they have had the resources and the incentives to lead the way. However, in this instance, many FEIs undertook large scale adoption of VLEs before their HEI partners as they saw the significant potential of the technology for their FE users. Consequently, these FEIs were already using VLEs before their HEI partners whereas others followed the HEI's example. The significance of this is that observations at Kingston Maurward suggest that students will show a strong preference for the VLE that they first encounter and it would take an extremely bad experience or loss of choice for them to change.

For students who are already studying at a college and who progress onto an HE programme, it could be particularly difficult for them to change to the HEI VLE or a combination of both. Conversely, students who have enrolled externally should feel that they are starting on a more level footing if all students are introduced to the HEI's VLE at the same time, adding to the barriers for internal progression described by Bathmaker and Thomas (2009).

Staff Perspectives

Student motivation to use or not to use a VLE, as discussed above, will also influence the motivation of staff. After all, there is no point in developing a resource that students either cannot or will not use. The Quality Assurance Agency (QAA) (2006) refers to the increasing significance of the learner voice on reviews, reinforcing the need to find student-focused solutions. The communication elements of the VLE are particularly useful to the HE in FE staff member as it provides a reliable method of communication wherever the student is located.

Encouraging students to interact with the technology and add their own ideas to a VLE allows staff to take advantage of the wide range of experiences and knowledge that many mature students bring to the classroom. This input can play a very positive role in enriching course material and resources.

For teaching and library staff, however, there are other considerations that need to be taken into account.

Among some teaching staff at both HE and FE level, there has been a reluctance to engage in VLEs at all. This is due to a number of factors including lack of confidence with the technology but the greatest barrier is time. Despite the ultimate time-saving potential of VLEs, the initial work can be time consuming, especially if the staff member wants to maximise the capabilities of the VLE. For staff who have both HE and FE responsibilities, this problem is magnified by their heavy teaching loads, longer terms and increasing pressures to become more research active.

Some staff are also concerned that use of the VLE may discourage students from attending lectures or engaging as fully with the programme as they would without the VLE. Students do not seem to share this perspective and are more likely to see the VLE as an additional strand to the learning experience to be used to complement other methods of learning (Heaton-Shrestha et al. 2009).

Library staff need teaching staff to engage with the VLE as they play a critical role in encouraging the students to use it. The number of teaching staff who do not make use of VLEs is at least starting to decrease as they start to see the benefits and/or are given no choice by their institution. This is particularly true for staff teaching HE level programmes in FEIs because they tend to use more innovative and creative teaching methods which they have developed as part of their FE teaching methods (Burkill et al. 2008).

Similarly, it has been suggested that the implementation of VLEs may have implications for the roles of academic library staff (Virkus et al. 2009). Again, this is perhaps less of a problem in FEIs where staff are used to being flexible and creative to support a very wide range of learning needs.

The impact on library roles will depend on the extent of the involvement of the library staff in developing and promoting the VLE. In some colleges, the library staff have cross-college responsibilities for the VLE whereas in others, they work with learning technologists or teaching staff, or other staff with overall VLE responsibilities. The role of learning technologist or its equivalent has developed in different ways across the sector depending on existing structures, staff availability and management approaches to e-learning.

The new challenge for HE in FE staff is choosing which VLE to use. Many FEIs may have more than one HE partner, each with its own VLE and they may also link in with local schools at 14–16 level where yet another VLE is in place. This is particularly problematic for library staff who, as part of a central service, are likely to need to use all these VLEs, but even teaching staff may find themselves using two or more.

Staff using two or more VLEs find that their efforts have to be duplicated. Resources with similar content may need to be put into entirely different formats depending on the VLE platform and structure. This has implications in terms of time and also training as staff will need to become literate in several VLE systems. This can lead to dissatisfaction and frustration and will ultimately discourage staff from engaging fully with the technology. Staff will also have to make sure that their students are literate in both the HE and FE VLE systems.

It could be argued that it is good for both students and staff to use different systems so that they become competent and confident in using any VLE regardless of the platform, but in reality it is likely to cause frustration and confusion for many.

In partnerships where the HEI enforces use of their institution's VLE, FE staff may feel that their creativity and academic freedom is being curtailed. In the FE environment, awarding bodies are often very prescriptive in their requirements so delivering HE programmes gives a greater sense of academic freedom. Consequently, they need to be able to focus on content and presentation rather than the technicalities of working around two or more different VLE platforms. They may also feel that the HEI is imposing something onto them that does not suit their style of delivery. Burkill et al. (2008) describe how HE in FE teaching staff tend to opt for more varied and creative delivery methods for which the college VLE might be better equipped.

The QAA makes it very clear that details of how learning resources such as VLEs are delivered is less important than the impact that they have on the student experience and ability to meet the required standard (QAA 2006).

Moving Forward

The first critical element for success in terms of VLEs in the HE in FE environment is cohesion. Students need to feel that they have their own identity and have a single source of access to the information and resources that will support their studies.

The ideal solution to this HE in FE VLE dilemma would be for students to access just one VLE which provides them with everything that they need from both the FEI and the HEI in a seamless way. Many institutions are working towards this but there is still a sense of reluctance in both the HE and the FE sectors to collaborate to the extent that they would need to for this to work. It is also hampered by the lack of standardisation and cross-functionality of platforms, the problem of multi-faceted partnerships and licensing issues.

For those colleges who have a separate university centre where there is little integration between the HE and FE environments in terms of teaching staff, location or support, it would seem logical to use just the HEI's VLE. However, this presents a number of difficulties, including loss of flexibility in terms of resourcing and, for some students and staff, depletion in the richness of the HE in

FE experience. It can also make it more difficult for colleges to encourage internal progression to HE if the two sections of the college community never integrate (Bathmaker and Thomas 2009).

HE students in all colleges could still access the either the HEI or the FEI VLE first and link through to its partner VLE. Bournemouth University (BU) began its VLE partnership with FEIs by suggesting that a minimum standard should apply to all BU courses. This required all staff across the university, including staff in partner colleges, to put a certain amount of information relevant to each course on its VLE. It was recognised that this could be problematic for colleges with different VLEs, so ways of linking the different platforms was agreed to be a prime focus of development, and BU is investigating ways to link from the University VLE to the College VLE and vice versa. Although not quite seamless, this solution would at least mean that the students access their information from a single starting point. There is however a risk that students may miss out on vital support and community information so the link needs to be carefully planned.

Another solution is for students to use the college VLE and link to the university's digital library rather than its VLE. There is a potential risk in this approach that students might miss material in one or other VLE so the linkage would need careful planning. If done successfully this solution would provide access for students to all the resources that they need and would also give them the information about the college community and services which are those that they are most likely to use. However, some university libraries no longer have a discrete digital library and this approach is unlikely to provide comprehensive access to information about the university campus should they wish to visit. Some students may prefer to identify with their HEI, and the use of the FEI VLE may discourage them. Fortunately, most FEIs support a wide range of learner profiles and ages so the FEI should still at least be suited to the mature HE in FE student in a way that a school VLE might not.

Many institutions, such as Kingston Maurward, are using both VLEs, which is ideal in terms of the amount of information available and the establishment of identity for students as members of both institutions. Where two different platforms are involved, it also allows staff to take advantage of the best features of each. However, it is less practical, requires literacy in both platforms and is confusing at times.

The second critical element for success is communication between the HEI staff and the FEI staff. This includes teaching and support staff. While the QAA explicitly does not favour any single, preferred model for relationships between FEIs and their awarding bodies, it highlights the importance of strong collaboration to deliver quality learning opportunities and meet appropriate academic standards (QAA 2006). Ultimately, the question of which VLE should be irrelevant and staff should be working together to create a totally student focussed, seamless platform for delivering information and enhancing the learning experience.

The final consideration is the role of the employer. Traditionally, partnerships in terms of VLEs and learning resources have mostly revolved around the educational players – HEIs and FEIs. The recommendations of the Leitch Review (Leitch 2006) pointed the way for colleges to engage more actively with employers and demand-led programmes at both FE and HE level. The current message coming from the QAA is that it now favours employer-led programmes. The prospect of this third commercial dimension may be a daunting prospect for some HE in FE partnerships, especially in relation to licences, but it is time to consider how employers and industry bodies, such as CITO, can engage in the VLE.

Conclusion

The VLE has many advantages for students studying for a degree in the FE environment. It can help to meet some of the very specific needs of these students who differ from other students both in terms of their profile as 'non-traditional' students and of the nature of programme delivery. As staff in both the FE and HE sectors start to engage more actively in the development of VLEs, many of the initial barriers to use are being overcome.

True to the way that HE in FE has grown up in a fragmented way, the new dilemma is whether the HEI VLE, the FEI VLE, both or a combined VLE should be adopted. Whatever the solution, it will require strong collaboration between HEI and its FE partners and a greater focus on the student experience and learner voice. Other parties, such as employers and industry bodies are likely to have an increasingly significant role in the development and delivery of Foundation Degrees, providing further challenges and opportunities for the delivery of learning resources.

References

Barber, D., Richardson, L. and Taylor, C., 2006. An introduction to higher education: supporting the needs of Foundation degree students. *Forward*, 10, 32–4.

Bathmaker, A.-M. and Thomas, W., 2009. Positioning themselves: an exploration of the nature and meaning of transitions in the context of dual sector FE/HE institutions in England. *Journal of Further and Higher Education*, 33 (2), 119–30.

Burkill, S., Dyer, S.R., and Stone, M., 2008. Lecturing in higher education in further education settings. *Journal of Further and Higher Education*, 32 (4), 321–31.

Challis, M., 2005. Challenging issues for Foundation degree providers: flexible delivery. *Forward*, 4, 18–21.

Cooper, M., 2006. Making online learning accessible to disabled students: an institutional case study. ALT-J, *Research in Learning Technology*, 14 (1), 103–15.

Dearnley, C., Dunn, G. and Watson, S., 2006. An exploration of on-line access by non-traditional students in higher education: a case study. *Nurse Education Today*, 26, 409–15.

Gerrard, C., 2007. Virtual learning environments: enhancing the learning experience for students with disabilities. *Campus-Wide Information Systems*, 24 (7), 199–206.

Golding Lloyd, M. and Griffiths, C., 2008. A review of the methods of delivering HE programmes in an FE college and an evaluation of the impact this will have on learning outcomes and student progression. *Journal of Further and Higher Education*, 32 (1), 15–25.

Heaton-Shrestha, C., May, S. and Burke, L., 2009. Student retention in higher education: what role for virtual learning environments? *Journal of Further and Higher Education*, 33 (1), 83–92.

JISC, 2003. *Managing the Future with MLEs*. Bristol: JISC. Available from: http://www.jisc.ac.uk/media/documents/publications/mlesreport.pdf (accessed 30 August 2009).

Leitch, S., 2006. *Prosperity for All in the Global Economy: World Class Skills*. Norwich: HMSO. Available from: http://webarchive.nationalarchives.gov. uk/+/http://www.hm-treasury.gov.uk/media/6/4/leitch_finalreport051206.pdf (accessed 11 August 2009).

QAA, 2006. *Outcomes from Institutional Audit: Learning Support Resources (Including Virtual Learning Environments)*. Gloucester: QAA. Available from: http://www.qaa.ac.uk/reviews/institutionalaudit/outcomes/learningsupport. asp (accessed 30 August 2009).

QAA, 2008. *The Handbook for Integrated Quality and Enhancement Review*. Gloucester: QAA. Available from: http://www.qaa.ac.uk/reviews/iqer/default. asp (accessed 30 August 2009).

Ryland J., 2006. Relating to further education: partners and franchises. In Dale, P. Holland, M. and Matthews, M., eds. *Subject Librarians: Engaging with the Learning and Teaching Environment*. Aldershot: Ashgate, 65–77.

Ryland, J. and Ball, D., 2005. HE-FE relationships. In: Ball, D., *Managing Suppliers and Partners for the Academic Library*. London: Facet, 84–103.

Smoothy, L., 2006. Cutting edge: the student experience. *Forward*, 8, 26–8.

Virkus, S., Agegn Alemu, G., Asfaw Demissie, T., Jakup Kokollari, B., Melgar Estrada, L.M. and Yadav, D., 2009. Integration of digital libraries and virtual learning environments: a literature review. *New Library World*, 110 (3/4), 136–50.

Warner, J., 2005. Foundation degrees FE and HE working together. *Update*, March, 12–24.

Chapter 12

Online Support Offered to International Students by UK University Libraries – What are we doing, and why are we doing it?

Frank Trew

When I embarked on this project I had thought to write about all of the efforts being made by university libraries to reach out to international students through their virtual learning environments (VLEs). My research did not uncover either a substantial body of literature on the topic, or evidence of a *huge* amount being done in this area. There is indeed a lot being done online to support international students, even if not specifically through a VLE, and I want to share some of what is being done in this chapter. But I also want to pose the question: 'Why are we doing it?' without necessarily having a ready answer to that question.

By 'international students' I am following the definition given by Arkoudis (2006, p. 5), where:

> international students will be those who have had the majority of their previous study in countries where English is not the main medium of instruction in education.

A similar definition is given by Carroll and Ryan, (2005 cited Bent et al. 2008, p. 2). So I am not focusing on distance learners, or on a cohort of home-grown, culturally diverse students, but on students who have come to the UK from abroad for their tertiary study. There are of course a substantial number of international students for whom English is their first language, for example those from North

America. There are also those students for whom English is not their first language but for whom it is the language in which they have studied, for example students from India and parts of Africa. For these students language is probably not the main difficulty; the challenges for them are differences in culture and learning styles. We need therefore to develop services and support mechanisms to enable international students to gain appropriate language skills and sufficient awareness of culture and customs to help them to study successfully.

The number of international students within UK universities has been on the increase over recent years, as data from the Higher Education Statistics Agency (HESA[1]) reveals. In 2006/7 there were 318,400 international students at UK universities (accounting for 13.4% of the student population), rising to 341,795 in 2007/8 (15%) and further rising to 368,970 in 2008/9 (18%). The increase in numbers owes something to the Prime Minister's Initiative (PMI), launched in 1999, (UKCISA 2010) and whose specific five-year strategy was to increase international student numbers by 70,000 in UK Higher Education (HE), double the number of countries sending 10,000 students per annum, and to improve international student satisfaction. What is significant about the increase in numbers however is the revenue that these students bring in to UK universities, some paying fees of more than £20,000 p.a. and propping up university finances (Shepherd 2009). Since these students are paying high fees they are also demanding value for money, something they are not always getting:

> 27% of international students from outside the European Union thought that UK universities offered poor or very poor value for money. (Sastry and Bekhradnia 2007, cited in SCONUL 2008, p. 3)

> 30% of overseas students … were dissatisfied with the value for money of their course. (Bekhradnia 2009, section 12)

When UK universities are also faced with competition from continental universities offering degree programmes taught in English for a fraction of the fees charged in the UK (Gale 2006, p. 37) it becomes a challenge to both recruit and to retain this lucrative market because "unless universities can satisfy their overseas students, those golden eggs will not continue to be laid indefinitely" (Bekhradnia 2009, section 12). What we see then is a concerted effort by UK universities to cater for their international students, and the library, as a service department within the university, is called upon to do its part. At which point I started to wonder whether, while there is a lot that we do, and a lot of what we do is very good, are we not just repackaging the services that we offer other students under an "International Student" label, as part of a wider university attempt to hang on to our golden eggs?

---

1   http://www.hesa.ac.uk/.

The SCONUL survey that was conducted prior to its 2008 report on services to international students found that 72% of respondents had university level International Strategies (as we might expect given what has just been said about how valuable a market international students are perceived to be) but that only 8% of libraries (14) had such a policy or action plan (Bent et al. 2008, p. 7). In 2007 the library at Durham University was about to devise an action plan to enhance its support for international students (Sunuodula 2007), and Anglia Ruskin University has a specific *Strategy for Supporting International Students 2009–11* (Anglia Ruskin University 2009). This document includes many policies for online support. It also states that a Faculty Liaison Librarian will be designated as 'International Support Librarian' who will take responsibility for championing and co-ordinating library services to international students. Again, this is a role that does not seem to be very common. When Helen Singer at the University of Hertfordshire took up a role offering Learning and Information Services support to international students she e-mailed Lis-link to find colleagues in a similar position. She received only nine responses, yet none of the respondents had full-time responsibility for international students (Singer 2005, p. 2). SCONUL (2008, p. 11) reports that only 25% of its respondents had someone looking after international students, and only one of these was full-time. It seems from all of this that libraries are being called upon to help the university recruit and retain international students, but that extra time and resources to do this are not always forthcoming and this in turn means that library support for these students can be patchy.

The most common online support on offer is the web-page (or pages) specifically for international students. Gale's (2006, p. 37) web survey found 'a web presence for international student library services was minimal' and Bent et al. (2009, p. 9), reporting on the SCONUL survey, report that only 4 libraries had specific web-pages for international students, and say a similar pattern was found when the project group accessed over 30 UK library websites.

Gale (2006) found that many of the web-pages simply gave the name of the university support officer, or had a single page of help and orientation information. This may not have changed that much. Many of the pages I came across do simply give students links to the university support offices/officers (non-library) or links to the (library) guides that had been produced for "regular" students, although packaged on a special 'International Students' page. For minimal effort therefore we can say that we are doing something to support them: we see you, you are special to us: look, we have a web-page designed especially for you!

Perhaps this is being too uncharitable. The library is a knowledge bank of information, and knowing where to send students to find that information is our speciality. So that may well mean our web-page to support international students directs them to the university support officers, or to information on visas and work permits, or to information on accommodation in the local area etc. Mehdizadeh and Scott's 2005 (p. 487) study of Iranian students in Glasgow found that they were very satisfied regarding academic issues, but that the majority of the students faced difficulties to do with employment while studying, or complained that they did not have enough realistic, statistical information about the city prior to their arrival. If our libraries are going to provide web-pages of information to support international students, then we should at least be giving them what they need, even if that means directing them to support services beyond the library.

In the 20 university webpages that I looked at, eight offer support specific to international students, often as links to help with their English language. Two linked to dictionaries, five to foreign language news/newspapers and four to glossaries of library jargon. These links may either direct students to traditional face-to-face resources (e.g. the English language classes) or to hardcopy and online resources (dictionaries, newspapers, glossaries).

Anglia Ruskin's strategy document recognises the use of jargon to be a hindrance to non-native English speakers and promises 'to use as little jargon as possible ... on our web-pages ... [and] within our website we will offer a glossary function to explain complex library terms'. Hilary Hughes' 'international-friendly library' will also compile a glossary of library/information jargon (Hughes 2001). But when Ayre et al. (2006) investigated the use of glossaries as a means for jargon-busting, these efforts were called into question. They looked at some 230 glossaries (the majority from the USA), and stated that the assumption would be that:

> Such a large number of glossaries suggests that many libraries consider such glossaries to be useful ... [as] using a "foreign language" (i.e. library vocabulary) without a context was a grave disservice [to library users]

However, they also questioned whether such glossaries were actually useful. Respondents were divided on the issue, but 'the largest group of respondents felt that glossaries were not useful, usually because [they] seemed rarely if ever consulted' (Ayre et al. 2006). In fact one librarian went so far as to state that librarians should be avoiding jargon in the first place rather than creating glossaries to solve the problems caused by its use.

Obviously opinion can be divided on this, and other issues, as we shall see. But it should also make us stop and question why we are doing what we are doing, and whether our efforts are indeed a valuable/valued-added resource, or a waste of time and effort. For example, there is ongoing debate about the use of multilingual resources. The University of Birmingham[2] has produced database guides in foreign languages and offers audio tours in English, French, Arabic and Mandarin. Gale (2006) reports that at the University of Exeter[3] a link was added to the AltaVista BabelFish[4] translation programme so that students could obtain an automatic translation of the web-pages into eight different languages. But the

---

2   http://www.library.bham.ac.uk/searching/infoskills/international_students.shtml.
3   http://as.exeter.ac.uk/library/using/international.
4   http://babelfish.altavista.com.

NELIG[5] blog on ideas for library instruction to non-native speakers explicitly recommends providing resources only in English with the traditional argument that students are expected to work in English as this will reinforce their learning of the language. A study at Virginia Tech in 2005 found that:

> since English proficiency level does not appear to be a barrier to successful library use, multilingual instructions may not be necessary in most cases. (Liao et al. 2007)

Which leaves me in somewhat of a quandary. Here at Rose Bruford College where I now work we have visiting groups of students from Latvia, the Czech Republic, and Spain (amongst other countries) and I am considering offering them some special support (to practise what I preach, if you like) perhaps in their own languages. While my knowledge of Spanish might be sufficient to get by, I certainly have no knowledge of the other languages and I would need to recruit student help in translations. But then I wonder whether my efforts would be either necessary or worthwhile. Perhaps the answer is that, if you have the time and inclination, and personnel and expertise, to offer these value-added services then go ahead and offer them. On the University of East London website[6] for instance there is a list of library staff and the languages they speak. Does this mean every library website should have one? Not at all. But if the resource exists and someone is keen and interested enough to make something of it then let it be encouraged. At Sheffield Hallam University[7], when staff were developing international student support to be delivered via mobile technologies, developing the necessary skills to do effective podcasts looked quite a hurdle to begin with, and the project may well have ended there. But members of the team acquired skills in scripting audio guides and study support podcasts, in audio recording and editing skills, and in using basic podcasting software such as Audacity, so that the project went ahead and proved to be quite successful[8]. Likewise at Glasgow University where staff were developing audio and visual materials for their VLE, Pringle et al. (2008) report that staff varied in their technical capabilities:

> The project involved considerable studio time simply to record video material. Editing time was then needed (with editing itself being a lengthy team effort), and thereafter several members of academic and technical staff were involved in transforming video data into a format that could be readily incorporated onto the website.

---

5   http://www.acrlnec.org/neligblog/?p=56.
6   http://www.uel.ac.uk/lls/users/InternationalStudents.htm.
7   http://students.shu.ac.uk/learning/support/index.html.
8   http://www.ukcisa.org.uk/files/pdf/pmi/pmi_reports_2009.pdf.

Library staff, although non-specialists, learned the new skills that were required and successfully completed the project. The conclusion I make here is that there is no one standard set of good practice for library support to international students. So much of it will depend on the skills and expertise of existing staff, and on the enthusiasm and willingness of staff to learn new skills.

Another major focus for library support to international students is during induction. Alison Lahlafi at Sheffield Hallam University asked on Lis-Link in 2010 about library orientation/induction activities for international students. Her summary of replies includes libraries developing a new induction DVD with lots of visual demonstrations, an audio guide to a library where the script can be downloaded to an i-Pod, and a library with video clips on its website on how to use the catalogue or find a journal etc. Increasingly many libraries are putting their inductions online: Heriot-Watt[9] have *International Student Orientation* on their website, Anglia Ruskin[10] have *Getting Started* and the University of Reading[11] offers a CyberLibrary course with a section on how to use the library.

Much has been written about the problems experienced by international students when they come to the UK and in *Serving Different Constituencies: International Students* I explored the literature on these issues in some depth (Trew 2006). But in addition to the language problems and culture shock that have been written about at length, there is also what Hughes (2001) terms "study shock" and Forland (2006) labels "learning shock", where students encounter differences in learning and teaching styles and where success is measured in different ways. While traditionally this shock is associated with Chinese and East Asian students coming from what is described as a Confucian heritage model of education, Gil Ortega (2003) reports similar shock amongst Spanish students: the Spanish educational system focuses upon rote learning and factual knowledge, discussion and argument in seminars and tutorials is unknown, and there is less individual contact with lecturers than is the case in the UK.

In answer to this several university libraries are developing resources for student access pre-arrival. Focus Groups among East Asian students at Roehampton University found that:

> all participants agreed it would be useful to gain insight into the expectations of the UK's education system and the university's policies of learning and teaching before arrival. (Forland 2006, p. 5)

At the University of Hertfordshire, Singer (2005) developed pages on StudyNet which include a pre-induction Powerpoint presentation with sound, and Pringle et

---

9   http://www.hw.ac.uk/home/dir/27/current-international-students.

10   http://web.anglia.ac.uk/inclusive_practice/getting_started/getting_started_00.html.

11   http://www.reading.ac.uk/library/contact/info-for/international/lib-international.aspx.

al. (2008) at the University of Glasgow reports on a project to develop materials both online and in a VLE to support international students prior to and on arrival at the university. Dundee College[12] has an online International Student Welcome Pack covering everything from climate and travel, the doctor and police, to places to worship and places to eat – as well as mention of the university libraries.

Julie Watson at the Centre for Language Study at the University of Southampton (University of Southampton/UKCISA 2010) reports on a project entitled Arrive UK, a pre-arrival online course within Moodle, on the development of 'learning objects' in the form of podcasts for this course, and on the proposal to further develop the course content by creating vodcasts (downloadable video files). Of note among the pre-arrival initiatives is *Prepare for Success* also developed by the University of Southampton, but now available as:

> an interactive web-learning tool for international students who are getting ready to come to the UK for study. (University of Southampton/UKCISA 2010)

It covers topics such as differences in university study, relationship with tutors, academic writing at university, ways of being taught etc. UKCISA has also produced an online document on study methods in the UK explaining about lectures, seminars, tutorials, written work, group assignments, examinations and plagiarism, and the Student Diversity and Academic Writing Project (SDAW) has a website entitled International Students, Academic Writing and Plagiarism[13], designed to help them with the transition from one university system to another, and including a short video on what to expect in UK higher education.

Another initiative recommended by UKCISA is that of an online pre-arrival mentoring service where current students can answer questions from new international students before they arrive[14]. This initiative has been adopted at Sheffield Hallam University where Naomi Ainge told me current students are interviewed to act as mentors, and new students email in their interest in having a mentor prior to arrival. Library staff then match up the two and the mentoring is conducted via email. At present this system is quite admin heavy and the library is looking at an alternative scheme that could almost run itself.

Finally, there is the computer/mobile game developed by Nipan Maniar at the University of Portsmouth. Entitled C-shock, it is an innovative approach to educate students on educational, cultural and social issues, comprising 12 games, 12 culture-shock elements, and five quizzes to combat UK culture shock. Students get graded on completion of a game or quiz, and end up with a PgC, PgD or MSc in C-Shock – Travel to UK.[15]

---

12   http://www.dundeecollege.ac.uk.
13   http://www.ukcisa.org.uk/files/pdf/about/material_media/mentoring.pdf.
14   http://www.ukcisa.org.uk/files/pdf/about/material_media/mentoring.pdf.
15   http://www.c-shock. com/index.html.

Linked with the issue of learning shock or study shock is the perception that international students do not participate fully in classroom or seminar discussions. At the University of Hertfordshire an attempt was made to overcome this reluctance by encouraging discussion through the StudyNet VLE. The aim was to help students improve their ability to read an academic article, to take part in discussions on the article and to experience this through StudyNet (Gillett and Weetman 2005). The assessment consisted of a combination of the quantity of contributions to the discussion (two being the minimum, and more if they wanted a good mark) and the quality of the contributions in terms of ideas, interaction and appropriate academic language. At the end of the exercise more than 50% of students responded positively to the exercise, while only 6% did not find it useful. In a similar vein, Arkoudis (2006, p. 11) states that:

> international students often report that they would like to participate but lack the confidence to do so.

Academics may need to create 'safe' learning environments where students feel that they can make a contribution, and perhaps the VLE is the place to do this.

There is however a danger of stereotyping international students, by adopting what has been termed the 'deficit' model, which overemphasises what international students might lack (Arkoudis 2006; Ottewill 2008; Pringle et al. 2008). Instead we are encouraged to focus on and accentuate the positive, building upon and celebrating their strengths and valuing their prior experiences. The colonial, 'us and them' model is to be replaced by one of 'cultural synergy' (Jin and Cortazzi 2001 cited Forland 2006, p. 4). That the deficit model may be outmoded becomes clearer when you consider the studies by Martin et al. (2009) and Liao et al. (2007). Each of these studied the information seeking behaviour and search skills of international compared to US students, and found that, contrary to expectations, the results were very similar. The computer and technological barrier identified in the 1980s and 1990s is no longer a major obstacle in finding and using information (Martin et al. 2009, p. 2) and:

> we have seen significant improvement in both English proficiency and information technology development worldwide (Liao et al. 2007).

Instead the two study groups exhibit similar proficiencies and problems: 91% of international students were as proficient as US students in identifying call numbers, and there was little difference between the two groups when asked to interpret a catalogue record. When asked to identify peer-reviewed or scholarly articles only 40% of all students accomplished this task (Martin et al. 2009). Although very similar, it does not mean that both cohorts are identical. The survey by Liao et al. (2007) reports these differences in detail, but the differences are slight, and their conclusion is that international students are using various online searching tools and resources as often as their American counterparts. Hughes (2005) in

Australia came to a very similar conclusion when exploring international students' use of online resources, stating 'in many respects the difficulties described by the participants would be similar to those common among non-international students'.

Furthermore when Liao et al. (2007) comment that 'though most international students do not find library services difficult to use, this does not mean they are using them correctly,' this could equally apply to any cohort of students at our university libraries. A lot of effort has been put into information literacy training for university students, and it seems that international students are not necessarily any worse than local students when it comes to research and critical thinking skills. Hughes' survey of international students' use of online resources at Central Queensland University found that participants reported extensive use of the Internet, moderate use of common journal databases and very limited use of specialist information sources:

> Across the board they displayed limited effectiveness in their online use, which was characterised by very basic approaches to planning and carrying out searches and processing results. (Hughes 2005)

These findings could apply equally to all students. My own experience teaching information literacy classes at Richmond: the American International University in London for at least the past ten years would certainly bear this out. While I might have expected the US students to be more competent in constructing a search strategy and thinking critically about the information resources they were using, this was not the case. All students seemed to have difficulty in putting together a meaningful search with which to interrogate a database that wasn't just some form of their assignment question, and when asked to evaluate the results they retrieved there was little difference between them and the large cohort of international students in terms of critical analysis. It may be significant that the Association of College and Research Libraries (ACRL) information literacy guidelines[16] make no mention of the needs of international students as a separate group. Maybe this is because:

> it is not the international students' cognitive skills that are in question ... as we know, developing critical thinking skills is equally challenging for domestic students. (Arkoudis 2006, p. 14)

This echoes a sentiment expressed by several libraries that there is little benefit in having specialist web-pages for international students since all the information is relevant to all students (SCONUL 2008, p. 17). Pringle et al. (2008, p. 3) make a valid point when they write that the differences reported by international students

---

16   http://www.ala.org/ala/mgrps/divs/acrl/issues/infolit/index.cfm.

may not be purely because they have come to the UK from abroad; all of the participants in their study:

> were also embarking on a higher level of study, whether going from undergraduate to postgraduate, or from high school to university and this transition alone may have been responsible for some of the changes they were experiencing.

Hughes (2005) found that most international students did not consider that being an international student greatly affected their use of online resources, but that when discussing cultural differences the participants tended to focus more on their wider educational experience than on their actual online use. When Badke (2002) advocates a programme for academic literacy, not merely information literacy,

> a compulsory, comprehensive, competency-based battery of training that will have them both understanding and showing skill in our Western approach to education,

perhaps this should be taught to all students, and not just international ones.

That said, there are several projects that are already providing online academic literacy support to international students. I have already mentioned *Prepare for Success* developed by the University of Southampton/UKCISA (2010), and most of the other pre-arrival projects mentioned above are aimed at providing international students with information about studying in the UK. More explicitly, Pringle et al. at the University of Glasgow developed quizzes for their VLE aiming to promote reflection on learning and teaching methods in UK HE, and produced videos highlighting, in students' own words, a variety of student experiences which put forward a wide range of techniques from which site users could select relevant options (Pringle et al. 2008, p. 5). Sheffield Hallam University[17] has a series of study support podcasts on their website covering topics such as culture shock, UK academic culture, essay writing, exams, and time management. Also at Sheffield Hallam University, a UKCOSA pilot project[18] developed a computer game as a means of addressing the same issues.

That information literacy skills need to be learnt equally by all students may account for the fact that I did not uncover many information literacy courses aimed specifically at international students. Anglia Ruskin's strategy for supporting international students, for example, mentions that information literacy is a key skill required by students and refers international students to the online tutorial PILOT[19] which provides support for off-site students. It makes no claim that this tutorial is explicitly for international students: rather it is a support for all off-campus students. However, there were exceptions. Hurley et al. (2006) report

---

17   http://students.shu.ac.uk/learning/support/podcasts.html.

18   http://www.ukcisa.org.uk/files/docs/pmi/shu_learning.doc.

19   http://libweb.anglia.ac.uk/pilot.

on a pilot information literacy course for international students at the Waterford Institute of Technology[20], and while the learning outcomes echo those of any information literacy course, there was some modification of content and means of delivery in order to address the needs of international students. Gil Ortega (2003) at the University of Brighton developed a set of online activities using a software package called *Hot Potatoes* which aimed to help overcome the common mistakes that Spanish students make.

One of the areas where international students are said to differ most is that of plagiarism:

> the amount of plagiarism in papers from international students is high, due to the philosophy that research is essentially reproduction of the work of others. (Badke 2002)

Alternatively, they may know what plagiarism is, but lack the English language skills required to read, extract relevant points and then put it into their own words (Arkoudis 2006, p. 13). If we broaden this issue to include intellectual property and copyright issues, all students seem to be equally ignorant of what UK academia expects and UK law requires. Students seem to think that anything on the Internet is fair game for them to use without acknowledgement, or will download music to their MP3 players at will. And, from my present experience, the fact that music scores have a different set of regulations to those of books and journals seems to be beyond their comprehension.

But these issues are not the exclusive preserve of international students as Jackson's (2006) paper reveals. Her study assessed undergraduate students' (not specifically international students') understanding of plagiarism, and found that there was a fundamental lack of understanding as to what constitutes plagiarism, and a lack of understanding of and ability to paraphrase. To overcome this she designed an interactive, online information literacy tutorial about plagiarism, which improved students' understanding of plagiarism and citing sources by 6% from pre- to post-test.

A project worth mentioning, that takes us from international students beginning at university to focus on their departure, is InterVisual at Brunel University[21] . This was conceived to provide a complete web-based package for international students to present themselves to overseas recruiters in a new and cost-effective way. Students can make short videos of their responses to pre-selected interview questions, and they can receive advice and feedback on their videos from Career Consultants before recruiters can view them. InterVisual has developed into an online interview coaching and recording package, with many other potential applications.

---

20   http://library.wit.ie/olas/.

21   http://www.ukcisa.org.uk/files/pdf/pmi/pmi_reports_2009.pdf.

At the University of Huddersfield research skills training and e-supervision is offered to international PhD students. A three-week-long training programme was provided focusing on research strategies and methodology, writing the research report and viva. Then flexible learning and supervision arrangements were set up through the use of Blackboard and Skype enabling students to return to their home countries and continue with their studies. (Jones and Hanson 2009).

This perhaps takes me beyond my original definition of international students and into the realm of distance learners. In this area I would like to mention the work of Enhancing Student Mobility through Online Support (ESMOS). Universities in the UK (Sheffield Hallam University) and in Austria, Italy, Poland, Lithuania and Bulgaria have been working together to develop online methods of supporting students who go abroad on study placements. So, not distance learners, but not exactly international students as I had defined them. However, there have been a lot of innovative projects to support these students both in terms of the VLE (Moodle, Blackboard, and First Class) and in terms of other social software (Serendipity, Blackboard Journal LX, Blogger, Edublogs and other synchronous chat tools etc.) Helen Keegan's (2006) article reports on two case studies where blogs have been used to support international 'mobility students', as they are called, and for further details I refer you to the work package by Morrone (2005), and to the ESMOS website[22].

In terms of social software, a number of universities are starting to explore this area as a means of support to students in general, and to international students in particular. Doncaster College[23], for example, has an International Students page on Facebook where current students can network and keep up-to-date with news, and former students can stay in touch with their friends. To date it has 624 'fans'. Dundee College also encourages its international students to become a 'friend' on Facebook, or Bebo, MySpace and Twitter. While joining groups which create a sense of identity is important, it is less clear what role the library should be playing in these groups, and any such initiative may depend more on the enthusiasm and willingness of individual staff members, and the time available to them. In my previous workplace a colleague joined Facebook on a personal level, but quickly became 'friends' with some of the students, and over time this network has grown. While she may not be posting items about the library, she is able to pick up on what interests students, what they are into and talking about, and she can use this to enhance her rapport with students in the face-to-face contact she has with them, especially in the Information Literacy classes she teaches. At Rose Bruford the college has a Rose Bruford Online site for students and staff to post tweets. I have yet to dip my toe into this water, mainly because I know that once in I would need to be tweeting on a regular basis if it is to be worthwhile, and I, like many of you, have to weigh up whether this would be time well spent, as opposed to other projects I could be working on.

---

22   http://www.esmos.eu/.
23   http://www.don.ac.uk/international_students.aspx.

One of the themes that arose from much of the literature on supporting international students concerned 'internationalisation'. The Higher Education Academy (2010) has worked on projects for the internationalisation of UK higher education and the tertiary curriculum, and has a resource bank of some 77 case studies in this area. Forland (2006, p. 1) reports that 'most institutions now have a commitment to internationalisation which includes internationalising the student body and the curriculum' and Arkoudis (2006) both looks at the difficulties of internationalising teaching and learning and offers some suggestions for overcoming these. But while most of this may be beyond my brief, which is to look at the online support given to international students, I did want to mention it in the context of the internationalisation of resources. Because while it is possible to acquire book and even journal resources that cater for the needs of international students, my experience of online resources is that they are still very much US and UK focused. I recall introducing students to our Lexis Nexis Executive subscription and while this covered all USA and UK newspapers (both national and local), there were only some European papers, and a few from the Pacific Rim. Africa and the Middle East didn't get a look in. Many of the large journal database suppliers tend to be US (primarily) or UK biased, which proved difficult when students were asked to write an argumentative paper about a social issue within their own country; there was just not the variety of online resources that they could be directed to from which they could collect the range of differing arguments and opinions that were required for their assignment. If we are to fully internationalise our resources then we need to convince our database suppliers that their content has to be more international as well.

At the beginning of the chapter I asked 'What are we doing?' The answer is that there are a lot of interesting initiatives and projects being undertaken, and here is a summary:

- Online webpages: in addition to those mentioned in this chapter, the following institutions also have online web pages:
  - Bournemouth University[24]
  - Edinburgh Napier University[25]
  - Glasgow School of Art[26]
  - Heriot Watt University[27]
  - London South Bank University[28]
  - Oxford Brookes University[29]

---

24   http://www.bournemouth.ac.uk/library/using_the_library/international.html.
25   http://staff.napier.ac.uk/services/library/userinformation/International/Pages/InternationalStudents.aspx.
26   http://www2.gsa.ac.uk/library/international_support.html.
27   http://www.hw.ac.uk/home/dir/27/current-international-students.
28   http://www1.lsbu.ac.uk/international.
29   http://www.brookes.ac.uk/library/guideintro.html.

- – University College Falmouth[30]
- – University of Bristol Language Centre[31]
- – University of Kent[32]
- – University of the Arts London[33]
- – University of the West of England[34]
- Glossaries (some multilingual)
- Orientations (online, with video or audio clips; a DVD)
- Pre-arrival support (online courses, packs, podcasts, vodcasts)
- Online mentoring
- Computer games (e.g. C-shock)
- StudyNet discussion (to enhance class participation)
- Information Literacy support (e.g. OLAS)
- Plagiarism course
- Social networking pages (e.g. Facebook, Twitter, blogs)
- Careers guidance (InterVisual)

I also asked 'Why are we doing it?' The answer to this is multi-layered. While we recognise that international students may need some special help and therefore devise pedagogic means of support, it also appears that libraries are being asked to play a role in the university's marketing strategy to recruit and retain students. But even these reasons are not straightforward. For in terms of pedagogy, there is debate about what actual help international students need: their information and academic literacy needs are also shared by what we term local students, so we are unsure whether to offer exclusive or inclusive support. There is debate about whether to make the students feel welcomed by offering services and resources in their own languages, or whether this does them a disservice by not focusing on improving their English language proficiency. In terms of marketing, we can readily create a web-page for our international students that simply directs them to pre-prepared guides and help that we have created for other students, or we can become enthusiastic about the new technologies and teach ourselves new skills in order to deliver special audio and video services to these students, but skills that will stand us in good stead for developing library services in general.

References

Anglia Ruskin University, 2009. *Strategy for Supporting International Students 2009–11*. Anglia Ruskin University. Available from: http://libweb.anglia.

---

30   http://ish.falmouth.ac.uk/.
31   http://www.llas.ac.uk/resources/mb/2575.
32   http://www.kent.ac.uk/library/students/international.html.
33   http://www.arts.ac.uk/international.htm.
34   http://www.uwe.ac.uk/library/info/international_students.htm.

ac.uk/policiesplans/files/University%20Library%20International%20Support
%20Strategy%202009-11.pdf (accessed: 29 March 2010).

Arkoudis, S., 2006. *Teaching International Students: Strategies to Enhance learning. CSHE (Centre for the Study of Higher Education)*. Available from: http://www.cshe.unimelb.edu.au/pdfs/international.pdf (accessed 29 March 2010).

Ayre, C., Smith, I.A., and Cleeve, M., 2006. Electronic library glossaries: jargonbusting essentials or wasted resource? *The Electronic Library*, 24 (2), 126-134. Available from: http://www.emeraldinsight.com/0264-0473.htm (accessed 29 March 2010).

Badke, W., 2002. International students: information literacy or academic literacy? *Academic Exchange Quarterly*, Winter. Available from: http://findarticles.com/p/articles/mi_hb3325/is_4_6/ai_n28969878 (accessed 29 March 2010).

Bekhradnia, B., 2009. *The Academic Experience of Students in English Universities: 2009 Report HEPI (Higher Education Policy Institute)*. Available from: http://www.hepi.ac.uk/466-1393/The-Academic-Experience-of-Students-in-English-Universities-(2009-report).html (accessed 29 March 2010).

Bent, M., Scopes, M. and Senior, K., 2008. *Discrete Library Services for International Students: How can Exclusivity Lead to Inclusivity?* University of Bolton Institutional Repository: Library Conference Papers. Available from: http://digitalcommons.bolton.ac.uk/library_conferencepr/1 (accessed 29 March 2010).

Forland, H., 2006. *The International Student Learning Experience: Bridging the Gap between Rhetoric and Reality*, Paper to Going Gobal 2, Edinburgh, 6-8 December 2006, Available from: http://www.britishcouncil.org/goingglobal-2_-_5e_-_heather_forland.pdf (accessed 29 March 2010).

Gale, C., 2006. Serving them right? How libraries can enhance the learning experience of international students: a case study from the University of Exeter. *SCONUL Focus*, 39 (Winter), 36-39.

Gil Ortega, M.C., 2003. *Spanish Students in British Universities: Developing a Support Resource to Improve their Academic Writing Skills*, Higher Education Academy: Subject Centre for Languages, Linguistics and Area Studies. Available from: http://www.llas.ac.uk/resources/paper/1423 (accessed 29 March 2010).

Gillett, A. and Weetman, C., 2005. Investigation of the perceived usefulness of a StudyNet group discussion facility by international students. *Journal for the Enhancement of Learning and Teaching*, 2(1). Available from: https://uhra.herts.ac.uk/dspace/bitstream/2299/2597/1/902908.pdf (accessed 29 March 2010).

Higher Education Academy, 2010. *Internationalisation of the Curriculum and Support for International Students*. Available from: http://www.heacademy.ac.uk/ourwork/teachingandlearning/Internationalisation (accessed 29 March 2010).

Hughes, H., 2001. *The International Friendly Library – Customising Library Services for Students from Overseas*, ALIA [Australian Library and Information Association] TAFE libraries conference, 2001. Available from: http://conferences.alia.org.au/tafe2001/papers/hilary.hughes.html   (accessed 29 March 2010).

Hughes, H., 2005. Actions and reactions: exploring international students' use of online information resources. *Australian Academic and Research Libraries* 36(4). Available from: http://alia.org.au/ publishing/aarl/36.4/hughes.pdf (accessed 29 March 2010).

Hurley, T., Hegarty, N. and Bolger, J., 2006. Crossing a bridge: the challenges of developing and delivering a pilot information literacy course for international students, *New Library World*, 107 (7–8). Available from: http://repository.wit.ie/321/ (accessed 29 March 2010).

Jackson, P.A., 2006. Plagiarism instruction online: assessing undergraduate students' ability to avoid plagiarism. *College and Research Libraries*, 67 (5). Available from: http://crl.acrl.org/content/ 67/5/418.full.pdf+html (accessed 29 March 2010).

Jones, A. and Hanson, S., 2009. *A Framework for Research Skills Training: Support and e-Supervision for International PhD Students*, PMI Student Experience. Available from: http://www. ukcisa. org.uk/pmi/case_studies_learning.php (accessed 29 March 2010).

Keegan, H., 2006. *Blogging to Enhance the Support of International Mobility Students. Learning Technology (IEEE)*, 8 (4). Available from: http://www.ieeetclt.org/issues/october2006/index.html#_Toc148658502 (accessed 29 March 2010).

Lahlafi, A., 2010. *Library Orientation for New International Students*, LIS-Link posting. (accessed 24 March 2010).

Liao, Y., Finn, M. and Lu, J., 2007. Information-seeking behaviour of international graduate students vs American graduate students: a user study at Virginia Tech 2005. *College and Research Libraries*, 68 (1). Available from: http://crl.acrl.org/content/68/1/5.full.pdf+html (accessed 29 March 2010).

Martin, C.K., Maxey-Harris, C., Graybill, J.O. and Rodacker-Borgens, E.K., 2009. Closing the gap: investigating the search skills of international and US students: an exploratory study. *Library Philosophy and Practice*. Available from:http://www.webpages.uidaho.edu/~mbolin/martin-maxeyharris-graybill-rodackerborgens.htm (accessed 29 March 2010).

Mehdizadeh, N. and Scott, G., 2005. Adjustment problems of Iranian international students in Scotland. *International Education Journal*, 6 (4). Available from: http://ehlt.flinders.edu.au/education/iej/articles/v6n4/mehdizadeh/paper.pdf (accessed 29 March 2010).

Morrone, F.L., 2005. *Guidelines for the Support of International Mobility Students. ESMOS*: Report for Work Package 7 – Protocols and Development. Available from: http://www.ae.salford.ac.uk/extras/esmos/publications.php (accessed 29 March 2010).

Ottewill, R., 2008. *Support for International Students: Guidance on Facilitating their Educational Transition*. Learning and Teaching Enhancement Unit, University of Southampton. Available from: http://www.soton.ac.uk/lateu/ institutional_development/international_students/guidelines.html   (accessed 29 March 2010).

Pringle, G., Fischbacher, M. and Williams, A., 2008. *Assisting International Students to Manage their Transition to UK Academic Culture*. Universitas 21 Teaching and Learning Conference, University of Glasgow, 21-28 February 2008. Available at: http://www.universitas21.com/TandL/Presentations/Thu3. pdf (accessed 29 March 2010).

SCONUL, 2008. Library services for international students. *SCONUL Access* Available from: http://sconul.ac.uk/groups/access/papers/international_students. pdf (accessed 29 March 2010).

Shepherd, J., 2009. Overseas students prop up university finances. *The Guardian*, 14 October. Available from: http://www.guardian.co.uk/education/2009/oct/14/ international-students-pay-20000 (accessed 29 March 2010).

Singer, H., 2005. Learning and information services support for international students at the University of Hertfordshire. *SCONUL Focus*, 35. Available from: http://www.sconul.ac.uk/publications/newsletter/35/20.rtf (accessed 29 March 2010).

Sunuodula, M., 2007. *Supporting International Students in Durham: A Library Perspective*. QED: Quality Enhancement at Durham. Available from: http://www.dur.ac.uk/resources/academicstaffdevelopment/dissemination/ newsletter/7_Final.pdf (accessed 29 March 2010).

Trew, F., 2006. Serving different constituencies: international students. In: Dale, P., Holland, M. and Matthews, M., eds. *Subject Librarians: Engaging with the Learning and Teaching Environment*. Aldershot: Ashgate.

UKCISA, 2010. *PMI: The Prime Minister's Initiative for International Education*, UKCISA. Available from: http://www.ukcisa.org.uk/pmi/index.php (accessed 29 March 2010).

University of Southampton/UKCISA, 2010. *Prepare for Success: Learning Activities to Prepare You for Study in the UK*. Available from: http://www. prepareforsuccess.org.uk (accessed 29 March 2010).

Watson, J., 2007. Integrating podcasts and learning objects in an online course for international students. *ALISS Quarterly*, 2 (4), 18–21.

Chapter 13
Library Performance Measurement in the Digital Age

Angela Conyers and Philip Payne

Why is Performance Measurement Important to Academic Libraries?

Library performance measurement has become increasingly important over the last 30 years. One of the major drivers has been the pressure for greater accountability in Higher Education (HE). Public services, including universities and colleges, have needed to demonstrate that their 'customers' are satisfied and that they represent good value-for-money. In the UK, we have seen the launch of the National Student Survey (NSS) where the views of final year students are solicited on their courses, the teaching, and the facilities available. The results of this survey (and other data on individual Higher Education Institutions) are made publicly available to inform prospective students' choices about where to study. HE libraries have needed to respond to this environment of greater accountability, but there have been particular pressures on them to take this seriously. In the digital age, the traditional activities of libraries are changing and library managers increasingly have to challenge the view that everything is now readily available via the Internet. This is a particular concern when the library's contribution may be less apparent. The provision of e-resources is not always associated with the library, whilst some users of e-services now have a limited need to visit the library itself. The increasing involvement by libraries in collaborative activity in support of learning and teaching, including the delivery of content and services through virtual learning environments, can also make the library's contribution less visible especially to senior institutional managers. Changes in perception of libraries coincide with significant financial pressures on Higher Education Institutions (HEIs), which are likely to become much greater as a result of the global economic downturn. There are also competing pressures on funding within institutions and the library can fare badly if it cannot demonstrate its value. In this environment, libraries must now be able to demonstrate that the investment made in them is worthwhile. They are approaching this in a variety of ways including the use of key performance indicators (KPIs), benchmarking with similar institutions, seeking the views of users, and attempting to assess their impact.

The rapid evolution of libraries in the digital world has been the other major driver for the increased emphasis on evaluation and performance. Rather than relying on subjective impressions, libraries need to develop a robust evidence base to inform internal management decision making and to support the management of change. Increasing sums are being spent by libraries on e-services and the digital infrastructure. Librarians need to know whether this represents good value-for-money as they are often making difficult choices between spending on new e-services and maintaining expenditure on traditional ones. Similarly, innovations need to be evaluated to see whether they meet users' needs and are cost-effective.

What have been the Traditional Measures of Performance?

Academic libraries have had a long tradition of keeping statistics and measuring aspects of their service. The number of books issued each year, number of visits to the library, number of new books or journals acquired, staffing and expenditure figures have traditionally been kept both for internal management purposes and for annual reporting. In the UK, HE libraries complete an annual return to the Society of College, National and University Libraries (SCONUL)[1] for inclusion in their annual library statistics. Similar data collection exercises are conducted by professional organisations in other countries. Two examples, amongst many, are the Association of Research Libraries (ARL)[2] in the United States and the Council of Australian University Librarians (CAUL)[3] in Australia. Such statistics have been valuable in demonstrating trends within the library and illustrating its economy and effectiveness. They continue to form the basis of any data collection. When the emphasis was on collection development, and on an assumption that libraries were unquestionably 'a good thing', these traditional input measures were sufficient. In the new digital environment and in an era of increasing accountability,

---

1   http://www.sconul.ac.uk/statistics/.
2   http://www.arl.org/stats/annualsurveys/arlstats/.
3   http://www.caul.edu.au/stats/.

new methods of measurement need to be found which reflect the changes taking place.

SCONUL first started collecting statistics from its university library members in 1987. The annual library statistics have been processed by LISU[4] at Loughborough University since 1995 and their large databank provides a valuable resource for libraries wanting to look at long-term changes and trends. One of the most valuable aspects of the SCONUL annual statistics has always been the ability to benchmark results with others. Most library directors will have used this facility in attempting to make the case for more money, more staff, or more space. Using this resource for trend analysis or for benchmarking has been greatly facilitated over the past few years by the availability of SCONUL statistics on the web, which enables libraries to directly interrogate the data via a web interface, and search and collate data using a range of variables. This includes the ability to compare results with others in the same group (post-1992 universities, Research Libraries UK[5] members etc.) or with those comparator institutions which the university itself has identified as potential 'competitors'. The availability of a range of consistent and reliable statistics over a long period can give confidence to those libraries that are using them for benchmarking. It also provides an invaluable tool in advocacy at the national level especially where evidence is required to demonstrate the changing nature of HE libraries.

Input measures (such as spending on books or e-books) or activity measures (such as loans or downloads) can rarely give the full picture on their own. Other variables such as full-time equivalent (FTE) staff and student numbers or expenditure figures are needed to produce meaningful ratios, particularly for benchmarking purposes. The SCONUL annual library statistics contain a selection of ratios on library provision and use, stock provision and expenditure, efficiency measures and expenditure ratios. Libraries can use these or adapt them to their own purposes to demonstrate effectiveness, and particularly cost effectiveness, in the running of the library service.

The evolving library digital landscape is leading to a re-evaluation of the statistics that should be collected and analysed. Data on log-ins and occupancy of publicly available PCs in the library are as likely to be as necessary as monitoring of study place occupancy. Libraries need to keep records of enquiries that are received online as well as those handled at an enquiry desk. There may be data to be collected relating to new library services such as number of items in the institutional repository, the number of published articles and chapters scanned, or the number of digital images made available. Libraries also need to measure the availability and use of electronic as well as print resources.

---

4   http://www.lboro.ac.uk/departments/dils/lisu/.
5   http://www.rluk.ac.uk/.

What do the Users Think?

With traditional library statistics, we are looking at the effectiveness of the library in terms of its internal management. However, they do not guide us on what the users actually think of the services provided. For this, qualitative data are needed. Libraries have always sought ways to obtain user views, and library surveys have a long history. Some libraries have produced their own, others use or adapt existing templates (e.g. the SCONUL satisfaction survey template), though increasingly now academic libraries worldwide are using LibQUAL+[6] either annually or every few years. This has the advantage of making it easier to compare results over the years, and to do some benchmarking with other LibQUAL+ libraries, though the benchmarking of qualitative data is much more difficult. These difficulties stem partly from the growth of student expectations of universities and their libraries in the context of them paying higher fees and contributing more towards their education. In the rush to find out users' opinions, there is a danger now that students are subjected to too many surveys, and suffer from survey fatigue. This is leading to more thought being given to what the library will get out of the results of a survey. It is also leading to greater consideration of alternatives to surveys, especially questionnaire surveys, for obtaining the views of service users.

To achieve greater robustness from survey data, more thought is now going into the questions that are asked in any student library survey. Sykes (2009) questions the value of a survey which finds that 70% of students are satisfied or very satisfied, where we do not know what aspects of the service they are satisfied with, and what they regard as important. The LibQUAL+ survey, by asking whether a service is seen as important as well as how it is rated, enables the library to identify the aspects on which they should be focussing. The Customer Value Discovery methodology was used at Nottingham Trent University to see what services and resources customers valued and which were seen as irritants (McKnight and Berrington 2008). The findings led to a number of changes in service delivery and resulted in a marked improvement in student satisfaction survey results. Significantly, library staff have been key stakeholders in this approach and have been involved at every stage in the process. Henwood and Norton (2008) describe the use of Profile Accumulation Technique (PAT) and focus groups at the Wellcome Library to move survey questions away from 'How satisfied are you?' to 'Tell us what matters'.

Putting the customer at the heart of the library service has become increasingly important. Some university libraries in the UK have applied successfully for the Customer Service Excellence Award,[7] a Government-backed scheme in which university staff and students are interviewed to ensure that the library meets the required level of service in each of five areas (customer insight, culture of the organisation, information and access, delivery and timeliness and quality of

---

6   http://www.libqual.org.
7   http://www.cse.cabinetoffice.gov.uk/homeCSE.do.

service). Such awards demonstrate that the library has thought through its service to customers and provides the opportunity for some publicity within the institution itself, all part of the need for greater accountability and for demonstrating the success of the library.

Value and Impact

Statistics can be used to show the efficiency and effectiveness of the service and surveys can demonstrate student satisfaction, but attempts to show the actual value and impact are much more difficult. Output measures or outcomes are now seen as of increasing importance, much more so than the traditional input measures. This was recognised by the SCONUL/LIRG impact initiative, in which 22 university libraries took part. For this, participating libraries identified an area of the service that they wanted to assess, and using an action research methodology, identified the objectives they wanted to achieve and the measures they would use (Payne and Conyers 2005). The approach to impact assessment was developed by David Streatfield and Sharon Markless of Information Management Associates who acted as consultants to the project (Markless and Streatfield 2006; Markless and Streatfield 2008). Using a team approach and selecting practical projects, libraries taking part were introduced to an action research model of impact assessment which would help demonstrate their contribution in a tangible way. Many of the projects related to the use and impact of electronic resources. For example, Glasgow Caledonian University looked at the impact of making available electronic information resources and developing an information literacy strategy (Crawford 2006) and Bournemouth University investigated equality of access to e-resources (Beard et al. 2007). The initial intention of the SCONUL/LIRG impact initiative had been to seek to develop sector-wide impact measures that could be used widely between libraries. Differences in institutional contexts and priorities meant that this was not possible. However, the overall initiative highlighted the importance of seeking to demonstrate the library's contribution to core business processes of the institution especially learning, teaching, or research (Poll and Payne 2006). The focus here is upon looking at real changes in knowledge levels, behaviour, and attitudes. The initiative has also helped to identify methodologies for assessing a library's impact. A variety of different evaluation methods were used in the projects. This included not only traditional research tools such as questionnaire surveys, analysis of existing statistics, focus groups, user diaries, and participant observation, it also included pre- and post-testing of information skills competency levels, analysis of bibliographies to see what resources had been used, and review of students' progress files (Payne 2006).

Attempting to assess the value and impact of the whole service is even more challenging, especially if you want to put a monetary value on it. Return on investment (ROI) is a recognised business technique appropriate for business enterprises, but how can you show the value of the library in these terms? The

British Library study (2004) used a method called Contingent Valuation (CV) to assess its economic impact and from this concluded that for every £1 of public money received by the British Library, £4.40 was generated for the UK economy. A similar attempt to set a monetary value on the library service at the University of Illinois at Urbana-Champaign (Luther 2008) looked at research income in relation to library expenditure. Using the ROI model, this case study used citation and survey evidence to demonstrate that for every dollar invested in the library in 2006 there was a return of $4.38 in grant income.

In both instances, with interestingly similar results, there was a pressure to come up with a financial statement. Questions such as 'What return do we get from our investment in the library?' are increasingly likely to be asked by senior institutional managers in times of budget cuts and answers need to be found, if not in actual money terms at least in terms of value. While it is questionable how far ROI can be used to set a monetary value on the library service, this and similar techniques can certainly be applied in a different way.

Using 'stories' or case studies is one good way forward and one that makes use of the web to enliven such traditional publications as the library annual report. Brophy (2008) argues the need for innovative but robust new methods to measure emerging library services. These, he suggests, should be based upon the use of ethnography, externally moderated self-evaluation, and composing narratives to capture the essence of our achievements within their contexts. The British Library provides an example of the use of 'stories' from a user and from a member of staff to introduce the web version of its annual report[8]. This is also a method that is much in tune with the way universities themselves are marketing their courses.

Performance Measures

Some libraries have developed service level agreements which describe the services offered and identify the level of service that can be expected. They consequently help to put in context any performance measures. Instead of looking back afterwards, for example at what percentage of inter-library loan requests have been satisfied, the library staff will have discussed and agreed in advance what it is reasonable for users to expect, so they can judge their performance against this standard. Birkbeck, University of London is an example of a library that spells out the services provided to its schools in this way, lists performance levels, and indicates how these performance levels will be monitored. For example, one service standard relates to requests for scanned readings: when requests for digitised readings are submitted two to three months prior to the date required, the readings will be made available at least one week prior to the date required. This standard is then monitored through a check of the status of items on a daily basis. The service level agreement also includes a generic set of KPIs for the library

---

8   http://www.bl.uk/about/annual/2008to2009/index.html.

which covers a range of quantitative and qualitative measures.[9] These include average number of hours open per week (during termtime and vacation), loans per FTE student, downloads per FTE student, and the percentage of respondents to the library survey satisfied with both the Birkbeck Library and Birkbeck eLibrary.

The Balanced Scorecard (Kaplan and Norton 1992) extends the use of KPIs and takes the process a stage further, by identifying a set of aims before identifying the KPIs that can meet them. This process ties the library service more closely into the institution's own strategic aims. An example of the use of the balanced scorecard within an academic library can be seen on the University of Hull library website.[10]

Measuring the e-Environment

The measures described above illustrate how libraries are adapting to the changing environment and recognising the need for greater accountability. What is equally important is to find a way of measuring the use of e-resources that are now taking such a large part of the library budget and influencing so much the way users interact with the library. It is no good maintaining records of traditional library services without setting alongside them evidence of use of the digital library if we are to continue to justify the library's role. SCONUL, through its Working Group on Performance Improvement, keeps a watching brief on all the SCONUL questions and aims to keep pace with change while also maintaining the integrity of the database. The introduction of e-measures questions has been a particular challenge. A set of new questions was introduced in 2003–04 following a pilot project run by Evidence Base[11] at Birmingham City University with HEFCE funding. Over the past few years, the number of libraries completing the e-measures questions has grown from 80 in 2003–04 to 110 in 2007–08, but at the same time there has been a recognition that the changing environment means that some of the original questions and guidelines are no longer appropriate. A new set of questions is now being piloted with plans to introduce these in 2010–11. These will include questions on e-journals, databases and e-books, and on numbers, usage and expenditure on each so that a set of performance measures in respect of each category (e.g. cost per use) can be drawn up.

Compared with print resources, the amount of information available on use of e-resources is daunting. Whereas usage of print journals was extremely difficult to capture, use of e-journals can show number of successful article requests, number of turnaways, number of pdf and html views, number of pageviews and more. When the e-measures questions were first introduced by SCONUL there was little

---

9   http://www.bbk.ac.uk/lib/about/strategy/servicelevel.pdf.
10   http://www.hull.ac.uk/lib/using_our_libraries/performance/balanced_scorecard/index.html.
11   www.ebase.bcu.ac.uk.

consistency, and pilot members reported widely different results from different publishers and even from the same publisher at different times. COUNTER is to be congratulated for introducing consistency and reliability into this previously unregulated world.[12] An excellent example of co-operation between the library and publisher communities worldwide, COUNTER was set up in 2002 and has developed a set of usage measures for e-journals, databases and e-books. By December 2009, there were over 100 publishers/vendors who were COUNTER compliant for e-journals and databases and over 25 for e-books and reference works. The Journal Report one (JR1) giving number of successful full-text article requests has become a recognised standard, making counting of use of e-journals much easier and more reliable. The SCONUL annual library statistics for 2007/8 showed 110 million full-text article downloads, compared to 98 million books issued across the UK HE sector, even though only 110 libraries reported on e-journal use compared to 143 giving book issues, an illustration of the importance of collecting full statistics on e-resource use.

As noted above, not all publishers are yet COUNTER compliant, and for databases and e-books in particular there are still significant omissions. New challenges continue to face those trying to introduce order. UKSG's JISCmail list[13] and the lib-stats list run from Newcastle University[14] both testify to the number of practical problems faced by e-resource librarians and provide excellent fora for discussion among librarians and publishers on an international basis. Another issue is that open access journals are likely to become more widespread and ways will need to be found to measure their usage. The Pirus 2 project is looking at article level use for material in repositories[15]. Identifying which articles are being read rather than identifying journal use is likely to be a future expectation. For journals themselves, the Journal Usage Factor[16] now being developed by UKSG is designed to identify which journals are the most used, a statistic to consider alongside the impact factor (IF)[17] which measures the frequency with which articles within a particular journal have been cited within a given period.

Collecting and Analysing Usage Data

While COUNTER has improved the consistency of the usage data, the task of collecting it from each publisher's website is very time consuming. COUNTER's requirement for the adoption of the SUSHI protocol[18] for harvesting the data

12   www.projectcounter.org.
13   lis-e-resources@jiscmail.ac.uk.
14   lib-stats@newcastle.ac.uk.
15   http://www.cranfieldlibrary.cranfield.ac.uk/pirus2/tiki-index.php.
16   http://www.uksg.org/usagefactors.
17   http://thomsonreuters.com/products_services/science/free/essays/impact_factor/.
18   http://www.niso.org/workrooms/sushi.

is likely in the long run to make this process easier, and there are commercial products that also help, but it remains a lengthy process. Baker and Read (2008) in a survey of library directors in US research libraries conducted in 2005 found that the time spent on collecting and analysing ranged from one to over 2,000 hours a year, with a median of 98 hours, with four libraries spending 20–40 hours a week. Any look at the queries raised on the lib-stats and lis-e-resources mailing lists will tend to support this. What is equally significant is that the process of collecting the data left little time for analysing:

> Generally, more time was spent on the non-intellectual processes of gathering and preparing vendor-supplied usage data than on the analytical processes that lead to an understanding of an institution's use of its electronic resources. (Baker and Read 2008, p. 52)

The publisher deals project at Evidence Base has worked with libraries on ways to analyse the usage data and produce reports that can be presented to management (Conyers 2007). Developing from this work, plans for a JISC Usage Statistics Portal will provide a one stop shop for getting access to usage statistics and also provide help with their analysis. Initially for NESLi2 deals, it is hoped that this can later be extended to other e-resources. Just having the statistics is not enough. Libraries need to be aware of how e-resources are being used, and most importantly whether they offer good value for money. If a library does not have that evidence to hand when asked 'What value do we get from the library?', they are on rocky ground.

What we do not know from the usage statistics is anything about the users. We may surmise, and anecdotal evidence will surely back this up, that students are making far more use of journal articles now that they are so readily accessible, but evidence on users is hard to come by. Some have tried to match up publisher usage reports with Athens or Shibboleth records or EZ proxy servers. While these can provide useful information, for example on time of day or type of user, any attempt to match them up with publisher usage will be fraught with difficulties. Other libraries record use of e-resources through authentication via their library management systems. This potentially provides greater granularity in the analysis of data. However, the data are unlikely to be COUNTER compliant and may well measure page hits rather than downloads. Others that try to measure usage of e-resources with their own systems experience problems with being able to include accesses which are on-site as they are IP address authenticated rather than requiring separate log-in. Another approach is to monitor hits for gateway pages to their e-resources. However, users who bookmark pages, or access the resources through other routes, will not be included in the counts.

Libraries sometimes use web forms to try to obtain user data on e-resources. However, this risks irritating users unless it is for a short period. It is therefore recommended that a sampling approach to data collection through web forms is adopted. It is also important to be aware when trying to estimate the type of user that not all will come through the library catalogue or web pages. Users again may have bookmarked a particular journal, or may have come upon it via a search on Google or Google Scholar.

The CIBER group at UCL[19] have used deep log analysis in a study of the information seeking behaviour and use of journals and journal articles by UK academic researchers (Research Information Network 2009). This study has provided valuable insight into usage patterns in different subject areas, searching techniques and value for money which though focussed on the research community has implications also for learning and teaching, with student use of e-journals being estimated at around 20% of total:

> It has not been possible to distinguish between use by students and faculty from the publishers' logs on this occasion, but on the basis of published survey findings we believe that use by undergraduate and Masters' students accounts for around 20 percent of the total. (Research Information Network 2009, p. 46)

In a study for JISC Collections (2009) on the national e-books observatory project, CIBER again used a mix of deep log analysis, user surveys and focus groups to explore the use of selected course text e-books by students and produced some important findings on likely future trends in e-book use within a library context.

User surveys have been mentioned earlier, and it must be stressed that the web offers new opportunities to conduct and analyse surveys with minimum effort on the library's part. Though response rates to web surveys such as LibQUAL+ are in general lower than those where more effort has gone into getting in replies, they are still valued for their ease of use and ability to highlight particular issues and trends. They also tend to encourage a larger number of comments when open-ended questions are asked.

Where gate figures showing those entering the library are in some cases going down with more use being made of the virtual library, it would seem sensible to find a metric which parallels the efficiency of the gate counter and looks at use of the library web pages. Google web analytics[20] or other web analytics tools are useful means of learning where library website visitors are coming from and which pages they are using. Black (2009), for example, demonstrates how web analytics (or web metrics) can be used to look at user behaviour in relation to timing and duration of visits, how users arrive at the website, the technology that users have, and the most popular content.

In a study commissioned by the British Library and JISC to identify how researchers of the future would access and interact with digital resources, CIBER (2008) looked at the 'Google Generation' or those born after 1993 who had 'little or no recollection of life before the web' but concluded that people of all age groups

---

19   http://www.ucl.ac.uk/infostudies/research/ciber/.

20   http://www.google.com/intl/en_uk/analytics/.

are using the internet and Web 2.0 technology. In an age when we all expect to give our opinions on anything we have bought on Amazon and use the opinions and star ratings given by others when making our buying decisions, or look up a hotel review on TripAdvisor when booking a holiday, it can surely only be a question of time before library catalogues adopt this approach too. Huddersfield University Library[21] catalogue now offers images of book covers, star ratings and comments. Web 2.0 offers many such opportunities to involve users in library activities. Joint (2009) explores options for the use of Web 2.0 services based on experiences at the University of Strathclyde library and stresses the importance of adopting a Web 2.0 strategy:

> Without such an approach, the risk is that your library service will become a jaded and unappealing mausoleum to the web as it was in the mid-1990s – a sort of online Miss Havisham's tea-party that increasingly few users will want to be part of in future. (Joint 2009, p. 174)

While there may be differing opinions as to how libraries themselves should be engaging with social networking sites such as Facebook, MySpace and Twitter, it is certain that Web 2.0 offers opportunities for more interaction with library users that will become increasingly prominent in the future.

Challenges of Measurement in the Electronic Environment

There has always been scope for error in the measurement of library service provision. In the past, traditional library measures have experienced the problem of inconsistent data collection often through the lack of clear definitions or the failure to use systematic methodologies for collecting the data. Similarly, user studies have suffered from poor design, inappropriate methodologies, imprecise question wording, or issues of whether respondents are answering questions accurately. Over time, many of these issues have begun to be addressed as evaluation expertise within the library world has grown and there is a greater appreciation of why these issues are important.

The digital environment has raised new data collection challenges. If we are counting enquiries, how do we handle queries through chat services or database-driven 'Ask a Librarian' services? Even counting the number of electronic resources available can be problematic. In counting the number of e-journals or e-books which we make available, do we include them if they form part of a database? If we provide access routes to open access material, do we count those resources amongst those that we have made available? The blurring of boundaries between the library and other service areas also makes data collection and reporting increasingly difficult. Where a library is part of a converged service

---

21   http://webcat.hud.ac.uk/.

with IT services, or even said to be 'superconverged' with other support services, it can be difficult to disaggregate figures relating to use or costs. Where 'library' space is shared with other services, the turnstile counts will not be comparable with a library which is not converged. Similarly, a single library and IT help desk may well find it difficult to distinguish between 'library' and 'IT' enquiries.

There are also challenges in terms of matching measures to the potential audience. Libraries, especially in institutions where there is devolved budgeting, are increasingly being expected to drill down and provide data relating to Schools or Faculties. Schools or Faculties may well want to know about usage of the library by their students and staff. The picture could be seriously distorted without data on their use of e-resources. If a School or a Faculty is contributing to the cost, there may also be a requirement to show that a particular e-book, e-journal, or database is actually used by their students or staff. This information is generally hard to obtain at the level that is required or with the degree of robustness that is expected.

What to Do with the Results?

With such a plethora of evidence to choose from, and so many opportunities for error in the detail, it is perhaps no wonder that many librarians find that the actual task of collecting the evidence is all consuming. Yet, the question 'what are we doing it for?' must remain in the forefront. An individual library's evaluation needs will be influenced partially by the service requirements for assessing efficiency and cost-effectiveness. We increasingly need to know whether services can be delivered more cheaply, to justify the costs of services, and to have an appreciation of best value-for-money in relation to different alternatives. Most academic libraries will also want to put the needs of the customer at the centre of service provision and development. So, increasingly, forward-looking libraries are likely to want to obtain the views of users not just when new services have already been put in place but in their development too. This limits the risk in relation to the investment that is made in new services as they are rolled out. However, although measurement of cost-effectiveness and satisfaction are valuable to us in managing our libraries, there is increasing pressure on libraries to be able also to demonstrate their value and impact.

Having the evidence available is only part of the picture though. The evidence needs to be systematically analysed and reviewed, before being presented to stakeholders. Detailed spreadsheets are unlikely on their own to impress or to increase anyone's understanding of the value of the library. Whatever statistics have been collected, whatever survey results are available, working out how best to present the results is vital. Actual presentation will depend on the particular audience, whether it be external stakeholders, senior managers, heads of schools, library users, library managers or library colleagues. The amount of detail will vary, but all those receiving information should have confidence in its reliability.

In an age where students are seen as consumers, and the library is far more accountable for its performance and value, presentation of evidence of how the library is performing in the digital age is of vital importance.

References

Baker, G. and Read, E.J., 2008. Vendor-supplied usage data for electronic resources: a survey of academic libraries. *Learned Publishing*, 21 (1), 48–57.

Beard, J., Dale, P. and Hutchins, J., 2007. The impact of e-resources at Bournemouth University 2004/2006. *Performance Measurement and Metrics*, 8 (1), 7–17.

Black, E.L., 2009. Web analytics: a picture of the academic library web site user. *Journal of Web Librarianship*, 3 (1), 3–14.

British Library, 2004. *Measuring our Value: Results of an Independent Economic Impact Study Commissioned by the British Library to Measure the Library's Direct and Indirect Value to the British Economy*. Available from: http://www.bl.uk/pdf/measuring.pdf (accessed 4 June 2010).

British Library, 2009. *Annual Report and Accounts 2008/09*. Available from http://www.bl.uk/about/annual/2008to2009/index.html (accessed 4 June 2010).

Brophy, P., 2008. Telling the story: qualitative approaches to measuring the performance of emerging library services. *Performance Measurement and Metrics*, 9 (1), 7–17.

CIBER, 2008. *Information Behaviour of the Researcher of the Future: A Ciber Briefing Paper*. Available from: http://www.jisc.ac.uk/media/documents/programmes/reppres/gg_final_keynote_11012008.pdf (accessed 4 June 2010).

Conyers, A., 2004. E-measures: ready for the count? *SCONUL Focus*, 31, 53–6. Available from:www.sconul.ac.uk/publications/newsletter/31/18.rtf (accessed 4 June 2010).

Conyers, A., 2007. What do publishers' usage statistics tell us? The analyzing publisher deal project from evidence base, *SCONUL Focus*, 40, 72–5. Available from: http://www.sconul.ac.uk/publications/newsletter/40/25.pdf (accessed 4 June 2010).

Crawford, J., 2006. The use of electronic information services and information literacy. *Journal of Librarianship and Information Science*, 38 (1), 33–44.

Henwood, J. and Norton, F., 2008. From "how satisfied are you?" to "tell us what matters": User evaluation at the Wellcome Library. *SCONUL Focus*, 43, 64–5. Available from: http://www.sconul.ac.uk/publications/newsletter/43/17.pdf (accessed 4 June 2010).

JISC Collections, 2009. *JISC National e-Books Observatory Project: Key Findings and Recommendations*. Available from: http://www.jiscebooksproject.org/wp-content/JISC-e-books-observatory-final-report-Nov-09.pdf (accessed 4 June 2010).

Joint, N., 2009. The Web 2.0 challenge to libraries. *Library Review*, 58 (3), 167–75.

Kaplan, R. and Norton, D., 1992. The balanced scorecard: measures that drive performance. *Harvard Business Review*, 70 (1), 71–9.

Luther, J., 2008. *University Investment in the Library: What's the Return? A Case Study at the University of Illinois at Urbana-Champaign.* Elsevier Library Connect, white paper 1. Available from: http://libraryconnect.elsevier.com/whitepapers/lcwp0101.pdf (accessed 4 June 2010).

McKnight, S. and Berrington, M., 2008. Improving Customer Satisfaction: Changes as a Result of Customer Value Discovery. *Evidence Based Library and Information Practice*, 3 (1), 33–52. Available from: http://ejournals.library.ualberta.ca/index.php/EBLIP/article/viewDownloadInterstitial/920/1074 (accessed 4 June 2010).

Markless, S. and Streatfield, D., 2006. *Evaluating the Impact of your Library Service: The Quest for Evidence.* London: Facet.

Markless, S. and Streatfield, D., 2008. Supporting self-evaluation in assessing the impact of HE libraries. *Performance Measurement and Metrics*, 9 (1), 38–47.

Payne, P., 2006. The LIRG/SCONUL Impact Initiative: assessing the impact of HE libraries on learning, teaching, and research. *Library and Information Research*, 30 (96), 2–12. Pre-print available at: http://eprints.bbk.ac.uk/447/1/payne3.pdf (accessed 4 June 2010).

Payne, P. and Conyers, A., 2005. Measuring the impact of higher education libraries: the LIRG/SCONUL Impact Implementation Initiative. *Library and Information Research*, 29 (91), 3–9. Available from: http://www.lirg.org.uk/lir/ojs/index.php/lir/article/view/180/225 (accessed 4 June 2010).

Poll, R. and Payne, P., 2006. Impact measures for libraries and information services *Library Hi Tech*, 24 (4), 547–62.

Research Information Network, 2009. *E-journals: Their Use, Value and Impact: A Research Information Network Report.* Available from: http://www.rin.ac.uk/our-work/communicating-and-disseminating-research/e-journals-their-use-value-and-impact (accessed 4 June 2010).

Sykes, P., 2009. Using Survey and Usage Statistics to Improve Libraries. *SCONUL Focus*, 45, 94–9. Available from: http://www.sconul.ac.uk/publications/newsletter/45/27.pdf (accessed 4 June 2010).

Chapter 14

Library Resources: Procurement, Innovation and Exploitation in a Digital World

Emma Crowley and Chris Spencer

Introduction

In retrospect the procurement of library resources in the twentieth century was relatively straightforward. The majority of resources were only available in print format and acquired in perpetuity. Key library activities revolved around ensuring that appropriate resources were acquired in time, on budget and that a robust collection management policy was in place to ensure that shelf-space was available for new acquisitions.

Whilst similar activity related to print materials can be observed in libraries today, the complete scenario for the 21st-century librarian is very different. Prospects for cost savings and technological advancement together signal a relentless shift towards electronic resources and away from print (Spinella 2008). The wealth of digital content increasingly being made available in a variety of forms and under a range of business models provides great opportunities for libraries to grow and develop their collections in ways previously not possible.

However, there are so many digital resources available that librarians require tools to ensure that they are able to manage the procurement process effectively whilst ensuring that the end-user is able to enjoy the full potential of the digital world.

It is also important that digital resources are not considered in isolation and that the remaining print legacy that most libraries still hold is exploited in a complementary way.

This chapter highlights the ways in which librarians and the suppliers of digital content are developing systems and services to meet the expectations of the 21st-century library user.

The Digital Resources

Digital content falls into two main categories:

- Digitised – analogue content that has been digitised;
- Born digital – originated and disseminated in digital form.

Digital content may take many forms, ranging from the well established, e.g. databases, e-journals and e-books to the more specific, e.g. theses, geospatial datasets, image libraries and digital broadcast audio/video. The wealth of digital content available can be demonstrated by the content listed below, currently available in a single full text business database – EBSCO's Business Source Complete:

- financial data
- books
- monographs
- major reference works,
- conference proceedings
- case studies
- investment research reports
- industry reports
- market research reports
- country reports, company profiles,
- SWOT analyses
- faculty seminars (videos)

In addition to the mixed economy of procured systems, subscriptions and in perpetuity content, freely available open access resources also offer libraries an abundance of data to support the work of their scholarly community. Researchers can more efficiently locate and review content that spans centuries and that extends across disciplines (Spinella 2008).

The range of digital resources continues to grow, with local availability dictated by an institution's collection strategy. A survey by the Association of Learned and Professional Society Publishers (ALPSP) of academic journal publishers found that over 90% of journals are online compared to 75% in 2003 (Cox and Cox 2008).

At the same time, users' expectations are that library resources should be available digitally by default with the same convenience, simplicity and power demonstrated by Google.

Selection and Procurement Processes and Onward Collection Management

Selection

For many university libraries, the subject specialist librarians are at the heart of the selection process. Their subject knowledge and contacts within the faculty they support are invaluable in ensuring a balanced collection strategy, whilst often operating within financially constrained budgets.

Using selection tools developed for print resources, subject specialist librarians increasingly rely on online tools provided by the suppliers and developed to facilitate selection of both print and digital resources. An example is OASIS™, supplied by Coutts Information Services, enabling selectors to order print and e-books within a single session. Other book suppliers provide similar tools e.g. Blackwell's Collection Manager, and Dawson Books' enterBooks. Subscription agents are also developing their applications in a similar way to streamline the selection and procurement processes whilst supporting collection development decisions, e.g. EBSCONET and EBSCO ERM Essentials, and Swetswise Selection Support.

New title notification and approval plans have been available for some time for print books but suppliers also now provide plans for e-books. Other supplier/ vendor initiatives include: interactive digital catalogues such as the IOP Journals Catalogue to help navigate the content; pre-purchase review of e-book content; Coutts Information Service's 'See Inside the Book'; collaborative sharing of selection activity across authorised groups of colleagues or institutions; integration within book supplier databases of out-of-print search and order such as 'iFound' from Coutts Information Services, and print on demand functionality; Joint Information Systems Committee (JISC) Academic Database Assessment Tool (2009a), an application that compares the content and functionality of bibliographic and fulltext databases; EBSCO Overlap Analysis Report, enabling librarians to compare coverage overlap in library e-collections, and Ulrich's Serials Analysis System that supports collection development activity.

Resource selection initiates the procurement process, and as such the two processes are interlinked. The ideal scenario is for the entire process to be integrated within a single workflow. This would have significant benefits for workflow efficiency and has been achieved to some extent for books and e-books by Coutts Information Service through OASIS™. A case study by Spencer (2009) describes the integration process and highlights the benefits and efficiencies achieved. Coutts will build on this further with the introduction of OASIS™ Lite in 2010 that will support resource selection by faculty.

Popular in US libraries, with some interest now being shown in the UK, are Patron Selection Plans for e-books. The library catalogue is populated with e-book records, but the library only purchases those e-books that are accessed by the library user.

Examples of other patron selection initiatives in UK institutions include:

- Box of Broadcasts (BOB)[1] a service that enables users to record programmes broadcast on selected TV and radio channels. At Bournemouth University BOB replaced the Library's Off-air Recording Service, where programmes were recorded onto DVD on demand and added to library stock;
- Electronic Theses Online Service (EThOS)[2], a British Library service aimed at providing digital copies of UK PhD theses on demand. This replaces the role of the traditional inter library loan service for the supply of PhD theses.

Management information generated by Inter-Library Loan (ILL) activity is often used to influence selection decisions and in some libraries the ILL activity is an integral part of the procurement process with detailed formulae in place to influence the buy or loan decision process.

Procurement

As the amount and range of digital content increases, procurement processes and collection maintenance increase in complexity. At the same time, the 'always available' nature of digital content increases the expectations of the end-user, whilst management expectations are for procurement teams to manage more resources with fewer staff.

Digital content is complex and expensive and therefore it is important that librarians and suppliers develop services and systems that procure, deliver and fully exploit the available content in the most cost-effective way.

Libraries have found that their existing Library Management Systems (LMS) are incapable of fully supporting the procurement and exploitation of available digital content and are resorting to plugging the gaps with a combination of local solutions, bought-in third party software and subscription agents' applications.

---

1   http://www.bobnational.net.
2   http://ethos.bl.uk.

The Life Cycle of Digital Content

Whilst there are similarities between the procurement and ongoing management of traditional print and digital library resources, there are additional facets unique to the life cycle of digital content.

The procurement life cycle of digital content can be described as follows:

1. Discovery and notification: similar processes to print and may utilise print notification processes.
2. Product consideration and trial processes: arrange; record details and promote the trial to faculty; gather licence and pricing information; seek and record feedback on the value of the resource.
3. Procurement: three distinct processes – licence negotiation; technical feasibility (e.g. software/hardware requirements etc.); business processes (e.g. funding and purchase).
4. Implementation: register; authentication set up; configure (including link resolver, proxy server set up); catalogue and add to portals/web pages; promote.
5. Ongoing maintenance: update holdings lists; check access; troubleshoot; usage statistics.
6. Preservation and archiving: strategies and procedures for preservation of access; risk management.
7. Evaluation: user feedback; usage data; downtime analysis; renegotiate licence.

Life Cycle Management Tools

Electronic resource management systems (ERMS) developed to manage this life cycle have been available for a number of years following the work of the Digital Library Federation's Electronic Resource Management Initiative (DLF ERMI) as reported by Jewell (2004) which specifies the requirements for an ERMS.

Papers by Collins (2005 and 2008) have provided updates on the major suppliers of ERMS and include comments from librarians on the benefits, challenges and future requirements of ERMS. Subscription agents such as EBSCO Information Services and Swets, with their knowledge of the market place and access to their customers' core data that is required to populate an ERMS, have seen an opportunity for developing a product for their library customers.

Commercial ERMS can be costly and out of reach for some libraries, who look to develop in-house solutions. Doering and Chilton (2008) describe how the University of Wisconsin-La Crosse's Murphy Library used Microsoft Access to develop an effective, but inexpensive ERMS.

Consortia and Library Collaboration

Consortia negotiation for the provision of library resources is well documented (Ashmore and Grogg 2009; Carbone 2007; Pye and Ball 1999). The benefits that can be achieved in terms of cost, content and service provision are significant and can be achieved at regional, national and international levels. The recent Joint Consortium Book Agreement, a multi-consortial agreement across six UK higher education purchasing consortia that included e-book provision, demonstrates the value of collaboration.

However, there can be tensions with such agreements, at national-regional consortia levels. It is important to be able to strike an appropriate balance between the requirements of an individual institution with those of a consortium as a whole (Kinner and Crosetto 2009; Kidd 2009).

Kidd's 2009 study highlights collaboration in electronic resource provision in libraries within Scottish Higher Education, a pioneering approach for the UK – The Scottish Higher Education Digital Library (SHEDL). The pilot has demonstrated benefits for all participating institutions in terms of increased content availability, administrative and cost savings and, importantly, demonstrating a contribution to the Scottish Funding Council's shared services and collaboration agenda for Scottish universities.

Bibliographic, Citation and Full-text Databases

The range of databases available covering similar subjects and across different vendor platforms is considerable. With budget constraints common in many institutions it is increasingly important to ensure that best value is achieved in terms of content, functionality and cost.

However, evaluation is complex and time consuming. A Joint Information Systems Committee (JISC) study (Andrews et al. 2006) identified the need for an online comparison tool to help libraries make informed decisions during the selection process. As a result the JISC Academic Database Assessment Tool (ADAT[3]) was developed. In addition, database vendors are also offering similar services for example the EBSCO Overlap Analysis Report.

E-journals

Procurement of e-journals is well documented (Carr 2008) and well established, ranging from direct purchase, the use of subscription agents through to the use of regional and national consortia. NESLi2 is well established in the UK for negotiating the Big Deals with the larger publishers, and with its SMP Initiative (Small and Medium Sized Publishers) launched in 2008.

---

3   http://www.jisc-adat.com/adat/home.pl.

Whilst the Big Deals are a quick and easy way of securing access to a critical mass of e-journals, there continues to be concerns about the sustainability of such agreements in the current economic climate. As early as 2006 Ball (2006) identified the potential dangers of the Big Deal. Baker (2008) also recognised that the difficulties in attributing cost and usage with bulk deals often lead to top slicing of budgets and a reduction in control for librarians over collection development. A survey of librarians by Taylor-Roe (2009) highlighted that, although there was a continuing satisfaction with the Big Deals, there was also need for change.

With the development of digital newspaper services such as Press Display[4], libraries have the opportunity of providing digital access to a wide range of regional, national and international newspapers in full facsimile. In addition to benefits for the users this allows libraries to rationalise their print collections, saving space and associated staff time.

E-books

The e-book market is not yet mature, but e-books are increasingly becoming the tool of choice for researchers and students. Librarians welcome core collections by subscription but increasingly wish to buy specific titles in perpetuity to meet local requirements, particularly indicative reading lists.

The recent Joint Consortium Book Agreement 2009–13 includes an e-book element that will help member institutions purchase individual e-books in subject areas that match curriculum needs within budget requirements.

Sourcing e-books has been problematical in the past largely due to suppliers' unhelpful purchasing processes and the unavailability of desirable content, particularly textbooks. With publishers such as Springer now more confident that higher visibility of its academic e-book content has resulted in an overall increase in print sales and e-book usage, more titles are being made available (van der Velde and Ernst 2009). Recent developments by book suppliers in consolidating print and e-book data into a single database not only help with sourcing issues but also allow librarians to use existing efficient workflows to select and order print and e-books simultaneously.

Generally speaking, we see a growth in print book sales in countries where Springer has reached a high e-book penetration. Although proof is hard to find, Springer believes that the larger visibility of the academic content draws attention to its books, and results in increased print-purchases, as well as growing e-book usage.

Inter-Library Loans

The increase in digital content has contributed to the dramatic decline in Inter-Library Loans (ILL) for photocopies of articles. However, a white paper by the

---

4   http://pressdisplay.co.uk.

US Association of Research Libraries indicates an increase in book loans across its member libraries (Beaubien 2007).

Initiatives in place to improve workflow and service to remaining ILL customers include:

- Secure Electronic Delivery: a service developed by The British Library for the supply of digital copies with the emphasis on speed of supply direct to the researcher's desktop (British Library 2009);
- E-book loans: an initiative developed by Canada Institute for Scientific and Technical Information (CISTI) and MyiLibrary (Woods and Ireland 2008);
- Use of electronic signatures for copyright (Titley 2007);
- Electronic Theses Online Service – a British Library service aimed at providing digital copies of UK PhD theses on 'demand';
- ILL staff developing new skills to better serve their customers (Buchanan 2009).

Free Content

The challenge to deliver freely available open access resources using resources such as the Directory of Open Access Journals (DOAJ)[5] and the Directory of Open Access Repositories (OpenDOAR)[6] in a coherent way may sometimes be as great as for procured services, since the funding can be time limited or the resource host non-commercial and therefore often cannot finance expensive new technological developments. Since 1996 the JISC funded Intute and its predecessor the Resource Delivery Network, have provided an easy route for students and researchers to access web content, identified and peer-reviewed by a network of subject specialists (Patrick 2010). Beyond August 2010, with JISC subject to its own funding reduction, financial support of Intute services in its current form will cease and librarians will need to innovate alternative information literacy tools (JISC 2009b).

Other Digital Content

Hypothetically, any learning material may be digitised and therefore the range of digital content a library might hold is limitless. This could include content digitised locally, from entire archives to individual book chapters or journal articles. For example, many UK universities have signed one of the two Copyright Licensing Agency's (CLA) higher education licences, either the *Basic HE Licence* or the *Photocopying and Scanning HE Licence* that permit the scanning of extracts from printed publications published in the UK, US, Australia, Canada, France, Ireland,

---

5   http://www.doaj.org/.
6   http://www.opendoar.org/.

South Africa and Switzerland. The digitised content must support teaching and learning and be stored securely so that it can be accessed only by those students for whom it was specifically digitised.

Resource Exploitation

The wealth of digital content has provided new opportunities for developing innovative systems to discover and strategies to share scholarly literature (Spinella 2008).

Web Pages, Portals and Virtual Learning Environments (VLEs)

Where and how to host digital content and the tools with which to exploit that content has concerned librarians since the emergence of the web in the early 1990s. Although early library web pages tended to be fairly sterile and functional environments they provided the main access point to procured resources. Now for many academic libraries the humble web page is simply a communication tool for external visitors and a springboard to other more tailored interactive platforms such as institutional portals and VLEs for home staff and students. At Bournemouth University, for example, reading lists and scanned articles were integrated at unit level into myBU (the institutional VLE provided by Blackboard). This step supports the N Gen Learner (Beard et al. 2007), whilst a 'Library tab' delivers direct access to a federated search tool, virtual enquiry service, library catalogue, e-books, e-journals, academic skills community, subject-specific databases, blogs and communication channels.

Library Management Systems or Unified Resource Management?

Research conducted by JISC and the Society of College, National, and University Libraries (SCONUL) concluded that existing technologies used to manage library information resources are not compatible with Web 2.0 priorities (Owen 2008). Librarians have become disenchanted with a stagnant market where libraries retain an unsatisfactory LMS due mainly to the perceived cost of change. LMS suppliers have been challenged to develop a different technology model to support library development. Whilst efforts have been made by vendors to develop associated 'quick win' tools they are only available at additional cost and the base LMS remains virtually unchanged. The exception to this strategy has been OCLC, which is continuing to implement and develop a 'web-scale cooperative library management service' (OCLC 2009), that expands WorldCat Local's existing cataloging and discovery tools to include the circulation and acquisition functions that have conventionally been performed by locally installed LMS. Other commercial vendors are now trying to catch up, with ExLibris due to introduce a Unified Resource Management (URM) in mid-2011, which it hopes will provide an open extensible platform to support future and emerging library needs. Also in the UK, SCONUL have commissioned a feasibility study which will address what opportunities exist to develop a shared service response for a next generation open source LMS for UK higher education libraries (SCONUL 2009).

Library Catalogues

Traditional library catalogues are usually just one component of an integrated LMS, which is adequate to deal with print content, but is unable to effectively display digital materials. The popularity of Web 2.0 technologies and social networking has led to user perception that providing information is an interactive and collaborative activity (Lancaster 2007). Although library catalogue vendors have recognised this development they have been slow to implement similar functionality in their existing products, and would rather commit resources to other products which incur a further charge for the customer. In comparison with alternative web destinations, most library catalogues lag way behind the expectations of users in terms of search capability, usability, visual attractiveness and user engagement (Mercun and Žumer 2008).

Some libraries have incorporated Web 2.0 technologies such as social bookmarking (tag clouds), user reviews and RSS capabilities into their existing library catalogue to heighten usability, such as Napier University Library and Huddersfield University Library. It is important, however, not to overemphasise the importance of Web 2.0 enhancements to next generation library catalogues. In their study Tam et al. (2009) found that international students preferred library catalogue features that fundamentally save time, are easy to use and improve their search experience, e.g. faceted browsing, tag clouds, borrower suggestions and relevance ranking. Conversely participants were less impressed by RSS feeds, user ratings and reviews. User participation can be viewed as a social activity when contributing to external web services; however it is less certain that students would be similarly motivated to share their views on potential assignment resources in the more competitive academic environment or indeed be confident of the credibility of entries.

Search and Discovery Tools

Search and discovery tools or 'nextgen catalogues' such as SirsiDynix's Enterprise, Serials Solutions' Aquabrowser, and Innovative Interfaces' Encore provide a discovery layer or interface for traditional integrated library catalogues. Aquabrowser purports to have been the first of its kind in the library market, is interoperable with any major LMS and library catalogue systems, and allows users to 'Search Discover Refine' rather than using more traditional library search strategies. Searches are performed via a single keyword search box and in contrast to traditional library catalogues are visually represented via a colourful 'cloud' of discovery terms. Perhaps more helpfully results may also be quickly refined using a faceted search tool depending on user needs, in the same way as has been developed by commercial websites such as Amazon.

Innovative open source initiatives such as VuFind, Backlight and eXtensible benefit libraries by allowing a level of customisation not possible with most commercial products; for example relevancy ranking can be amended according to user or collection profile. However, it is important to consider that implementation involves staff and hardware costs as well as possible sustainability issues.

Since search and discover tools are, at present, merely more intuitive catalogue interfaces, institutions are either unable to or are unwilling to completely abandon their more traditional integrated library catalogues. Those who have implemented such products such as Harvard University, University of Edinburgh and University of Sussex, are perhaps offering both traditional and nextgen catalogues to satisfy the differing search needs of their patrons. However, the principal reason for persisting with the older interface, even in a minimalist way, is that the underlying traditional catalogue is still required to perform obligatory tasks such as reservations.

Federated Search Engines

The concept of searching multiple silos on the library's website is no longer acceptable to patrons in a Google-obsessed world (James et al. 2009). Providing a single-search-box that can quickly retrieve information from all library-supplied sources is substantially more desirable to students who may be suffering the effects of procrastination, information overload and under pressure to meet assignment deadlines (Medeiros 2009). Federated search engines such as MetaLib, WebFeat and 360 Search have been widely adopted by university libraries to search multiple databases, library catalogues, e-book platforms, e-journals, newspapers etc. at the same time.

In theory one single all-encompassing search facility should also be popular amongst librarians, due to the superior accessibility and predicted time saved in information literacy training. However, federated search tools are not without their problems. Results can be disappointing as they rely on how the data are supplied by individual commercial database providers, who appear to deliberately structure their search queries differently to gain competitive advantage. Furthermore search granularity is limited, indexing is inconsistent, duplication exists, speed can be poor, relevancy is sacrificed for number of hits and results are presented in contradictory ways: for example a reference where a keyword appears on page 24 may appear to have a higher rating than a reference where the same keyword appears in the title.

The WebFeat and 360 Search products have recently been combined into a 'more powerful' 'feature pack' 360 Search service[7] but it remains to be seen whether future Web Discovery products will ultimately replace federated searching, rather than being a requirement for their implementation.

---

7   http://www.serialssolutions.com/360-search.

Web Discovery Tools

Are web discovery tools the answer to student procrastination in the research process? Medeiros (2009) predicts that Serials Solutions' web-scale discovery service product, Summon, is likely to be more successful as a one-stop solution in retrieving information from a multiplicity of library supplied sources than federated search tools. As with its principal competitors, Ex Libris' Primo and EBSCO's Discovery Service, Summon harvests most of the content in advance from library catalogues, repositories, contracted providers, and by leveraging federated search, rather than connecting to them in response to user queries. The resulting searchable index makes the retrieval mechanism faster and capable of normalised relevancy ranking (Hadro 2009). Web Discovery Tools are also able to exploit OpenURL and Digital Object Identifiers where a content partnership does not exist. Results are displayed in a single integrated list which can be navigated using the ubiquitous faceted browsing present in all new search tools.

Some libraries are taking a proactive approach, designing and implementing their own tools to meet users' needs for search and data discovery (James et al. 2009). The HAM-TMC Library chose Vivísimo's Velocity 6.0, with a search engine, a federated search tool, and a clustering engine, to build a discovery tool.

Link Resolvers

For researchers wishing to utilise the full functionality of individual bibliographic databases an OpenURL link resolver, e.g. ExLibris' SFX, OCLC's WorldCat Link Manager, SwetsWise Linker, EBSCO LinkSource, is invaluable. Being able to link to all procured full text content from within other suppliers' databases or catalogues such as COPAC provides instant gratification, negating the need for searching separate catalogues or journal A–Z tools.

Where link resolvers fail to deliver is in the number of steps required to access content, the confusing way that data can be displayed, especially when there is a multiplicity of suppliers, and as with federated search engines their success is reliant on the connectivity and indexing of the source. Most frustrating for users is the frequent realisation of 'zero results', as the misconception of one hundred percent resource discovery seems to be heightened with this tool, whatever the magnitude of library budget.

Web 2.0 and Beyond

With the wider community adoption of social media and other Web 2.0 applications, librarians must embrace new technologies that assist users and promote libraries as being at the forefront of information retrieval (Webb and Nero 2009). In researching usage of Web 2.0 applications in university library web sites Harinarayana and Raju (2010) discovered that RSS feeds and Instant Messaging (IM) were most extensively utilised. RSS feeds are easy to implement and provide an excellent way of disseminating library product news, events and search updates to researchers, whilst IM allows librarians to provide immediate reference services. Many libraries are also utilising Facebook, the popular social networking site, to create applications and engage with students in their own environment. Whist universities are experiencing limited success with this approach, the British Library has attracted in excess of 10,000 fans.

Web 2.0 applications are so prevalent beyond the library community that they appear instinctively more attractive as enhancements for library web pages than semantic technologies (Burke 2009). Thomson Reuters have invested in semantic web technology with their Calais service – it can provide content-driven analytics, interactive data segmentation and search engine optimisation that is difficult to achieve with keyword-based searching. It is, however, hoped that Talis Platform's role in the high profile data.gov.uk project will inspire Talis to incorporate semantic web (or Web 3.0) features in its forthcoming library products.

Mobile Devices

Since mobile devices are more or less ubiquitous among library users it will become increasingly crucial to ensure that online resources such as e-book platforms, federated search tools, library catalogues and library web pages are compatible. Indeed Cummings et al. (2010) discovered that more than 58% of mobile device owning survey respondents at Washington State University specified that they would use their device to search the library catalogue.

Liston (2009) compared the performances of three nextgen catalogues (SirsiDynix's Enterprise, Innovative Interfaces' Encore and Serials Solution's Aquabrowser) using three smartphones (BlackBerry, Windows Mobile and iPhone), discovering for example that only the iPhone supported Aquabrowser. Personal experience supports Liston's findings, successfully using the alternative 'high accessibility version' of the Aquabrowser interface using a BlackBerry. However, although most interface functionality exists, title entries were absent. This demonstrates the need to apply pressure on vendors to provide support for a wider variety of devices. How smartphones and other Windows Mobile-compatible devices display content, enable micro-browsing and respond to accessibility guidance may ultimately decide the future success of competing library interfaces.

E-book readers such as Amazon's Kindle and Sony's Reader are the current 'must have' device of choice; to the extent that on the 25th December 2009 Amazon reached a new landmark when their e-book sales outstripped print sales for the first time and in the US Kindle was Amazon's best selling product during the Christmas period (Anon. 2009). The launch of Apple's iPad in April 2010 further propagated this market. Libraries and their vendors must therefore ensure they respond to this phenomenon. At the Texas A & M University Libraries the Kindle e-book lending program has been tremendously popular with readers, although patrons rarely selected scholarly titles, preferring to use e-books for social or general reading

(Clark 2009). With a more targeted academic development the VLE suppliers Blackboard have created a 'Building Block' for e-readers that will allow users to send course documents available on Blackboard to their Kindle.

Prominent academic book suppliers Ingram Digital have also introduced MyiLibrary Audio, which allows digital audio-books to be experienced via PC, Mac, iPod, iPhone and other MP3 devices. They intend that their library procured e-books will shortly be viewable in the same way.

Student Incentives

A popular strategy amongst some UK universities has been to make equipment such as laptops, PDAs, e-readers, and content available freely to new students as a way of marketing courses and encouraging student retention. In partnership with John Smith's Campus Bookshops, Anglia Ruskin University and the University of East London offer free and discounted books by way of a bursary scheme.

Researcher Tools

Research repositories are of paramount importance in ensuring that institutional research outputs, including e-theses, are available open access. These repositories can be integrated into internal web discovery and external metasearch tools to improve content and institutional visibility. A proliferation of free and paid-for web-based tools to aid researchers in collaborative activity continue to appear, including social networking services such as Academia.edu, ResearchGATE and ResearcherID. Guidance must be given to ensure that researchers comply with copyright and are utilising the services that provide the most valuable payback. Libraries also need to make their research management and collaboration tools such as EndNote, EndNote Web, Zotero and RefWorks easily available, and ensure that all search interfaces incorporate a straightforward citation export function.

Scanning

Since nearly 100% of all new information is purported to be generated and stored digitally, scanning could be regarded as merely a transient phenomenon (Mestl et al. 2009). Until the majority of content is no longer largely textual, however, the CLA's HE licences necessarily provide UK institutions with the opportunity to scan existing print materials where digital copy is unavailable or unaffordable. Beard and Dale (2008) highlight how, under the pilot version of the licence, Bournemouth University was able to scan book chapters and journal articles and make them available at unit level via the institution's VLE. Subsequently this allowed the short loan collection that was unpopular and rarely used by students to be phased out.

It is hoped that in the near future e-book publishers will overcome their reluctance to make chapter level content purchasable and that aggregators will develop the technology to allow embedding within VLEs or other forthcoming platforms.

UK Research Reserve

The UK Research Reserve (UKRR) is a distributed national research collection of high value, but low-demand journals, managed collaboratively by the British Library and 29 UK Higher Education libraries. This innovative project has allowed libraries to de-duplicate their journal holdings, whilst ensuring continued access to titles where archive digitisation is not commercially viable. UKRR hope that by 2013, a hundred kilometres of valuable shelf space will have been released to meet the changing needs of library researchers.

Communication Innovation

'How do you communicate information to your customers?' is a question that continually occupies librarians' thoughts. Simply adding content to a web listing, portal or VLE page is not sufficient, and patrons receive so much spam that emails are rarely read and tutorials only attended at point of need. Students in particular do not use resources unless they virtually leap from the page and shout 'Use me!'; therefore librarians have needed to embrace communication tools that meet customers in their own personal digital worlds.

Librarians are regularly blogging, 'tweeting' (micro-blogging) and creating profiles in social networking sites e.g. Facebook, to connect often quite informally with users about new acquisitions, resource developments, trials and emerging technologies. Some libraries are also beginning to use mobile technology to engage with their student population: for example Huddersfield University recently implemented delivery of a series of ten succinct 'library tips' to mobile phones of new students via SMS (text message). Typical messages contain advice and a link to a mobile device-friendly web page or online resource (Walsh 2009). Other libraries are utilising patrons' phones to facilitate audio tours and text messaging reference services (Buczynski 2008).

Informing Decisions: Making Use of Quantitative and Qualitative Data

Libraries have traditionally collected data from all areas of library activity to assist with performance metrics. With the growth of digital content there is an opportunity not only to build on library performance measurement but also to quantify more accurately library operations whilst supporting collection development and funding decisions.

Most vendors and publishers routinely supply libraries with a wide range of reports on the use of subscribed content. In addition, the increasing use of industry standard COUNTER-compliant reports gives libraries the opportunity to consistently compare data across resources and vendors.

Bucknell (2008) highlighted how COUNTER-compliant usage data and MS Excel can be utilised to aid a library's decision-making processes when reviewing the renewal of large e-journal collections.

Whilst the availability of COUNTER-compliant reports has created a more reliable basis for data analysis, it is still not entirely consistent, as evidenced by Baker and Read (2008) and it is important to understand how the data are collected and reported.

In addition, data collection is time consuming and there is a danger that more time could be spent on collecting the data than is actually spent analysing the findings. The Standardised Usage Statistics Harvesting Initiative (SUSHI) (NISO 2009) aims to simplify the collection process through automation and direct data transfer to a library's ERMS.

JISC Collections (2009) are investigating the development of a usage statistics portal to "help librarians make informed decisions about their collections through the provision of tools to aid analysis".

Combining quantitative data with the results of qualitative research can provide a powerful tool for analysing library services. Qualitative methods may incorporate feedback from individuals, focus groups and structured surveys or questionnaires such as LibQUAL+.

Fidel (2008) highlights the use of mixed methods research (MMR) as a mechanism for integrating qualitative and quantitative methods into a single study to improve its quality by the use of triangulation to verify accuracy.

Partnerships and Opportunities

Home Institution

Given frequently challenging budgetary conditions, a pragmatic view of procuring library resources is essential, as is liaising with both library and faculty colleagues within institutions. Compromise is often key to ensuring budget spend is optimised, particularly where they have been devolved to faculty and Big Deal products predominate. Librarians are also excellent collaborative partners, working together in teams to devise new ways to utilise existing systems, innovating novel functionality and evolving processes.

Young people frequently have a poor understanding of their own information needs (Rowlands et al. 2008), so it is vital that libraries carefully observe and frequently engage with their student and research communities. Product analysis, user needs surveys, targeted focus groups and feedback help to improve platforms, services and ultimately produce library advocates.

Partner Institutions

It is essential to liaise with faculty and partner institutions to ensure resources are available where licences permit, for example, where a degree validated by a university is being delivered at a college. Vigilant monitoring is required to make certain that network infrastructure, and local security settings, do not prevent users from accessing all the resources to which they are entitled. Marriott (2005) identifies students on NHS placements as being particularly vulnerable to problems with PC access, network access, software and firewalls. There is also often a training issue, where resource provision by more than one permissible provider gives access to different groups of tools and datasets, therefore causing confusion for the student.

Other Higher Education Institutions

As discussed previously, the influential role of library consortia in collectively negotiating beneficial deals is a prime example of the value of collaboration within the UK higher education community.

Another popular and valuable form of communication between higher education partners is through the use of long-established discussion groups. Via JISCmail, JISC hosts a number of dynamic procurement and digital resource related discussion groups. JISC-E-COLLECTIONS[8], for example, is a helpful open environment for information professionals to disseminate knowledge and share good practice in matters concerning negotiation, licensing, access management and agreements for digital content. The Chartered Institute of Library and Information Professionals (CILIP[9]) also provide training opportunities and forums to exchange information on digital developments. More sensitive issues such as current offers from journal publishers are communicated to the NESLi2 community via a closed discussion list (LIS-NESLI-REPS).

Discipline-linked library groups can also be powerful players in the procurement world, exerting considerable influence on traditionally non-academic suppliers. The Business Librarians Association (BLA), for example, has dealt directly with companies like Thomson Reuters, on behalf of the higher education library community, to broker favourable deals for products such as Thomson ONE Analytics. In contrast, whilst the British and Irish Association of Law Librarians (BIALL) are encouraged to provide feedback on the content and functionality of systems, commercial suppliers of legal information appear traditionally less inclined to negotiate broader deals for the academic market, preferring to contact institutions individually.

---

8   https://www.jiscmail.ac.uk/cgi-bin/webadmin?A0=JISC-E-COLLECTIONS.
9   http://www.cilip.org.uk.

The UK Serials Group (UKSG) has a slightly different focus in that its events, training, journal and open discussion list (LIS-E-RESOURCES[10]) provide forums for all parties involved with e-resources to discuss matters relating to e-resource provision. More broadly UKSG's mission is to connect librarians, publishers, intermediaries and technology vendors and encourage the exchange of ideas on scholarly communication. This group sits at the forefront of emerging library technologies.

Working with Vendors

Increasingly both libraries and their suppliers are benefiting from working together strategically to build enhanced systems and desirable collections (see Figure 14.1). This symbiotic relationship manifests itself most productively within the many company or product focussed advisory groups that have been formed by companies such as Coutts, EBSCO, Ingrams and LexisNexis®. These mutually beneficial forums allow librarians to share quality advice and feedback, face-to-face or via web conferencing software. Beta testing of new interfaces gives the vendor the opportunity to modify their platforms and introduce functionality that best serves the library community.

Challenges

Whilst the benefits of digital resources are self-evident, the challenges in ensuring their provision, discovery and use are complex. The exponential shift towards digital content requires library staff to adapt, take on new roles and acquire or develop new skills and expertise in areas such as licence negotiation, IT applications deployment, budget management and analysis, marketing and promotion and usage analysis and reporting.

Vendor Benefits	Library Benefits
• Beta testing of new interfaces	• Influence on functionality of new interfaces
• Quality feedback	
• Usability studies	• Influence on content
• Advice on content	• Introduction of cutting-edge systems
• Opportunity to integrate with internal library process	• Shared experiences with other colleagues from other institutions
• Advocacy	• Technical help from colleagues at other institutions
• Sales	

Figure 14.1   Benefits of vendor and libraries working together

---

10   https://www.jiscmail.ac.uk/cgi-bin/webadmin?A0=LIS-E-RESOURCES.

Negotiating contracts and licences for digital resources can be complex and time consuming. Organisations such as Eduserv, JISC and consortia have gone some way towards minimising the financial, consultation and legal burden by negotiating on behalf of the academic community and by introducing model licences. Eduserv estimated that their Chest agreements saved the UK academic community £28 million on the cost of software and data products in the period from January to September 2009 (Eduserv 2010).

Shared E-resources Understanding (SERU), a US initiative, is a document of understanding between libraries and publishers who have an established history of co-operating in a non-litigious manner. Published in 2008 by NISO, the document aims to minimise the effort and expense involved in licence negotiation.

Maintaining access and the preservation of digital content in perpetual usable formats are a primary concern both in terms of immediacy of access and availability of a future digital archive. As libraries subscribe to a large number of e-journals, maintaining access can be problematic. Because of staffing constraints, many libraries will adopt a fix upon failure approach to maintaining access. Collins and Murray (2009) describe a proactive strategy (SEESAU) to access verification implemented by the University of Georgia's library. Initiatives such as LOCKSS (Lots of Copies Keep Stuff Safe[11]); CLOCKSS (Controlled LOCKSS[12]) and more recently PeCAN (Pilot for Ensuring Continuity of Access via NESLi2[13]) aim to provide sustainable archives for the long-term preservation of scholarly publications.

Making users aware of the wide range of digital resources will continue to be a challenge, especially as users expect a "Google-like" experience. Lauridsen and Stone (2009) highlight the challenge and reflect on how librarians might cope.

Breeding (2009) stresses the need to maximise the impact of libraries' digital collections, especially rare, historic, or local material, to ensure relevance of libraries in the future. Libraries should aim to remain uniquely relevant by providing access to born-digital materials created by their own community e.g. research papers, conference presentations, theses, audio files, streamed lectures, blogs, wikis etc. Law (2009) highlighted this and other areas of strength and core activity that libraries should be exploiting. Breeding (2009) suggests using next-gen discovery tools and interfaces to improve the library's standing in the community it serves.

Publishers and suppliers are increasingly eager to collaborate with librarians to build and supply the content and systems that best meet library needs: however, there is a caveat; vendors' ultimate aim is to maximise profit which can conflict with library-driven innovation, the open-access movement, institutional roles and perpetually challenging budgetary environments. Some publishers, concerned about a possible decline in sales of textbooks to students, refuse to make library

---

11 http://www.lockss.org/lockss/Home.
12 http://www.clockss.org/clockss/Home.
13 http://development.jisc.ac.uk/whatwedo/programmes/infl1/pecan.aspx.

acquirable e-copies of their titles, whilst attempting to sell interactive course cartridges (for VLEs) directly to lecturers on the understanding that the book will be adopted as core reading. Alternatively an e-copy of a book or access to an associated teaching resource site may be purchasable by an individual, but not a library, causing discontentment for academics, librarians and students alike. In 2009 Elsevier also caused outrage when it was reported that they had been approaching university vice-chancellors directly about taking full text open access research repositories out of universities' hands (Corbyn 2009). A repository operated by a journal publisher could set access conditions that undermine the needs of researchers and make it hard to search the data.

Periods of economic recession add significantly to the challenges already highlighted, as does the continuing tax aberration whereby e-content procured by libraries incurs VAT, although print does not. A report by JISC (2009c) documents the impacts that a recession might have on libraries, ranging from budgetary cuts through to difficulty in retaining and recruiting staff.

Conclusions

In the former print-only world, the expectations of users and librarians were lower; paradoxically now that content is proliferating rapidly, patrons expect everything to be free of charge and to be immediately and easily accessible. It should, therefore, be both the librarian's and vendor's aim to create systems that provide total integration and a seamless experience for a diversity of users.

Librarians and customers still need to engage with a multiplicity of digital and print formats. Libraries are currently spending the majority of their under-pressure budgets on e-content, but most library environments remain hybrid, due to higher costs of some digital materials, small society print titles, publisher entrenchment over textbooks, and legacy print.

Working collaboratively there are opportunities for libraries and vendors, perhaps using artificial intelligence, semantic web and cloud technology, to evolve the discovery and analysis capabilities of future search tools (Mestl 2009). The key challenge in the digital world is keeping pace with shifting internet sociologies, technologies and 'choosing the winners'.

References

Andrews, N., Monday, J. and Williams, A., 2006. *A Study Evaluating Bibliographic and Citation Databases in Use in the UK Higher Education Community*. London.

Anon, 2009. *Amazon Reports Higher Sales of e-Books than Physical Books on Christmas Day*. Bath: Best Books (M2).

Ashmore, B. and Grogg, J.E., 2009. The art of the deal. *Searcher*, 17 (1), 18–25.

Baker, D., 2008. 'Inside every fat man': Balancing the digital library budget. *Interlending and Document Supply*, 36 (4), 213–17.

Baker, G. and Read, E.J., 2008. Vendor-supplied usage data for electronic resources: A survey of academic libraries. *Learned Publishing*, 21 (1), 48–57.

Ball, D., 2006. Signing away our freedom: The implications of electronic resource licences. *Acquisitions Librarian*, 18 (35/36), 7–20.

Beard, J., Cheshir, K. and Davey, A. 2007. *Supporting the N Gen Learner by Integrating e-Resources within a University VLE.* Paper presented at the Supporting the Net Generation Learner: Proceedings of the Second International Blended Learning Conference, 17 June 2007, University of Hertfordshire, Hatfield, UK.

Beard, J. and Dale, P., 2008. Redesigning services for the net-gen and beyond; a holistic review of pedagogy, resource, and learning space. *New Review of Academic Librarianship*, 14, 99–114.

Beaubien, A.K., 2007. *ARL White Paper on Interlibrary Loan.* Washington DC: Association of Research Libraries.

Breeding, M., 2009. Maximizing the impact of digital collections. *Computers in Libraries*, 29 (4), 32–4.

British Library, 2009. *Secure Electronic Delivery.* Available from: http://www.bl.uk/sed (accessed 9th October 2009).

Buchanan, S., 2009. Interlibrary loan is the new reference: Reducing barriers, providing access and refining services. *Interlending and Document Supply*, 37 (4), 168–170.

Bucknell, T., 2008. Usage statistics for big deals: Supporting library decision-making. *Learned Publishing*, 3, 193–9.

Buczynski, J.A., 2008. Libraries begin to engage their menacing mobile phone hordes without shhhhh! *Internet Reference Services Quarterly*, 13 (2/3), 261–9.

Burke, M., 2009. The semantic web and the digital library. *Aslib Proceedings*, 61 (3), 316–22.

Carbone, P., 2007. Consortium negotiations with publishers – past and future. *Liber Quarterly: The Journal of European Research Libraries*, 17 (1–4), 98–106.

Carr, P.L., 2009. From innovation to transformation: A review of the 2006–7 serials literature. *Library Resources and Technical Services*, 53 (1), 3–14.

Clark, D.T., 2009. Lending Kindle e-book readers: First results from the Texas A & M University project. *Collection Building*, 28 (4), 146–49.

Collins, M., 2005. Electronic resource management systems: Understanding the players and how to make the right choice for your library. *Serials Review*, 31 (2), 125–40.

Collins, M., 2008. Electronic resource management systems (ERMs) review. *Serials Review*, 34 (4), 267–99.

Collins, M. and Murray, W. T., 2009. SEESAU: University of Georgia's electronic journal verification system. *Serials Review*, 35 (2), 80–87.

Corbyn, Z., 2009. Publisher 'threat' to open access. *Times Higher Education*, 18 June 2009.

Cox, J. and Cox, L., 2008. *Academic Journal Publishers' Policies and Practices in Online Publishing*. Clapham.

Cummings, J. Merrill, A. and Borrelli, S., 2010. The use of handheld mobile devices: Their impact and implications for library services. *Library Hi Tech*, 28 (1), 22–40.

Doering, W. and Chilton, G., 2008. A locally created ERM: How and why we did it. *Computers in Libraries*, 28 (8), 6–48.

Eduserv, 2010. *What are Chest Agreements?* Available from: http://www.eduserv. org.uk/licence-negotiation/about (accessed 15 March 2010).

Fidel, R., 2008. Are we there yet? Mixed methods research in library and information science. *Library and Information Science Research*, 30 (4), 265–72.

Hadro, J., 2009. Summon aims at one-box discovery. *Library Journal*, 134 (3), 17–18.

Harinarayana, N.S. and Raju, N.V., 2010. Web 2.0 features in university library web sites. *Electronic Library*, 28 (1), 69–88.

James, D., Garrett, M. and Krevit, L., 2009. Discovering discovery tools evaluating vendors and implementing Web 2.0 environments. *Library Hi Tech*, 27 (2), 268–76.

Jewell, T. D., 2004. *Electronic Resource Management: Report of the DLF Initiative*. Washington, DC.

JISC, 2009a. JISC Academic Database Assessment Tool (ADAT). Available from: http://www.jisc-adat.com/adat/home.pl (accessed 16 November 2009).

JISC, 2009b. JISC reviews its Intute service. Available from: http://www.jisc. ac.uk/news/stories/2009/12/intute.aspx (accessed 31 March 2010).

JISC, 2009c. Impact of the economic recession on university libraries and it services. Available from: http://www.jisc.ac.uk/publications/documents/ libsitimpacts.aspx (accessed 1 December 2009).

JISC Collections, 2009. Usage statistics portal – demonstrator built. Available from: http://www.jisc-collections.ac.uk/news_and_events/newsletter.aspx?ke ywords=usage+portal (accessed 5 November 200).

Kidd, T., 2009. Collaboration in electronic resource provision in university libraries: SHEDL, a Scottish case study. *New Review of Academic Librarianship*, 15 (1), 97–119.

Kinner, L. and Crosetto, A., 2009. Balancing act for the future: How the academic library engages in collection development at the local and consortial levels. *Journal of Library Administration*, 49 (4), 419–37.

Lancaster, N., 2007. Information futures: The library as cockpit. *Managing Information*, 14 (5), 42–5.

Lauridsen, H. and Stone, G., 2009. The 21st-century library: A whole new ball game. *Serials*, 22 (2), 141–5.

Law, D., 2009. Academic digital libraries of the future: An environment scan. *New Review of Academic Librarianship*, 15 (1), 53–67.

Liston, S., 2009. OPACs and the mobile revolution. *Computers in Libraries*, 29 (5), 6–47.

Marriott, R., 2005. Access to learning resources for students on placement in the UK: What are the issues and how can we resolve them? *Health Information and Libraries Journal*, 22 (4), 262–6.

Medeiros, N., 2009. Researching the research process: Information-seeking behavior, summon, and Google books. *OCLC Systems and Services*, 25 (3), 153–5.

Mercun, T. and Žumer, M., 2008. New generation of catalogues for the new generation of users: A comparison of six library catalogues. *Program: Electronic Library and Information Systems*, 42 (3), 243–61.

Mestl, T., Cerrato, O., Ølnes, J., Myrseth, P. and Gustavsen, I.-M., 2009. Time challenges – challenging times for future information search. *D-Lib Magazine*, 15 (5/6).

NISO, 2008. *SERU: A Shared Electronic Electronic Resource Understanding.* Available from http://www.niso.org/workrooms/seru (accessed 15 July 2010)

NISO, 2009. *Standardised usage statistics harvesting initiative.* Available from: http://www.niso.org/workrooms/sushi/ (accessed 5 November 200)].

OCLC, 2009. *OCLC Announces Strategy to Move Library Management Services to Web Scale.* Available from: http://www.oclc.org/news/releases/200927.htm (accessed 1 March 2010).

Owen, T.B., 2008. Preparing the ground for library 2.0. *Library and Information Update*, 7 (11), 22-22.

Patrick, M., 2010. Disentangling the web: A guide to online resources for theology. *Expository Times*, 121 (5), 213–17.

Pye, J. and Ball, D., 1999. *Library Purchasing Consortia Benefits in the UK: Activity, Benefits and Good Practice.* Bruton.

Rowlands, I., Nicholas, D., Williams, P., Huntington, P., Fieldhouse, M., Gunter, B., Withey, R., Jamali, H.R., Dobrowoiski, T. and Tenopir, C., 2008. The Google Generation: The information behaviour of the researcher of the future. *Aslib Proceedings*, 60 (4), 290–310.

SCONUL, 2009. Consultants appointed for major study of library systems. Available from: http://www.sconul.ac.uk/news/lms_apr09 (accessed 29 March 2010).

Spencer, C., 2009. Improving procurement workflow. *Panlibus Magazine* (14), 1.

Spinella, M., 2008. JSTOR and the changing digital landscape. *Interlending and Document Supply*, 36 (2), 79–85.

Tam, W., Cox, A.M. and Bussey, A., 2009. Student user preferences for features of next-generation OPACs: A case study of University of Sheffield international students. *Program: Electronic Library and Information Systems*, 43 (4), 349–74.

Taylor-Roe, J., 2009. 'To every thing there is a season': Reflections on the sustainability of the 'big deal' in the current economic climate. *Serials*, 22 (2), 113–21.

Titley, G., 2007. Electronic signatures for copyright in the UK: A solution to the "Holy Grail" of document delivery. *Interlending and Document Supply*, 35 (1), 6.

van der Velde, W. and Ernst, O., 2009. The future of ebooks? Will print disappear? An end-user perspective. *Library Hi Tech*, 27 (4), 570–83.

Walsh, A., 2009. They all have them – why not use them? Introducing mobile learning at the University of Huddersfield Library. *SCONUL Focus*, 47, 27–8.

Webb, P.L. and Nero, M.D., 2009. OPACs in the clouds. *Computers in Libraries*, 29 (9), 18–22.

Woods, B. and Ireland, M., 2008. eBook loans: An e-twist on a classic interlending service. *Interlending and Document Supply*, 36 (2), 105–15.

Chapter 15

Continuing Professional Development and Workplace Learning

Sheila Corrall

Introduction

A commitment to continuing professional development (CPD) is one of the defining characteristics of being a member of a profession, rather than having an occupation or doing a job. Professional bodies have always stressed its importance, but have recently placed more emphasis on formally recording and validating CPD activities. The pace of change in the digital environment has made continual updating of knowledge and skills even more important. In addition, political, economic, social and technological developments have influenced changes in professional work, which has generally become more specialised. However, professional work has also become less differentiated along other dimensions, as a result of overlaps among different levels of jobs and between previously distinct specialist groups, requiring renewed effort to define the core competencies of librarianship. New micro-specialties or niche sub-specialties have also emerged within areas that were already specialised, such as subject librarianship and systems librarianship. This chapter reviews developments in CPD in relation to university library practice and (like Chapter 4) highlights particularly the impact of technology on content and delivery.

Current Drivers of Continuing Professional Development

Numerous professional associations and special interest groups in the library sector have produced formal statements of the knowledge, skills and understanding that practitioners are expected to display in their work, which typically also highlight the responsibility of individuals to maintain and develop their competencies, illustrated here by the preamble to the Medical Library Association's (2007, p. 4) policy statement:

> MLA believes that lifelong learning must be a cornerstone of every individual's professional development plan to achieve success in the health sciences environment and that individuals must assume greater personal responsibility for defining their ongoing learning goals, increasing their competencies, and improving their professional performance.

Many professional bodies in different fields now also require their members to provide formal evidence of their CPD to retain their qualifications. Within the library sector, the Chartered Institute of Library and Information Professionals (CILIP) currently offers a voluntary Revalidation Scheme enabling members to demonstrate their commitment to CPD formally on a three-year cycle, by submitting a portfolio of evidence including a CV, a CPD log and a personal statement providing a critical evaluation and reflection of the learning outcomes from training and development since their previous submission (CILIP 2004). CILIP's recent commitment to replacing revalidation with the phased introduction of a mandatory CPD scheme provides further evidence of the necessity for library and information professionals constantly to refresh their knowledge and skills in a volatile digital world (Broady-Preston 2009).

Specialisation is another significant driver of CPD. New professionals often work in roles requiring broadly-based expertise at the start of their careers and then need or want to specialise in a particular field as they identify job opportunities and/or recognise personal interests that they are keen to pursue. In addition, there has been a general trend for professional work to become more specialised, driven on the one hand by the growing complexity of the operational environment and on the other hand by non-specialists undertaking tasks previously seen as the work of professionally-qualified practitioners (Cheetham and Chivers 2005; Corrall and Cox 2008; Watkins et al. 1992). In university libraries, this is exemplified both in the shift towards online searching by end-users and in the redistribution of responsibilities between professional, paraprofessional and other library staff, which in turn has drawn attention to the training and professional development needs of library assistants (Corrall 2004; Webb 2004).

Traditional work boundaries have become blurred not only within professions, but also between professions and other specialist groups, giving rise to labels such as 'hybrid' and 'blended' librarian (as noted in chapter 4), with the result that new specialties have emerged requiring practitioners to develop skills, knowledge and understanding drawn from more than one domain in a trend that has become more common in the digital world. Examples in university libraries include growth of new specialties in the area of library technologies and information systems, such as digital library specialists and institutional repository managers, who need to combine library/information and information technology/media expertise; academic liaison librarians and information literacy educators are a more extreme case of hybrid or blended professionals, requiring information-related, subject-based, pedagogical and technological know-how to fulfil their roles effectively in subject-specific digital learning environments (Bell and Shank, 2007; Corrall and Cox 2008).

Professional organisations have recognised this need for greater breadth and depth in their formal definitions of the competencies that librarians are expected to possess and enhance throughout their careers. The American Library Association's Core Competences of Librarianship includes a whole section devoted to 'technological knowledge and skills' and the following points related to pedagogical understanding (ALA 2009, p. 4):

- The role of the library in the lifelong learning of patrons, including an understanding of lifelong learning in the provision of quality service and the use of lifelong learning in the promotion of library services.
- Learning theories, instructional methods, and achievement measures; and their application in libraries and other information agencies.
- The principles related to the teaching and learning of concepts, processes and skills used in seeking, evaluating, and using recorded knowledge and information.

The ALA (2009) statement is intended only to provide 'a general foundation' for professional practice and the ALA website[1] refers practitioners to other more specialised knowledge and competencies statements developed by relevant professional organisations. A notable example here is the Medical Library Association's (2007) competencies statement, which again specifies competence in both information technology/systems and curricular design/instruction, in addition to information resources and services, scientific research methods, managerial areas and the specific subject context for health information work. Another highly-specialised example is the ALA Association of College and Research Libraries Standards for Proficiencies for Instruction Librarians and Coordinators, which defines 41 core proficiencies in 12 categories for instruction librarians and an additional 28 proficiencies for coordinators, illustrating the level of expertise now reckoned as 'needed to be excellent teachers' (ACRL 2008, p. 2).

---

1   http://www.ala.org/ala/educationcareers/careers/corecomp/corecompspecial/ knowledgecompetencies.cfm.

Multiple Routes to Continuing Professional Development

CPD can be experienced in many different ways, both on the job and away from the workplace. The term Continuing Professional Education (CPE) or 'professional continuing education' is also used, notably in the US, for both formal award-bearing programmes and short courses (Lynn et al. 2010). There are overlaps between initial and continuing professional education programmes: some academic programmes are intended as 'professional preparation' programmes for new entrants to the profession, while others are designed specifically as professional development or enhancement for experienced practitioners wanting to upgrade their qualifications and/or develop their expertise in new specialisms (e.g. the part-time distance learning MSc in Health Informatics at Sheffield), but many programmes can be used for either purpose; for example, the MSc in Electronic and Digital Library Management at Sheffield attracts both recent graduates seeking careers in a dynamic specialist field and experienced professionals wanting a deeper understanding of the digital environments that characterise the contemporary library landscape.

In addition, schools and departments of information and library studies often promote individual modules or clusters of modules from their standard education programmes as standalone or packaged offerings, either on a traditional model of weekly sessions or as intensive blocks of teaching and learning over one or more days, enabling practitioners to take modules on topics not covered in their previous education or subjects that have changed significantly or emerged in the interim. Some information schools also offer short courses on more advanced or specialised topics related to their research interests as open programmes or bespoke provision tailored to the needs of particular institutions or professional communities; for example, the Centre for Information Literacy Research at Sheffield has provided workshops on information literacy strategy development for university and college libraries as part of our ongoing work on the application of strategy tools to information literacy activities (Corrall 2008; Corrall and Sen 2010).

The importance of work-based or workplace learning for staff development is evidenced by the formation in 2003 of a new section of the International Federation of Library Associations (IFLA) specifically to focus on Continuing Professional Development and Workplace Learning (CPDWL). LIS schools are experiencing growing demand for part-time professional education from people who want to combine learning with a full-time job and can see the benefits of being able to relate theory to practice in a more direct way than can be done when studying full-time away from the workplace. Traditional weekly day-release attendance and distance education via e-learning are both popular modes. Educational institutions are also experimenting with different, often innovative, models; for example, a new two-year part-time Foundation Degree in Library and Information Practice is being delivered in four one-week residential sessions per year, with the rest of the programme being taught online through blogs, interactive learning and social networking. The course has been deliberately designed as 'work-based and

Table 15.1   Continuing professional development activities

External activities	Internal activities
• Committees and meetings	• Task forces and working groups
• Multi-institutional/cross-sectoral projects	• Cross-departmental/multi-professional projects
• Establishing new formal partnerships	• Negotiating new internal collaborations
• Professional networks/special interest groups (in-person and virtual)	• Knowledge exchange with colleagues (e.g. events, best practice websites)
• Formal education programmes (including online learning)	• Mentoring schemes and coaching programmes
• Summer schools/immersion programmes	• Action learning/learning by doing
• Training courses	• Training hours and in-house courses
• Conferences and seminars	• Trial and error, problem-solving
• Benchmarking clubs	• Testing new products and services
• Study visits	• Work shadowing
• Job exchange	• Job rotation
• Preparing and presenting talks for professional meetings	• Preparing and delivering training for library staff
• Preparing and teaching courses for library professionals	• Conducting service evaluations and in-house research projects
• Peer support groups	• Reading professional literature
• Writing for publication	• Learning logs and reflective journals

grounded in practice, with the firm belief that you learn better by doing' (Glyndwr University 2009). Practitioners at all levels from library assistants to senior managers are increasingly recognising the value of work-related learning that takes place on or around the job, from both economic and educational viewpoints.

Larsen (2006) provides a list of different methods of CPD, which she splits into external and internal activities. Table 15.1 adapts and expands her examples to show the variety of options and how CPD can be incorporated in the operational tasks of university libraries without necessarily requiring substantial funding, although several of the external activities listed may incur significant costs. Some of the examples (e.g. mentoring programmes and training courses) can be undertaken as either internal or external activities, but are listed only once to avoid duplication.

Technological Impacts on Work and Learning

The impact of the digital environment on CPD activities can be seen here in some of the methods included, such as online/e-learning, professional networking experienced through virtual environments and websites for knowledge exchange. Technology-related developments have also set the agenda for CPD through their impact on all areas of university library practice, notably in relation to collection development and information resource management, information literacy education and liaison activities, where the skills, knowledge and understanding needed by library staff have expanded significantly. The technology-related skillset not only extends across an expanded range of library-specific and other related systems (e.g. electronic resource management systems, repository software and virtual learning environments), but arguably must also include familiarity with the discipline-specific and generic tools used by researchers, teachers and students. Social media competencies have emerged as a hot topic in this context (as noted in Chapter 2). Murphy and Moulaison (2009, p. 328) explain the multi-faceted skillset needed:

> Librarians need a new branch of skill sets specific to utilizing and leveraging social networking sites to provide quality services and maintain their role as information experts in a Web 2.0 world … These include skills for interacting with patrons within the sites, understanding and articulating the nature of social networking sites and their potential roles related to library services, creating presences and content, evaluating and applying information, and having the ability to assist patrons with gaining and applying these skills.

Many academic librarians have adopted a learning-by-doing method to learn about Web 2.0/Library 2.0 technologies, thus applying the classic action learning philosophy to a digital learning environment. Gross and Leslie (2008) provide a good example of learning-by-doing in their account of implementing and evaluating a successful Learning 2.0 '23 things' programme in an Australian academic library; Appleton (2009) describes a large-scale implementation of Learning 2.0 in the UK, which involved 140 learning and information services staff working in groups via a virtual learning environment (Blackboard); and Wilson (2008) describes how academic librarians can incorporate the use of Web 2.0 tools, such as podcasts, RSS and Twitter, into their daily routines to keep up with technology developments. Academic librarians are also using Web 2.0 tools for CPD related to other areas of practice, engaging virtually in external activities without incurring the costs of travel: for example, by attending talks on professional interests and communicating with people already practising in the area through Second Life, which can be more engaging than simply reading an article, while also stimulating participants to explore topics further through reading (Jennings 2009). Similarly, they have used virtual learning environments to deliver training on topics not directly related to technology: Forrest (2007) describes the delivery of a self-paced five-part module to raise awareness of disability issues among university library staff, which demonstrated increased understanding and attracted favourable comment.

However, conventional methods of CPD are still popular, as shown by the extensive programmes of short courses offered by CILIP and other professional organisations. A recent US survey of practitioner opinions of different modes of CPD revealed face-to-face instruction as the most preferred (and frequently experienced) option, with blended learning ranked second (but least frequently experienced), followed by asynchronous and synchronous web-based learning and finally webcasts. Many respondents commented positively on web-based synchronous instruction, citing access to instructors and interactions with other learners as benefits. They also liked the idea of webcasts and asynchronous instruction, but reported that the former often failed to engage their interest and the latter tended to be pushed aside by daily work. Cost was stated as the key factor influencing their CPD choices, followed by immediate access to instructors (Lynn et al. 2010). Libraries can reduce cost by combining external and internal education activities, for example Beaubien et al. (2009) describe how a university library educated liaison librarians in scholarly communication by sending a small group to a regional institute prior to organising a series of discussion sessions within the institution.

Summer schools and other intensive courses are now well established in the sector and continue to attract applicants: for example, the International Summer School run by Tilburg University since 1996, which has a digital library focus and attracted more than 1,000 individuals over a ten-year period, some of whom have attended more than once (Prinsen 2007) and the Immersion Program offered annually by the Association of College and Research Libraries since 1999, which now offers four different one-week tracks intended to give teaching librarians 'the intellectual tools and practical techniques to help your institution build or enhance its instruction program' (ACRL 2010a). The expansion of this programme shows how teaching ability is no longer regarded as an add-on for subject/liaison librarians, but recognised as a core competence, as information literacy efforts have gained momentum. A UK survey of subject librarians found the majority had attended short courses on teaching, almost one third had taken an extended programme and nearly a fifth had gained a formal qualification in teaching (Bewick and Corrall 2010). Whatley (2009, p. 30–31) confirms the need for continual updating of pedagogical abilities to perform effectively in digital learning environments, as she outlines how technology has affected her role as a liaison librarian and her professional development needs:

> I now need robust continuing education to enhance the effectiveness of my teaching and expose me to smart instructional design techniques. I need to hone my skills in developing achievable learning outcomes and in assessing those outcomes, and I need to understand what I can accomplish using online tutorials, podcasts, and research guides and what I cannot.

Summer schools have had a crucial role in relation to special collections, which are attracting renewed interest and usage as a result of digital library developments and have been identified by trend watchers as a likely future focus for the profession (Jefcoate 2007; ACRL 2010b). Lynch (2009, p. 4) argues that:

special collections are a nexus where technology and content are meeting to advance scholarship in extraordinary new ways ... Information technology is reshaping both stewardship and use of these collections.

Schreyer (2004) reports that few US schools offer comprehensive coverage in their programmes – although archives education is better – but many practitioners participate in the range of one-week introductory and advanced courses provided by the Rare Book School at Charlottesville[2], hosted by the University of Virginia. The London Rare Books School[3] is the UK version of the Charlottesville programme, offered similarly as a series of one-week courses in the summer by the University of London as UK educational provision is similarly limited, though national initiatives in archives and developments in digital libraries are influencing curriculum developments; for example, Sheffield now offers electives on Archives and Records Management and on Digital Multimedia Libraries as part of the MA Librarianship.

Mentoring and Reflection as Professional Meta-competencies

A significant trend over the last ten years is the growing recognition within the library profession of the benefits of mentoring relationships, the importance of critical reflection and the value of reflective writing to professional development. In the UK, mentoring and reflective practice have both been actively promoted by CILIP through their incorporation as essential features of its framework of qualifications. Candidates for all qualifications – from Certification for paraprofessionals, through Chartership for new professionals to Revalidation and Fellowship for experienced practitioners – must submit a personal reflective statement as a required element in the portfolio of evidence that forms the basis for the award. The CILIP guide to *Building Your Portfolio* (Watson 2008) includes practical guidance on reflective writing and sample extracts from personal statements of successful candidates. CILIP also provides supporting courses on portfolio building through its Career Development Group. Mentoring is a compulsory requirement for all Chartership candidates, strongly advised for Certification candidates and also available to applicants for Revalidation and Fellowship (CILIP 2006).

Professional organisations in other countries have also recognised the role of mentoring and reflection in professional development by featuring these practices in their competency statements (Abels et al. 2003; ACRL 2008; ALIA 2005; MLA 2007). In addition, mentoring relationships and reflective journals are common features of the library leadership institutes that have become a global phenomenon over the past 20 years (Mason and Wetherbee 2004). Mentoring and reflection can

---

2   http://www.rarebookschool.org/.
3   http://ies.sas.ac.uk/cmps/events/courses/LRBS/index.htm.

both be classed as 'meta-competencies'. Cheetham and Chivers (2005, p. 109) define a meta-competency as 'a competency that is beyond other competencies, and which enables an individual to monitor and/or develop other competencies' and actually give reflection the status of a 'super-meta-competency', because of its potential to help people step beyond their other competencies and then analyse, modify and develop them. Many commentators have observed wider benefits from reflection beyond the personal and professional development of the individual as it can also lead to improvements in work practices and service delivery and thus contribute to quality enhancement and organisation development (Forrest 2008; Sen 2010).

Forrest (2008) describes the different purposes and types of reflection that are relevant to practitioners who need to evaluate their own personal performance and the overall service performance of their library (for example, to build a portfolio for a professional qualification or more immediately to improve the quality of a teaching session). She provides several models and examples as guidance, noting that people often find reflection hard, but that the process (and specifically the physical act) of writing can help people to progress their thinking, deepen their understanding and eventually improve their practice. Reflection can also often form an integral part of other staff and educational development initiatives, such as peer observation of teaching, as shown by Brewerton's (2004, p. 36) informative account of the triad process used at Oxford Brookes University Library; one of the specific objectives of the scheme was 'to encourage all Subject Librarians/ Assistant Subject Librarians to reflect on the effectiveness of their own teaching sessions and identify their developmental needs'. Cipkin and Stacey's (2009, p. 31) comparative analysis of the skills, development and evaluation needs of liaison librarians operating at entry level and middle management also confirms the value of reflective practice at different career stages:

> Although we operate at different levels within the organisation, we conclude that success depends, in large part, on reflective practice and recognition that subject liaison skills also interface with a host of other generic skills, including managerial and technological abilities.

Recognition of the central role of reflection in professional practice has led to its formal introduction into higher education, notably for students on vocational courses to prepare them for reflective practice in the workplace. Sen (2010) describes how students on the MA Librarianship programme at Sheffield are helped to develop skills in reflective writing through lectures, readings, workshops and an assessed task that involves an online journal where they reflect on their own development as a manager throughout a two-semester module on Management for Library and Information Services. Students have found this assignment particularly valuable in preparing them for the demands of the CILIP Chartership process. Library and information educators have also introduced mentoring into their practice in collaboration with practitioners. Hallam and

Newton-Smith (2006) describe two examples of 'transitional mentoring' initiated with the Australian Library and Information Association to ease the transition from professional education to the workplace: an individual mentoring scheme that begins during the final semester of the education programme and a group scheme to support students in their first year of employment. Other contemporary examples of library mentoring include programmes designed to support diversity within the profession and in-house leadership development initiatives (Moore et al. 2008; Murray 2007).

Power (2006) offers additional insights into the theory and reality of reflective workplace learning in an academic library, concluding with practical advice on the use of tools such as learning logs, learning plans, learning lines and portfolios to organise and record learning. Joint's (2003) discussion of writing for publication explains in practical terms how the process of reflecting and writing can be taken to a next stage of publishing in a professional or academic journal, offering the potential to enhance practice at a deeper and broader level by sharing personal or institutional insights and contributing to the professional knowledge base. In this context, the development of new open-access peer-reviewed journals, such as the US-based *Communications in Information Literacy* and UK-based *Journal of Information Litera*cy, which have practitioners involved as editors or members of editorial boards, demonstrates the present high level of engagement of information literacy practitioners in CPD.

Leadership Institutes and Organisational Development Programmes

Leadership development has been flagged as a priority for the library profession since the 1980s. Within the UK, it featured prominently in the Fielden report on human resource management in academic libraries, whose recommendations argued that

> programmes on leadership and associated issues are required for those middle or senior managers in LIS who have major staff management responsibilities, and aspire to head of service positions (John Fielden Consultancy 1993, s. 4.41).

Ten years later, when converged library and computing services had become common in the UK, the HIMSS report similarly identified leadership among the key skills gaps and unmet development needs for aspiring service heads (Abbott 2003). The same concerns have been reported in other countries, notably Canada, where the '8 Rs report' identified leadership potential as the most important and most elusive competency for academic libraries recruiting professional staff and also argued that 'Leadership … is a competency that should be held by staff throughout the organization' (8 Rs Research Team 2005, p. 19). Leadership in the present environment is even more challenging with the need to operate and influence across traditional boundaries as library and information organisations continue to expand and collaborate with an array of diverse partners, including academic writing centres, careers services, educational development teams, multimedia production units, study skills tutors and university presses.

A common response to the perceived leadership problem is the 'leadership institute', a particular form of development programme that generally combines an intensive, multi-day residential element with a challenging practical assignment, diagnostic and reflective exercises, peer networking and coaching or mentoring. Mason and Wetherbee (2004) identify more than 30 programmes of this type launched over the last 20 years, mainly in the mid to late 1990s and predominantly in North America. Continuing demand is indicated by Arnold et al.'s (2008) survey of 230 participants in leadership institutes, which lists websites for 30 examples across the globe. Such institutes can be cross-sectoral or sector-specific, with several well-known examples in the academic library field, notably the ACRL/Harvard Leadership Institute (ALHI) and the Frye Leadership Institute, which is aimed at both library and IT professionals (Gjelten and Fishel 2006). UK initiatives in this area also date back to the 1990s, when the former British Library Research and Development Department sponsored an experimental cross-sectoral strategic management development programme that eventually led to a programme for the higher education sector managed by the Society of College, National and University Libraries (SCONUL) with other partners (Noon 1997).

The latest example in the UK is the Future Leaders programme for academic information services, run by the Leadership Foundation for Higher Education, with support from SCONUL and the Universities and Colleges Information Systems Association (UCISA), which is 'based on the assumption that excellent leadership cannot be taught but can be learned' (Stevenson 2006, p. 19). Cox et al. (2006) identify other distinctive characteristics of the Future Leaders programme, for example:

- year-long format, including two residential modules and three meetings of learning sets, culminating with a capstone day to share and review achievements and learning;
- emphasis on self-awareness and ongoing reflection, including a regular supply of stimulating readings and strong encouragement to maintain a reflective journal;
- pre-course interaction at an individual level with facilitators, including interview, analysis of Myers-Briggs Type Indicator data and presentation of 360-degree feedback report;
- execution of a self-selected project, aligned with institutional priorities, regularly reported and supported at learning sets during the year;
- availability of ongoing supports, including VLE forum and resources list, teleconferences and access to programme facilitators and participants.
- highly supportive network of contacts with similar aspirations and challenges, cemented by sharing of experiences and the atmosphere of openness, honesty and trust.

Key features of contemporary library leadership programmes thus include the use of technology-supported learning to supplement face-to-face interactions. As an alternative to externally-provided programmes, some academic libraries have opted to develop and implement their own in-house leadership development programmes, a notable example being the University of Saskatchewan Library in Canada. Williamson's (2009) case study describes how her programme was deliberately not designed as an intensive immersion programme, but instead structured into six shorter (two-day) off-site modules, each covering a particular theme: leadership and relationship building; team building; leading change; performance planning and accountability; leadership and organisational culture; and personal mastery and organisational effectiveness. Williamson (2009, p. 623–4) explains that this less intensive model:

> is intended to help reduce the resource impacts on the participants, provide time in between modules to reflect upon, practise and implement what has been learned and to provide time to complete reading or practical leadership assignments.

Murray (2007) also recognises the need for individual libraries to take responsibility for leadership development, specifically in relation to succession planning. Advocating a strategy of 'grow your own', she suggests various tactics (including leadership institutes and project-based assignments), but places particular emphasis on internal systems and processes to support development, describing the use of formal mentoring and personal development plans at the University of Cambridge.

Although leadership institutes are evidently well established and well liked within the sector, such programmes have been criticised for their short-term nature and failure to cover in sufficient breadth and depth the knowledge, understanding and skills needed to lead change in complex digital environments. Hernon and Schwartz (2006) argue for a more cohesive and comprehensive approach, represented by the new PhD in Managerial Leadership for the Information Professions initiated by Simmons College in Boston[4]. Developed with a grant from the Institute of Museum and Library Services under its 2005 Librarians for the 21st Century programme, the Simmons PhD combines doctoral-level study with leadership development in a distinctive and novel way. It differs from leadership institutes in its strong research focus, much longer duration (enabling fuller exploration of leadership theories and their application) and the recognised academic qualification awarded on completion. It also differs from a standard PhD in library and information science in its concentration on managerial leadership, emphasis on contribution to the theory of organisational behaviour and management and the involvement of leaders in the profession as 'professors of practice' working alongside Simmons faculty members.

---

4   http://www.simmons.edu/gslis/academics/programs/phd-mlip.php.

Practitioner Doctorates for Advanced Professional Development

Doctoral degrees have not traditionally been a popular CPD strategy for practising librarians. Powell et al.'s (2002) survey of ALA, ASIST, MLA and SLA membership involvement in research found only 21 of their 615 respondents had a doctorate in library and information science. However, Johnson (2009) argues that more LIS Masters graduates will wish to progress to the next rung on the qualification ladder as the status of both Bachelors and Masters degrees declines following the massive global expansion of higher education. Anecdotal evidence supports this claim, particularly in relation to academic librarians, with a trend towards research-based career development already evident among practitioners in North America, where deans of university libraries often prefer candidates for senior positions to have a doctorate or be willing to obtain one. Academic status is an acknowledged issue for academic librarians that affects their credibility with the academic staff that they aspire to partner in the teaching and learning process. Growth in postgraduate research student intakes, particularly from overseas, has resulted in many subject/liaison librarians spending more time supporting research students and led some to conclude that they would be better equipped for this role if they had personal experience of research at a higher level than the typical Masters dissertation project.

The trend of LIS practitioners studying for higher degrees reflects a more general trend among professional disciplines as practitioners in all domains are faced with continually expanding knowledge bases and the need for enhanced skills in data handling and analysis to support evidence-based practice in the workplace. There is a widespread view that traditional PhD programmes do not adequately prepare people for senior positions in the professions, hence the need for new forms of degree programmes that combine doctoral-level research with practice-based learning (Wormell 2004). New models of research degree have emerged to meet the needs of practitioners seeking advanced professional development, the most significant being the 'professional doctorate' (also known as a 'practitioner' or 'practice-based' doctorate), which is typically a highly-structured subject-specific degree of shorter duration than the traditional PhD with the name of the profession in the title, for example Doctor of Education (EdD) or Doctor of Business Administration (DBA). The first EdD was awarded at Harvard University in 1921, but professional doctorates did not appear in Australia and the UK until the 1990s; Bourner et al. (2001) record the University of Bristol's EdD as the first British example in 1992, but report rapid growth thereafter, with 109 programmes identified at 38 institutions by 1998.

Specialist doctoral degrees have now been introduced in many subjects. A notable example is the structured, part-time Doctoral Programme in E-Research and Technology Enhanced Learning at Lancaster University[5] introduced in 2008, which combines two four-day residentials with online learning and normally takes

---

5   http://csalt.lancs.ac.uk/csalt/tel_docprog.htm.

four years to complete, involving six taught modules and a thesis of around 50,000 words. Within LIS, Wormell (2004, p. 117) outlines plans for a professional doctorate at the Swedish School of Library and Information Science, arguing that the new degree will:

> fit the needs of libraries, business and industry for research oriented, but broadly educated senior managers and technologists, who – with a doctoral training – can perform more effectively in their working environment.

The model includes half-day workshops on Saturdays, combining taught elements and reflective sessions run as action learning sets, supplemented by a virtual research community. The thesis here consists of a portfolio (c.50,000 words) with a prescribed structure based on three studies of issues within the candidate's organisation (written as journal articles and refereed externally), supported by a context-setting introduction, a literature review, a concluding chapter and appendices including a reflective report (5,000 words) and three case studies (2,000 words each).

In the US, in addition to the Simmons College initiative, Syracuse University[6] has established a Doctorate of Professional Studies in Information Management, described as 'a part-time executive degree program for working professionals' and as 'a scientist-practitioner degree, focused on training future leaders in applied areas of the information professions'. This is a three-year programme aiming to prepare practitioners with at least five years experience for 'senior leadership jobs in business, government, libraries, and elsewhere'. Highlighted features include the flexible online, hybrid, limited-residency format; the applied focus, with customisable areas of study; and a strong peer support network. The thesis project again is on a smaller scale than the standard doctoral project: it is expected to be completed in a single year and to have the format, tone and style of a publishable trade book. In the UK, Robert Gordon University[7] introduced a Professional Doctorate in Information Science (DInfSc) in 2010 as a practice-based alternative to the traditional PhD for practitioners with a minimum of three years managerial experience in information or knowledge management, which can be taken part-time or full-time, on campus or online, but requires a thesis closer to the standard PhD length (c.80,000 words). In addition, the Information School at Sheffield[8] will shortly offer a four-year taught doctorate similar to the Lancaster model and the successful EdD offered by the School of Education at Sheffield.

Professional doctorates conform to the same academic standards as a traditional PhD, but have additional features likely to appeal to university librarians, namely:

---

6   http://ischool.syr.edu/academics/doctoralprograms/DPS.

7   http://www.rgu.ac.uk/information-communication-and-media/study-options/postgraduate-research/professional-doctorate-in-information-science.

8   http://www.shef.ac.uk/is/research/phd_mphil/index.html.

- a focus on work-related issues, working on real problems/projects
- rapid application of learning and research within the workplace
- generation of publishable work as part of the submitted thesis (e.g. journal articles)
- participation in action learning sets and support from a peer network/online community.

In addition, as a form of in-service (rather than pre-service) professional development, they differ from the traditional doctorate in the period typically set for completion, which is shorter than the pro rata six years usually suggested for a part-time PhD, reflecting the experiential learning already gained by specialist practitioners and managers. The modular structure with its larger taught element and division of submitted work into smaller publishable outputs make this an attractive and manageable option for busy professionals who are committed to evidence-based practice and keen to raise their game academically. There are similarities with leadership programmes, but the practitioner doctorate offers a more sustained period of reflective personal development.

Conclusion

CPD is one of the distinguishing characteristics of a professional practitioner, which is particularly important in the context of continuing rapid technology-driven change in university libraries. Staff development is a shared responsibility of individuals and employers that is being pursued through numerous diverse routes, from conventional external courses and summer schools on special interests to managed learning in the workplace using virtual environments and innovative work-based education programmes. Reflection and mentoring are more widely practised as a result of their incorporation in professional qualification schemes and leadership programmes. The preparation of future leaders remains a global concern for the profession that is being addressed by university libraries collectively and individually with in-house initiatives being introduced alongside established leadership institutes. Practice-based taught doctoral degrees are emerging as a promising new method of advanced professional development, illustrating the growing professional recognition of the need to see education, research and development as a continuum informing, enhancing and advancing university library practice.

References

8 Rs Research Team, 2005. *The Future of Human Resources in Canadian Libraries*, Edmonton: University of Alberta. Available from: http://www.ls.ualberta.ca/8rs/8RsFutureofHRLibraries.pdf. (accessed 12 July 2010).

Abbott, C., 2003. HIMSS (Hybrid Information Management: Skills for Senior Staff): Final Project Report, Birmingham: University of Birmingham. Available from: http://www.himss.bham.ac.uk/Documents/final/ProjReportfinal.pdf (accessed 12 July 2010).

Abels, E., Jones, R., Latham, J., Magnoni, D. and Marshall, J.G., 2003. *Competencies for Information Professionals of the 21st Century*, rev. ed., Alexandria, VA: Special Libraries Association. Available from: http://www.sla.org/PDFs/Competencies2003_revised.pdf (accessed 12 July 2010).

ACRL, 2008. *Standards for Proficiencies for Instruction Librarians and Coordinators*, Chicago, IL: American Library Association, Association of College and Research Libraries. Available from: http://www.ala.org/ala/mgrps/divs/acrl/standards/profstandards.pdf (accessed 12 July 2010).

ACRL, 2010a. *Immersion Program*, Chicago, IL: American Library Association, Association of College and Research Libraries, Institute for Information Literacy Available from: http://www.pla.org/ala/mgrps/divs/acrl/issues/infolit/professactivity/iil/immersion/programs.cfm (accessed 12 July 2010).

ACRL, 2010b. 2010 top trends in academic libraries: a review of the current literature, *College and Research Libraries News*, 71 (6), 286–92.

ALA, 2009. *Core Competences of Librarianship.* Available from http://www.ala.org/ala/educationcareers/careers/corecomp/index.cfm (accessed 15 July 2010).

ALIA, 2005. *The Library and Information Sector: Core Knowledge, Skills and Attributes*, rev. ed., Canberra: Australian Library and Information Association Available from: http://www.alia.org.au/policies/core.knowledge.html (accessed 12 July 2010).

Appleton, L., 2009. Learning 2.0 @ LJMU: a staff development programme for learning and information services staff, *SCONUL Focus*, 46, 59–63. Available from: http://www.sconul.ac.uk/publications/newsletter/46/15.pdf (accessed 12 July 2010).

Arnold, J., Nickel, L.T. and Williams, L., 2008. Creating the next generation of library leaders, *New Library World*, 109 (9/10), 444–56.

Beaubien, S., Masselink, L. and Tyron, J., 2009. Recasting the role of comprehensive university libraries: starting points for educating librarians on the issues of scholarly communication and institutional repositories, *Push the Edge: Explore, Engage, Extend: ACRL Fourteenth National Conference, March 12–15, 2009, Seattle, Washington*, pp. 95–109. Chicago, IL: American Library Association, Association of College and Research Libraries. Available from: http://www.freedomtoread.org/ala/mgrps/divs/acrl/events/national/seattle/papers/95.pdf (accessed 12 July 2010).

Bell, S.J. and Shank, J.D., 2007. *Academic Librarianship by Design: A Blended Librarian's Guide to the Tools and Techniques*, Chicago, IL: American Library Association.

Bewick, L. and Corrall, S., 2010. Developing librarians as teachers: a study of their pedagogical knowledge, *Journal of Librarianship and Information Science*, 42 (2), 97–110.

Bourner, T., Bowden, R. and Laing, S., 2001. Professional doctorates in England, *Studies in Higher Education*, 26 (1), 65–83.

Brewerton, A., 2004. How I joined the Triads: the launch of a peer observation and review scheme at Oxford Brookes University Library, *SCONUL Focus*, 31, 35–44. Available from: http://www.sconul.ac.uk/publications/newsletter/31/13.pdf (accessed 12 July 2010).

Broady-Preston, J., 2009. Professional education, development and training in a Web 2.0 environment: a case study of the UK, *New Library World*, 110 (5/6), 265–79.

Cheetham, G. and Chivers, G., 2005. *Professions, Competence and Informal Learning*, Cheltenham: Edward Elgar.

CILIP, 2004. *Revalidation Scheme Handbook*. London: Chartered Institute of Library and Information Professionals. Available from: http://www.cilip.org.uk/jobs-careers/qualifications/cilip-qualifications/revalidation/pages/default.aspx (accessed 12 July 2010).

CILIP, 2006. *Mentor Scheme Guidelines*, London: Chartered Institute of Library and Information Professionals. Available from: http://www.cilip.org.uk/filedownloadslibrary/mentorschemeguidelines080806.pdf (accessed 12 July 2010).

Cipkin, C. and Stacey, D., 2009. Reflecting roles: being a successful subject liaison librarian in a changing environment, *SCONUL Focus*, 45, 27–31. Available from: http://www.sconul.ac.uk/publications/newsletter/45/8.pdf (accessed 12 July 2010).

Corrall, S., 2004. Rethinking professional competence for the networked environment, *In:* Oldroyd, M., ed. *Developing Academic Library Staff for Future Success*, London: Facet. 15–99.

Corrall, S., 2008. Information literacy strategy development in higher education: an exploratory study, *International Journal of Information Management*, 28 (1), 26–37.

Corrall, S. and Cox, A., 2008. Capturing the hybrid ground, *Library and Information Update*, 7 (7–8), 42–4.

Corrall, S. and Sen, B., 2010. *Learning to Plan and Planning to Learn: An Action Learning Approach to Information Literacy Strategy*, 6th Librarians' Information Literacy Annual Conference, 29-31 March 2010, Limerick, Ireland. Available from: http://www.lilacconference.com/dw/programme/Presentations/Tuesday/Henihan_Suite/Corrall-Sen-longpaper-Planning.pdf.(accessed 12 July 2010).

Cox, J. Kilner, A. and Young, D., 2006. Taking steps that make you feel dizzy: personal reflections on module 1 of the Future Leaders programme, *SCONUL Focus*, 38, 26–29. Available from: http://www.sconul.ac.uk/publications/newsletter/38/7.pdf (accessed 12 July 2010).

Forrest, M.E.S., 2007. Disability awareness training for library staff: evaluating an online module, *Library Review*, 56 (8), 707–15.

Forrest, M.E.S., 2008. On becoming a critically reflective practitioner, *Health Information and Libraries Journal*, 25 (3), 229–32.

Gjelten, D. and Fishel, T., 2006. Developing leaders and transforming libraries: leadership institutes for librarians, *College and Research Libraries News*, 67 (7), 409–12. Available from: http://crln.acrl.org/content/67/7/409.full.pdf+html (accessed 12 July 2010).

Glyndwr University, 2009. *New Foundation Degree in Library and Information Practice at Glyndwr University.* Press release, available from: http://www.glyndwr.ac.uk/en/Contactus/PressOffice/Pressreleases2009/NewfoundationdegreeinLibraryandInformationPractice/ (accessed 12 July 2010).

Gross, J. and Leslie, L., 2008. Twenty-three steps to learning Web 2.0 technologies in an academic library, *The Electronic Library*, 26 (6), 790–802.

Hallam, G. and Newton-Smith, C., 2006. Evaluation of transitional mentoring for new library and information professionals: what are the professional and personal outcomes for the participants? *Library Management*, 27 (3), 154–67.

Hernon, P. and Schwartz, C., 2006. Leadership: a unique focus, *Journal of Academic Librarianship*, 32 (1), 1–2.

Jefcoate, G., 2007. European research libraries and special collections, *Liber Quarterly*, 17 (2). Available from: http://liber.library.uu.nl/publish/articles/000198/article.pdf (accessed 12 July 2010).

Jennings, L., 2009. Virtual CPD: professional development at a distance, *Impact*, 12 (1), 7-9.

John Fielden Consultancy, 1993. *Supporting Expansion: A Report on Human Resource Management in Academic Libraries, for the Joint Funding Councils' Libraries Review Group,* Bristol: Higher Education Funding Council for England. Available from: http://www.hefce.ac.uk/pubs/hefce/1994/m3_93.htm (accessed 12 July 2010).

Johnson, I.M., 2009. Education for librarianship and information studies: fit for purpose?, *Information Development*, 25 (3), 175–7.

Joint, N., 2003. Writing for publication in a library journal, *SCONUL Newsletter*, (28), 61–6. Available from: http://www.sconul.ac.uk/publications/newsletter/28/ART21.RTF (accessed 12 July 2010).

Larsen, G., 2006. Preparing for new and changing roles in research libraries – the need for continuing professional development, *Liber Quarterly*, 16 (3/4). Available from: http://liber.library.uu.nl/publish/articles/000184/article.pdf (accessed 12 July 2010).

Lynch, C., 2009. Special collections at the cusp of the digital age: a credo, *Research Library Issues*, 267, 3–9. Available from: http://www.arl.org/bm~doc/rli-267-lynch.pdf. (accessed 12 July 2010).

Lynn, V.A., Bose, A. and Boehmer, S.J., 2010. Librarian instruction-delivery modality preferences for professional continuing education, *Journal of the Medical Library Association*, 98 (1), 57–64.

Mason, F.M. and Wetherbee, L.V., 2004. Learning to lead: an analysis of current training programs for library leadership, *Library Trends*, 53 (1), 187–217.

MLA, 2007. *Competencies for Lifelong Learning and Professional Success: The Educational Policy Statement of the Medical Library Association*, Chicago, IL: Medical Library Association, Chicago, IL. Available from: http://www.mlanet.org/education/policy/ (accessed 12 July 2010).

Moore, A.A., Miller, M.J., Pitchford, V.J. and Jeng, L.H., 2008. Mentoring in the millennium: new views, climates and actions, *New Library World*, 109 (1/2), 75–86.

Murphy, J. and Moulaison, H., 2009. *Push the Edge: Social Networking Literacy Competencies For Librarians: Exploring Considerations and Engaging Participation Explore, Engage, Extend*: ACRL Fourteenth National Conference, March 12–15, 2009, Seattle, Washington, Chicago, IL: American Library Association, Association of College and Research Libraries, 328–30. Available from: http://www.freedomtoread.org/ala/mgrps/divs/acrl/events/national/seattle/papers/328.pdf (accessed 12 July 2010).

Murray, A., 2007. Growing your own: developing leaders through succession planning, *Liber Quarterly*, 17 (3/4). Available at: http://liber.library.uu.nl/publish/articles/000217/article.pdf (accessed 12 July 2010).

Noon, P., 1997. Managing for success – perhaps, *Librarian Career Development*, 5 (4), 128–35.

Powell, R.R., Baker, L.M. and Mika, J.J., 2002. Library and information science practitioners and research, *Library and Information Science Research*, 24 (1), 49–72.

Power, G., 2006. Workplace learning for busy information professionals, *Legal Information Management*, 6 (4), 260–64.

Prinsen, J.G.B., 2007. The International Ticer School: getting inspired to shape your library of the future, *Liber Quarterly*, 17 (1). Available from: http://liber.library.uu.nl/publish/articles/000193/article.pdf (accessed 12 July 2010).

Schreyer, A., 2004. *Education and Training for Careers in Special Collections, A White Paper Prepared for the Association of Research Libraries Special Collections Task Force*. Available from: http://www.arl.org/bm~doc/sctf_ed.pdf (accessed 12 July 2010).

Sen, B.A., 2010. Reflective writing: a management skill, *Library Management*, 31 (1/2), 79–93.

Stevenson, V., 2006. Future Leaders Programme, March 2006–2007, *SCONUL Focus*, 37, 9–20. Available from: http://www.sconul.ac.uk/publications/newsletter/37/5.pdf (accessed 12 July 2010).

Watkins, J. Drury, L. and Preddy, D., 1992. *From Evolution to Revolution: The Pressures on Professional Life in the 1990s*, Bristol: University of Bristol.

Watson, M., 2008. *Building Your Portfolio: The CILIP Guide*, London: Facet.

Webb, J., 2004. Developing routes for academic support staff, *In:* Oldroyd, M., ed. *Developing Academic Library Staff for Future Success*, London: Facet. 95–111

Whatley, K.M., 2009. New roles of liaison librarians: a liaison's perspective, *Research Libraries Issues*, 265, 29–32. Available from: http://www.arl.org/bm~doc/rli-265-whatley.pdf (accessed 12 July 2010).

Williamson, V., 2009. Developing leadership to transform our library: the Library Leadership Development Program (LLDP) at the University of Saskatchewan, *Library Management*, 30 (8–9), 619–26.

Wilson, D.W., 2008. Monitoring technology trends with podcasts, RSS and Twitter, *Library Hi Tech News*, 25 (10), 8–12.

Wormell, I., 2004. Professional doctorate – a new and widened perspective for professional and personal development within LIS, paper presented at *Knowledge and Change: 12th Nordic Conference on Information and Documentation*, Aarlborg, Denmark, 1–3 September, 2004. Available from: http://www2.db.dk/NIOD/wormell.pdf (accessed 12 July 2010).

Chapter 16

Librarians as Midwives of Change in Scholarly Communication

David Ball

'Force is the midwife of change' – Karl Marx

Introduction

History testifies to two ICT revolutions. In my reckoning scholarly communication is now in the grip of a third. The point of this chapter, to paraphrase Marx, is to show that librarians are in a position not simply to interpret the world of scholarly communication, but to change it, or at least to act as the midwives of that change.

The first ICT revolution was the development of writing. Beforehand the only vehicle for storing information was the human memory. Transmission relied on speech and signs; if content was not to perish with the individual, replication needed time and personal contact. After the invention of writing, portable storage media decreased the restrictions imposed by time and space. Knowledge became much less vulnerable; more could be stored and passed from generation to generation or carried across long distances; critical thinking was enhanced.

While writing represented a huge advance, scholars in the world of manuscripts knew severe limitations. They tended to travel to manuscripts, which were often in jeopardy: witness the destruction at Alexandria. It was very difficult to determine provenance and authority, and to compare texts. Dissemination by copying tended to corrupt texts.

It is almost impossible for us now to appreciate the scale and impact of the second ICT revolution – printing with movable type – we have spent our lives during its maturity. Scholars in the late 15th and early 16th centuries were however under no illusions about its nature. We hear of Johann Fust having to flee Paris: its inhabitants believed that only someone in league with the devil could produce so many perfect copies of the bible. Later Fust was conflated with Georg (subsequently known as Johann) Faust, who was of course reputed to have sold his soul to the devil in return for knowledge (Eisenstein 1993, p. 19–20). Particularly telling is the association of a technology, so marvellous that it could only be achieved through necromancy, with the pursuit of that most dangerous commodity – knowledge.

For the scholar the advances represented by printing were marked. The possibilities of obtaining texts were hugely enhanced. By 1503 8 million books had been printed, more, it is estimated, than the number of manuscripts produced between 330AD, the founding of Constantinople, and 1453, when it was captured by the Turks; the cost of copying one manuscript equated to the cost of producing over 300 printed books (Eisenstein 1993, p. 13–14). Provenance and authority were enhanced by the use of title pages; texts became more organised and exploitable through indexes, tables of contents etc. Later editions improved texts through corrections; they did not corrupt them as copying had corrupted manuscript texts.

Looking forward 200 years from the birth of printing, Guédon (2001) discusses one of its major outcomes: the invention of scholarly communication by Oldenburg with the *Philosophical Transactions of the Royal Society of London*. He also notes the fluidity at that time of boundaries between the various players in publishing (writers, printers, book dealers). Under Oldenburg's direction the achievement of the *Philosophical Transactions of the Royal Society of London* was twofold. First they acted as a register of intellectual property: publication there was equivalent to establishing title to that property. Secondly acceptance by an editor or peer review panel conferred status and credibility through the backing of the journal's name.

Today's third ICT revolution has been predicted for at least a century. At the end of the 19th century, Octave Uzanne (1894) was writing of the demise of the book:

> I do not believe (and the progress of electricity and modern mechanism forbids me to believe) that Gutenberg's invention can do otherwise than sooner or later fall into desuetude as a means of current interpretation of our mental products... You will surely agree with me that reading, as we practise it today, soon brings on great weariness; for not only does it require of the brain a sustained attention which consumes a large proportion of the cerebral phosphates, but it also forces our bodies into various fatiguing attitudes. If we are reading one of our great

> newspapers it constrains us to acquire a certain dexterity in the art of turning
> and folding the sheets; if we hold the paper wide open it is not long before the
> muscles of tension are overtaxed ...

Uzanne did not foresee the move from broadsheet to tabloid newspapers. His substitute for print was more radical: the phonograph, playing wax cylinders. In more recent times microform was hailed as the successor to print.

What we recognise as today's electronic revolution is not new in the scale or nature of its impact. Luther nailed his 95 Theses to the door of Wittenberg's *Schloßkirche* on 31 October 1517. Within two weeks they were translated and known throughout Germany; throughout Europe in a month (Eisenstein 1993, p. 153). For contemporaries this lightning speed was as fantastic as the speed of electronic communication today.

Eisenstein (1993, p. 45) also notes that printing fostered social and intellectual combinatory activity. Much innovative scholarly work was undertaken outside the established academic centres. Printers developed networks of contributors and researchers, to improve their texts and give a competitive edge. Again this strikes a chord today with the development of virtual research communities and the sharing of research data (Borda et al. 2006).

Eisenstein (1993, p. 80) quotes Thomas Jefferson on the preservative powers of print:

> How many of the precious works of antiquity were lost while they existed only
> in manuscript? Has there ever been one lost since the art of printing has rendered
> it practicable to multiply and disperse copies? This leads us then to the only
> means of preserving ... that is a multiplication of printed copies.

This points forward to the current LOCKSS initiative – Lots Of Copies Keeps Stuff Safe.[1]

These echoes of very current concerns and issues remind us that there is every reason to believe that the current, third ICT revolution will indeed at last replace print, bringing as far-reaching effects as the first two.

The Information Value Chain

A strong echo of the past is the fluidity of roles in Oldenburg's time, which Guédon compared above to the fluidity evident today. A firm taxonomy of roles will highlight the changes that have taken place since the 1990s, and may help us to predict future possibilities and directions. Bide's useful taxonomy (Ball 2005) identifies the following activities or functions in the information supply chain: creation, publication, aggregation, access and use. To a greater or lesser degree,

---

1   http://www.lockss.org/lockss/Home.

each of the activities, or links, adds value to the information, until it is used and the value realised.

This account is simplified, concentrating on the key players in the chain. Some of the main concepts applied during this discussion are: branding, authority, monopoly, and the product-to-service shift. Each link in the chain confers an element of branding or authority on the information. Authority has to do with reliability, informed opinion, having status or expertise. One thinks for instance of the BBC: news broadcast in the World Service carries a great deal of authority. Branding has to do with consistency and quality. Coca-Cola and Pepsi Cola are different brands, with different qualities, consistent in themselves and having different adherents. Each link in the chain also has a greater or lesser degree of monopoly. This is obviously particularly important for the information marketplace.

One major factor differentiating electronic from printed information is the shift from product to service. With printed information, much labour and cost are tied up in producing, distributing, storing and handling a physical product: books and journals. With electronic information, libraries and other intermediaries generally provide or facilitate only access to information held elsewhere, a service not a product. It is worth noting that this shift follows a general trend, as companies and public bodies outsource or disaggregate activities.

Creation

The first link in the chain is creation. Creators may be authors or compilers. They may be directly employed by publishers, as are journalists and technical writers. They may be employed as academics, and hence expected to produce articles and monographs as part of their employment. Alternatively they may be independent agents.

In literature or fiction, the creator confers authority. In picking from the shelf one of Anthony Powell's novels, one knows what one is getting. The creator is also a monopolist; this monopoly, recognised and protected by copyright, is then generally transferred to a single publisher.

Publication

The publication link is essentially concerned with the selection and editing of information into consumable and buyable form (titles, series, journals). In one sense it is a form of quality control. Publishers also market the product, and undertake, or subcontract, physical production and distribution or electronic storage.

For librarians, authority is conferred in part at least by the imprint – Oxford University Press, for instance, or Butterworths. The end-user is more likely to focus on the brand – e.g. Who's Who. In scholarly communication, the editorial and refereeing process creates authority, and is concentrated at the level of the title. The publisher's monopoly, often transferred from the creator, is also jealously preserved.

As we all know, the delivery of information in electronic form embodies some important differences from delivery in printed form. There is essentially no physical production and distribution of electronic information. There is a physical realisation at the moment of use – as an image on a computer screen or a print-out. But this occurs only at the end of the information chain, not close to the origin, as happens with print. For the rest of the chain we are talking about access to the information, not a physical product containing the information. Librarians, as purchasers, are therefore now buying, on behalf of our users, a service as opposed to a physical product.

This of course has many and quite far-reaching repercussions. In the days of print, libraries and their users were bound only by the law. For instance, the law of copyright for printed works is complex but generally well understood by librarians in terms of fair dealing for research or private study. However the information provider or intermediary is now able, through licences, to impose restrictions on the use of the electronic form of the information far beyond the limits outlined in copyright legislation. The balance of rights between users and copyright owners enshrined in the legislation has therefore shifted in favour of the publisher.

We should also note that, with electronic information, authority is potentially diluted. It is easy to publish and disseminate information on the web, far easier than publishing and disseminating in print, which require considerable investment of money and time.

Aggregation

One may define aggregation as bringing together in a coherent collection disparate information sources. Libraries have conferred authority by virtue of selecting printed material. Users perceive a certain warranty of fitness for purpose if a book is in their library's collection.

Libraries have had a perhaps unrecognised near monopoly on aggregation of printed information. With electronic information, there is no physical product to acquire or handle. The role of aggregator therefore moves elsewhere in the supply chain, to the publisher or intermediary such as the serials agent.

Libraries' collective near monopoly, evident for printed information, is therefore lost: users need set foot nowhere near a library to have access to aggregators' sites; they simply need a network connection, and either the appropriate permissions or deep pockets.

A relatively new area of aggregation is of course the institutional repository, bringing together the citation, and full text of a university's research output. In many institutions the repository falls within the remit of the librarian, as the custodian of the aggregate of its research output, who, as in the context of print, confers authority by virtue of selection and preservation.

Access

Facilitating and controlling access to aggregated printed information has been core territory for libraries, a perhaps unrecognised near monopoly. Tools have been developed: catalogues, bibliographies and indexes aid discovery and location; library management systems control access to collections.

Providing access to electronic information is however fundamentally different. New tools have been developed, as the focus has switched from controlling physical access to identity management. Libraries have lost the monopoly on access: the majority of our users can connect to information resources as easily from a living room, or a train, or a beach, as through a library. Perhaps paradoxically, the open access movement and the mushrooming of repositories have sidelined the librarian: search engines such as Google Scholar and free access to pre-prints have circumvented the traditional library, allowing the researcher direct unmediated access to texts. The coming generation of search tools may also sound the death knell of the abstracting and indexing services so familiar to our profession.

The hybrid stage that we have experienced since the start of the new millennium – having to maintain a rump of print unavailable in electronic form while the majority of usage is electronic – somewhat obscures this development. It is a distraction – uncomfortable, time-consuming and expensive. Much attention is devoted for instance to the systems architecture that evolved in the print era: it is no longer fit for purpose, but it has not yet been replaced by an architecture for the hybrid or solely electronic library.

Use

Finally we arrive at the end of the chain and its reason for existence, the user, who of course, particularly in the academic sector, may also be the start of the chain.

Hitherto we have stressed that, for traditional printed resources, we have been dealing with a physical product. What we provide to the user in the electronic environment is a service – access to the information – not the physical product itself. However, Ranganathan's Five Laws of Library Science (1931), slightly paraphrased, are just as applicable to electronic resources:

- Resources are for use.
- Every user his or her resource.
- Every resource its user.
- Save the time of the user.
- The library is a growing organism.

There are anomalies of course. Academics have immediate access to a far greater corpus of material, yet licences impose restrictions on non-academic use. The library is a shrinking organism of information held directly and physically, but a vastly expanded and growing organism in terms of access to information.

The Economic Background

This section attempts to identify, in broad terms, the costs associated with the links in the information value chain just discussed. It concentrates on academic journal publishing, utilising Research Information Network's 2008 report. The figures rely on many assumptions, disputed by publishers and others. However, even if they do not give a completely accurate picture, they are extremely valuable in providing an overall indication of the costs of publishing and how they are distributed. As librarians, intermediaries, purchasers, we tend to concentrate on the visible costs, those associated with subscription and access for instance. It is salutary to have one's mind focused on the hidden costs.

Publication

The report's breakdown of the costs of the publishing link of the chain for journals is as in Figure 16.1.

'First-copy costs' are the fixed costs for peer review, editing etc., and amount to 57% of the total costs. Variable costs arise from distribution, printing and subscription management. Indirect costs are overheads for marketing, hosting, investment etc.

Per article first-copy costs are estimated to be £2,330, and total costs to be £4,057. It is worth noting that the first-copy costs arise whatever the method of publication – subscription or open access, or form – print or electronic.

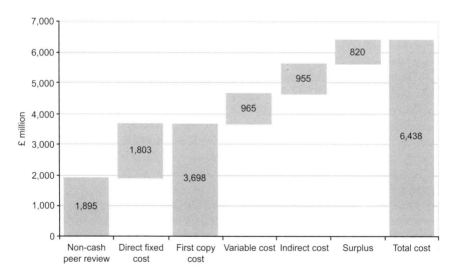

Figure 16.1   Total publishing and distribution cost incurred in the global scholarly communication process by activity

Source: Research Information Network, 2008. Reprinted with permission of RIN.

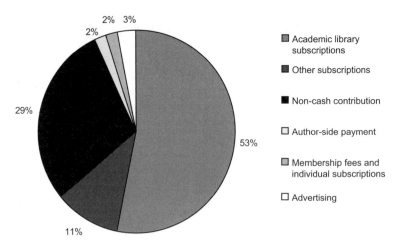

2%   3%

2%

29%

53%

11%

■ Academic library
  subscriptions

■ Other subscriptions

■ Non-cash contribution

□ Author-side payment

■ Membership fees and
  individual subscriptions

□ Advertising

**Figure 16.2   Funding contribution to meet global publication and distribution
incurred cost (all journal types)**

Source: Research Information Network, 2008. Reprinted with permission of RIN.

Figure 16.2, from the same source, illustrates the contributions made to meet these costs. Academic library subscriptions cover 53% of the costs; non-cash contributions (peer review and editing) cover 29% of the costs. Thus 82% of the costs are borne by higher education institutions.

These contributions recognise that higher education institutions benefit from scholarly publication in two ways: first from the peer review process that recognises the quality and impact of their research; second from access to the research of other scholars.

These calculations of course take account only of costs; they ignore the value in intellectual property rights (IPR) donated by scholars to publishers.

The profile for funding scholarly monographs will be somewhat similar: high first-copy costs with a non-cash contribution from the author in terms of the IPR, and the bulk of the revenue from academic libraries. One difference is that authors will generally receive a royalty; however the number of copies sold will generally be small, although print-on-demand may increase the time that the monograph remains in print and hence the number of copies sold.

The economics of textbooks are however very different. The study by Content Complete and OnlyConnect (2009) records the publishers' view that sales to students account for 70–90% of overall revenue from textbooks, with the remainder coming from libraries. Librarians may dispute these figures, but, despite the second hand trade amongst students, there is a large element of 'repeat business', with each new cohort of students buying new copies of the same titles. According to Content Complete (2009), the Publishers Association in the UK estimates undergraduate spending on books in 2006/07 at £220 million. Library budgets would be hard pressed to match this spending, so publishers' reluctance to make textbooks available as e-books to libraries is quite understandable.

With textbooks a further difference is the high volume of sales, compared with that of the scholarly monograph. The royalties passed to academic authors of textbooks will be correspondingly large in terms of volume.

Access and Use

The Research Information Network report also provides useful data on the access and use links of the chain, at least for the UK.

Figure 16.3 shows that the total cost of access provision, excluding subscriptions at about £117 million, borne by libraries, is £72 million, 12% of the total in this link. The bulk of access costs (£530 million, or 86%) is made up by the time spent by researchers in locating, displaying, downloading and browsing articles. The report excludes here the cost of reading.

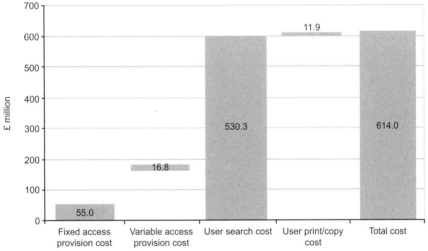

Figure 16. 3   Total annual access provision and usage cost incurred in the UK scholarly communication process

Source: Research Information Network, 2008. Reprinted with permission of RIN.

Figure 16.4 shows the total UK contribution, including peer review and subscriptions, to the total cost of scholarly communication.

These figures may not give a completely accurate picture. However there is a stark message for academic libraries. We have concentrated much intellectual effort on trying to contain subscription increases, in negotiating deals for content. Yet at £117 million, subscriptions account for only 12% of the UK's contribution; even peer review is larger, accounting for nearly 14%.

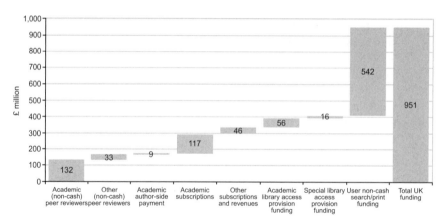

Figure 16.4   UK funding contribution to the total cost of scholarly communication UK

Source: Research Information Network, 2008. Reprinted with permission of RIN.

But the really remarkable figure is the £542 million cost of the final (use) link of the chain in locating and downloading articles – 57% of the total. Remembering Ranganathan, should we not as a profession be paying more attention to saving the time of our users? In purely economic terms, saving 10% of costs here is the equivalent of saving 46% of subscription costs or 41% of the costs of peer review, both completely unachievable.

Trends in Pricing and Negotiation

Despite the figures just quoted, subscription costs remain important: they constitute an actual outflow of cash and they are directly measurable. However, in negotiating we have let ourselves be manoeuvred into a weak position *vis-à-vis* the academic publishers. We are producers for and consumers in a mature, profitable, multi-million pound business. Yet we donate our intellectual property, donate staff time for peer review etc., and then buy the resulting product through subscriptions.

Negotiating with journal publishers is problematic. They are monopoly providers: *Nature* for instance is only available, ultimately, from Nature Publishing Group. There is little competition in the academic market, since generally one cannot substitute one title for another. Publishers will only reduce prices if they see a cost saving or some other benefit. They may offer additional content for the same price, but with any price reduction the saving by the university could go directly to other publishers. As far as the publishers are concerned, reduced prices equal decreased surplus and loss of market share.

In the UK higher education negotiations with publishers for electronic content began in 1995 with the Pilot Site Licence Initiative (PSLI). This set the model for later 'big deals' negotiated by the Joint Information Systems Committee (JISC) through the National Electronic Site Licence Initiative (NESLi, subsequently NESLi2). NESLi2 offers a licence and a framework agreement negotiated with publishers; individual higher education institutions may then opt in to the agreement. The big deals generally allow access to all of a publisher's content issued in a defined time-span. Pricing has been based on historical print spend. Thus higher education institutions with low historical spends on print journals have benefited disproportionately. There has however been some equalisation of charges over the last years.

Practice in the USA has been different from the opt-in model: a consortium will often make a one-off payment to a publisher to make content accessible to all members. Costs are allocated to individual higher education institutions according to an agreed formula. This model is now being seen in the UK, for instance the Scottish Higher Education Digital Library (SHEDL) makes a single payment; the entire publisher's content becomes available to all Scottish higher education institutions.

Doubts about the long-term effects of the big deal have been expressed for a number of years (Ball 2003). In the short term it offers a huge amount of content for information-hungry scholars. However, it reinforces the monopoly position and advantage of the big publishers: journal prices rise faster than inflation, and library budgets; librarians have understandably felt unable to cancel their big deals; spending has been cut elsewhere, on non-big deal publishers, putting them at risk, or the bookfund. Agreements also run for three or five years, and have strict no-cancellation clauses covering the content; freedom of manoeuvre is very restricted.

Although it may offer some cost benefits, the single-payment big-deal model, such as SHEDL's, seems to reinforce the monopoly even further. If it is difficult for a single academic library to cancel a big deal, how much more difficult will it be to cancel a deal for a whole country's academic libraries? It seems that for the sake of limited cost savings on subscriptions, as we have seen, a relatively inexpensive link in the chain, we are willing to place yet more power in the hands of the publishers.

Following the pain inflicted by exchange-rate fluctuations, there are indications that librarians are for the first time seriously considering cancelling big deals when they come up for renewal. Some publishers (generally the smaller ones) have moderated price increases. However the big ones are refusing to moderate price rises or to allow cancellations. They are also making clear that moving away from the big deals will bring no price advantage. The implication is obvious: they are confident that, in the majority of cases, cuts will fall on their competitors, further strengthening their position in the market.

Finally mention must be made of the part played by the regional purchasing consortia for HE in the UK, such as the Southern Universities Purchasing Consortium (SUPC). They have traditionally negotiated with intermediaries, such as subscription agents, rather than with publishers. Their effect is limited in terms of scholarly communication: negotiations are restricted to the services offered by intermediaries and, in terms of cost, to the intermediaries' margins, which are on average under 8% of the subscription price.

What Is to Be Done?

It has long been recognised (Ball and Spice 1996) that the electronic age offers the potential to turn academic library practice on its head. University libraries until now have promised to collect or gain access to the research outputs of all other universities and research institutions, a task that is both impossible to accomplish and costly to attempt. With the widespread introduction of institutional repositories, however, it is now feasible for each university or research institution to collect all the research outputs of its own scholars, and make them available to all other universities. This task, by contrast, is finite and achievable; the costs are commensurate with the research standing and income of the academic institution.

Universal access is therefore achievable; recent approaches to universities by publishers, offering themselves as an alternative to the institutional repositories, indicate some nervousness at this prospect.

However, at the moment, apart from a very small number of open access journals and an even smaller volume of author-paid articles in subscription journals, what is lacking outside commercial publishing is peer review. This is the key to higher education's weak position *vis-à-vis* the academic publishers.

There are some measures that might be taken to weaken the power of the publishers and facilitate change:

- Copyright – As has been noted already, the academic world has for too long given away rights to its intellectual property. On the other side of the coin, electronic journals have also enabled publishers to alter the balance of rights to the detriment of the casual, non-affiliated user. For the future we should ensure that academics/higher education institutions grant publishers only a non-exclusive right to publish, and retain their right to publish through repositories (for further discussion see Chapter 8 by Alma Swan).
- Repositories – Critically these allow us to take back the monopoly on aggregation and lay the foundation for open access. We should continue to develop the infrastructure of institutional repositories and foster a culture of academics depositing research outputs as an integral and automatic part of the research and publication process.
- Support open access journals – The first-copy costs identified above (for peer review etc.) do not disappear. However the cost and value of these services are more transparent, and open to competition, if the author or higher education institution bears them (the 'author pays' model). See below for some of the cost implications.

- Create overlay journals – These are virtual journals, the content of which is not collocated but remains distributed across institutional repositories throughout the peer review and publication process.

What can be achieved is demonstrated by the University of California's flagship eScholarship programme, which

> provides a suite of open access, scholarly publishing services and research tools that enable departments, research units, publishing programs, and individual scholars associated with the University of California to have direct control over the creation and dissemination of the full range of their scholarship'.[2]

Here it might be noted that repositories and open access are hospitable to the scholarly monograph, as well as to the journal article or conference paper. They enable us once again to function as university presses.

Recent work by Swan (2010) of Key Perspectives for the JISC has highlighted the cost implications of some of the above measures. She indicates that there are cost savings for many universities in open access models; however universities publishing large numbers of articles may incur additional costs. At a cost of £1,000 per article for an open access journal, the three smaller of four universities surveyed would save between £0.17 million and £1.4 million per annum; the largest, most research-intensive would face additional costs of £1.86 million per annum. At a cost of £1,127 per article in an overlay journal, savings for the two smaller universities ranged from £0.38 million to £1.25 million per annum; the two larger universities would face additional costs of between £0.35 and £2.67 million.

However, as in Research Information Network's 2008 report cited above, Swan also identifies major additional saving in the efficiency of the research process. Here we need to play a full part in the core library business of saving the time of the user.

Conclusion

What is clear from the above discussion is that we are caught up in an ICT revolution as momentous as the birth of printing. New structures are taking shape, breaking the mould that has been familiar to us for 300 years. At the moment we perceive them only dimly, and there are many practical, cultural and financial impediments to their development. However our duty is to embrace, lead and harness change. We have a unique opportunity to act as midwives, delivering a new age of scholarly communication by, to return to the Marxist metaphor, reclaiming the means of production.

---

2   http://www.escholarship.org/.

References

Ball, D., 2003. *Beware Publishers Bearing Gifts: Why the 'Big Deal' is a Bad Deal for Universities*, Libraries and education in the networked information environment: proceedings of the 24th Annual International Association of Technological University Libraries 2003 Conference, Middle Eastern Technical University, Ankara, June 2–5, 2003. Available from: http://eprints.bournemouth.ac.uk/215/ (accessed October 2009).

Ball, D., 2005. Signing away our freedom: the implications of electronic resource licences. *The Acquisitions Librarian*. 18 (35–36), 7–20.

Ball, D. and Spice, C., 1996. *The Big Flame: A Model for a Universal Full-text Electronic Library of Research*, in Libraries and associations in the transient world: new technologies and new forms of co-operation: conference proceedings: Third International Conference "Crimea 96" ([Foros: The Organizing Committee]), vol. 2, pp. 12–15. Available from: http://eprints.bournemouth.ac.uk/1/ (accessed October 2009).

Borda, A. et al., 2006. *Report of the Working Group on Virtual Research Communities for the OST e-Infrastructure Steering Group*. London, UK, Office of Science and Technology, 46pp. Available from: http://eprints.soton.ac.uk/42074/ (accessed March 2010).

Content Complete and OnlyConnect Consultancy, 2009. *Study on the Management and Economic Impact of e-Textbook Business Models on Publishers*, e-book aggregators and higher education institutions: phase one report (public version), London, JISC. Available from: http://www.jiscebooksproject.org/archives/211 (accessed March 2010).

Eisenstein, E.L., 1993. *The Printing Revolution in Early Modern Europe*. Canto ed. Cambridge: Cambridge University Press.

Guédon, J.-C., 2001. *In Oldenburg's Long Shadow: Librarians, Research Scientists, Publishers, and the Control Of Scientific Publishing*, Washington, Association of Research Libraries. Available from: http://www.arl.org/resources/pubs/mmproceedings/138guedon.shtml (accessed March 2010).

Ranganathan, S. R., 1931. *The Five Laws of Library Science*. Madras Library Association: Madras.

Research Information Network, 2008. *Activities, Costs and Funding Flows in the Scholarly Communications System in the UK*, London, RIN. Available from: http://www.rin.ac.uk/our-work/communicating-and-disseminating-research/activities-costs-and-funding-flows-scholarly-commu (accessed October 2009).

Swan, A., 2010. *Modelling Scholarly Communication Options: Costs and Benefits for Universities*, London, JISC. Available from: http://ie-repository.jisc.ac.uk/442/ (accessed April 2010).

Uzanne, O., 1894. The end of books, *Scribner's Magazine Illustrated*, 16 (July to December), pp. 221–31. Available from: http://www.uiowa.edu/~obermann/endofbooks/ (accessed March 2010).

Index